OHIO'S FIRST PEOPLES

OHIO BICENTENNIAL SERIES
Editor: Clarence E. Wunderlin, Jr.

H. Roger Grant, *Ohio on the Move: Transportation in the Buckeye State*

Phillip R. Shriver and Clarence E. Wunderlin, Jr., eds., *The Documentary Heritage of Ohio*

Stephane Elise Booth, *Buckeye Women: The History of Ohio's Daughters*

Catherine M. Rokicky, *Creating a Perfect World: Religious and Secular Utopias in Nineteenth-Century Ohio*

James H. O'Donnell III, *Ohio's First Peoples*

OHIO'S FIRST PEOPLES

James H. O'Donnell III

OHIO UNIVERSITY PRESS / ATHENS

Ohio University Press, Athens, Ohio 45701
© 2004 by James H. O'Donnell III
Printed in the United States of America
All rights reserved

Ohio University Press books are printed on acid-free paper ⊗ ™

12 11 10 09 08 07 06 05 04   5 4 3 2 1

The publication of this book was made possible in part
by the generous support of the Ohio Bicentennial Commission.

Library of Congress Cataloging-in-Publication Data
O'Donnell, James H., 1937–
  Ohio's first peoples / James H. O'Donnell III.
    p. cm. — (Ohio bicentennial series)
Includes bibliographical references and index.
  ISBN 0-8214-1524-7 (cloth : alk. paper) — ISBN 0-8214-1525-5 (pbk.: alk. paper)
  1. Indians of North America—Ohio—Antiquities. 2. Indians of North America—
    Ohio—History. 3. Hopewell culture—Ohio. 4. Fort Ancient culture—Ohio.
    5. Ohio—History—18th century. 6. Ohio—History—19th century. 7. Ohio—
    Antiquities. I. Title. II. Series.
E78.O3 O26 2004
77.1004'97—dc22

                                                        2003018114

Contents

List of Illustrations   vii

Acknowledgments   ix

Introduction   1

1   Peoples of "Ingenuity, Industry, and Elegance"   14

2   Ohio Sanctuary   28

3   The Noise and Miseries of War   46

4   The War for Ohio   73

5   "No Resting Place"   110

Ohio's First Peoples: A Bicentennial Afterthought   127

Notes   129

Works Cited   159

Index   169

Illustrations

Philo Archaeological District 3

Rufus Putnam's map of the mounds at Marietta, 1788 7

Map of Delaware settlements drifting westward into Ohio 8

Map of the Ohio frontier, 1772–81 9

Plan of the Marietta earthworks, 1837 10

Map of Granville subregion 23

Gustavus Hesselius's portrait of Lapowinsa, 1735 30

Return of English captives to Colonel Bouquet, ca. 1764 40

Henry Hamilton's sketches of chiefs, 1778 54

Sketch of Pacane by Hamilton, 1778 55

Moravian Delaware village 69

Map of invasions of Ohio Indian country, 1774–82 70

Death of Colonel Crawford, 1782 71

Fort Harmar 76

Gilbert Stuart's portrait of Joseph Brant, 1786 79

Campus Martius and mounds 81

Map of westward movement of tribes after 1782 85

Little Turtle 87

Benjamin Lossing's portrayal of Tecumseh 99

George Catlin's portrait of Tenskwatawa, the Prophet 104

Between-the-Logs 112

Mononcue 116

Acknowledgments

While it may be said that movies involve casts of thousands, almost every book includes a support system far beyond the author's adequacy to thank. For suggestive guidance, I am indebted to Professor Clarence Wunderlin of Kent State University, series editor of the Bicentennial Series, and also to David Sanders, director, Ohio University Press. At Marietta College, I am appreciative of the moral and financial support given by President Jean Scott, Provost Sue DeWine, and the Faculty Development Committee. At the Dawes Memorial Library of Marietta College, I wish especially to thank Professor Sandra Neyman, the Marietta college librarian, and Ms. Linda Showalter, library special collections associate in the Slack Research Collection, for their amazing knowledge of the collection and their uncanny ability to locate sources. No historian today dares try to prepare an overview like this without the aid of patient archaeologists. In my case I am grateful to Wesley Clarke, Registered Professional Archaeologist, an environmental planner with the Ohio Department of Transportation who protects endangered sites in southeastern Ohio. My enormous and eternal debt, however, is to one who is not only my professional colleague but also my friend, wife, and source of all things beautiful, Mabry O'Donnell. Each day her supporting love makes possible whatever I accomplish. To her I say *Je t'aime, toujours, je t'aime.*

OHIO'S FIRST PEOPLES

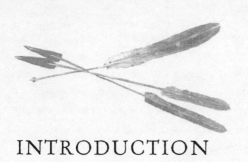

INTRODUCTION

TWO HUNDRED YEARS AGO A NEWLY ARRIVED VISITOR TO OHIO WOULD have almost immediately encountered the presence of Native American peoples. Villages, camps, trails, and the remnants of ancient mounds were visible markers on the land. Indeed, one could borrow the once-popular Ohio travel slogan "Ohio, the heart of it all" to describe the long periods of Native American residence there. By 2003, however, a traveler crossing Ohio by car during the state's bicentennial may not have recognized many Native American names on the road signs. Neither Marietta nor Newark reveals through its name the rich complex of mounds located in each. Nor on the other hand will the signs to either Indian Mound Mall or Wyandot Lake direct the curious to repositories of information. If one is truly dedicated to exploring the remaining evidence of early Ohioans, one of the best guides is *Indian Mounds of the Middle Ohio Valley: A Guide to Adena and Ohio Hopewell Sites.*[1] Written by Susan Woodward and Jerry McDonald, this easily portable volume gives not only a description of but also driving directions to each of the "forty-one mounds, earthworks, and affiliated sites" it describes. Thirty-one out of the forty-one sites are within the boundaries of the modern state of Ohio.

Both the archaeological and historical records indicate, moreover, that native groups have flowered, flourished, and faded in Ohio for thousands of years. Even today the remnants of these cultures lie literally beneath our feet. For the past sixty years in Marietta, the first organized settlement in Ohio, citizens have strolled, picnicked, observed crew races, heard band concerts, and enjoyed the green space in East Muskingum riverside park, poised only inches above a Hopewell hamlet near the mouth of the Muskingum River. Beneath them lay buried the characteristic Hopewell indicators of maygrass and nutshells, carbonized in silence along with pottery shards and projectile points (often made of the fine-grained flint native to Ohio known as Flint Ridge chalcedony).[2] Rock shelters, flint knapping sites, caches of projectile points and blades, hunting camps, agricultural hamlets, mound-oriented ceremonial centers, and place names like the historic Mahican John's Town reflect the presence of Native Americans over the millennia. Illustrative of this continued presence over time in one place is the Philo Archaeological District in southern Muskingum County, which includes villages of a number of different phases within a span of over thirteen hundred years (1260 B.C. to A.D. 82) along a two-mile stretch of Muskingum River bottomland.[3] Only a relatively short distance away, in the valley of the Licking River is a multicomponent site used for hundreds of years by flint knappers and nut processors. Despite frequent visits by collectors to the well-known location (even during the time of professional retrieval there!), archaeologists still gathered more than seventeen thousand pieces of archaeological evidence.[4] One wonders what might have been discovered had the site been found in an undisturbed state.

It seems appropriate, therefore, that as part of Ohio's bicentennial statehood celebration we survey the story of the Native American presence in the state. Modern readers are inclined to ask about the first person to live in Ohio, but like most questions in archaeology and prehistory, this one is not easily answered. The settlers known as Paleoindians were present in Ohio at least 10,890 years ago, according to the research of archaeologist David Brose. His investigations of a Paleoindian site in Medina County, Ohio, complement the work of an archaeological team's findings at Newark, Ohio. While Brose's findings document the presence of Paleoindian components, the team working at Newark was confronted with an even greater

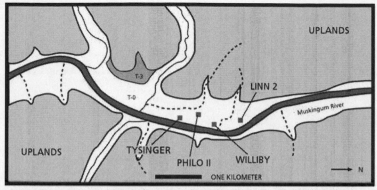

CLASSIC HOPEWELL HABITATION SITES - PHILO ARCHAEOLOGICAL DISTRICT

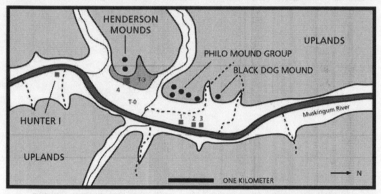

EARLY LATE WOODLAND SITES - PHILO ARCHAEOLOGICAL DISTRICT
1) TYSINGER HAMLET   3) PHILO II NORTH VILLAGE
2) PHILO II SOUTH VILLAGE   4) HENDERSON EARTHWORK

Philo Archaeological District, showing the locations of Hopewell habitation sites (*top*) and early Late Woodland habitations and burial mounds (*bottom*). From Paul J. Pacheco, ed., *A View from the Core: A Synthesis of Ohio Hopewell Archaeology* (Columbus: The Ohio Archaeological Council, 1996), 321. Reprinted by permission of the Ohio Archaeological Council. Copyright © 1996.

surprise in 1989. During the deepening of a golf course pond, the contractor encountered unusual bones in the bottom muck that turned out to be those of a mastodon (*Mammut americanum*). The fully grown male mastodon evidently had been killed elsewhere and somehow transported to the pond (a testimony to the cooperative strategies of these hunters), where it lay until the late twentieth century.[5]

Although its primary emphasis will be on the so-called historic period from the seventeenth to the nineteenth century, this study will begin with an overview of the first peoples whose handiwork permanently altered the landscape of Ohio, specifically the cultures labeled with the modern names Adena (500 B.C. to A.D. 100, Early Woodland) and Hopewell (100 B.C. to A.D. 500, Middle Woodland). Of concern also will be the Ohio Valley peoples designated Fort Ancient (some of whom lived as late as 1635), successors to the Hopewell and, as some scholars argue, predecessors to the historic Shawnees. Although the term "Fort Ancient" is no more of native origin than is "Adena" or "Hopewell," it identifies those peoples who provided a transition from the age of non-European dominance to the earliest precontact influences through the impact of trade. One scholar has even suggested that some of these Ohio Fort Ancient settlements resulted from the ripple effect of the early beaver wars that drove populations southward, away from the southern shore of Lake Erie to the relative safety of southwestern and southeastern Ohio. His interpretation gains credence from the presence of a seventeenth-century French iron axhead found in a Fort Ancient village on Blennerhassett Island in the Ohio River, transported there either by Native American traders or newly arrived kinsmen of the villagers. The presence of the European felling ax—found during the summer of 1974 in a refuse pit along with a "Madisonville Grooved-Paddled sherd and a crude triangular point base"—certainly reflects the creation of what historians call the "middle ground."[6] Whatever the reasons, the south shore of Lake Erie was more or less emptied of settlement by the middle of the seventeenth century.[7] If we accept the "beaver wars" paradigm, Ohio becomes a kind of western hunting ground for the Iroquoian imperialists (and for both the English and the French, who shifted from adversaries to allies and back again with ease) seeking to dominate the blossoming trade with the Europeans.

That trade and its ramifications built on the foundations of intertribal trading and rivalries, which existed long before the arrival of the Europeans in North America. It is argued that the first contacts between the French and the Iroquois took place in 1534 as the French slowly worked their way up the St. Lawrence River valley. Although the earliest exchanges may have been a swapping of furs by Native Americans for goods they considered exotic, the interchange rapidly took on new meaning as the market for skins needed for making fashionable beaver hats was balanced by the native

Ohio's First Peoples

peoples' demands for the superior technology of iron tools and weapons. In the early years of the trade, the highway for goods was the St. Lawrence River valley, hence the orientation of the tribal alliances toward that area. Eventually the most desirable trade item was the gun, which all the warriors prized; unfortunately, alcohol was no less in demand. Before the arrival of the Dutch and the English, the French enjoyed a monopoly in providing European goods.[8] Alliances forged on the anvil of the Anglo-French wars affected forest diplomacy from the middle of the seventeenth century through the next one hundred years. Native American diplomats, who called the French "father," only reluctantly addressed the English likewise after the French vacated the continent in 1763, but ultimately they would have to adjust to a "Great Father" in Washington, D.C.

Another legacy of the seventeenth-century trade rivalry was the strengthening of the League of the Iroquois. Although the precise origin of this arrangement is the subject of much speculation, it seems clear that by the middle of the seventeenth century, five Iroquoian tribes in present-day New York—the Oneida, Mohawk, Onondaga, Cayuga, and Seneca—had bonded into a confederation able to cooperate at a level previously unknown in the story of Native American politics. This league, or confederacy, allowed its members the freedom of peace within the league and the combined power of allies when war erupted. It was the strength of the Five Nations and their allies that resulted in the catastrophic losses suffered by Huron-related groups in present-day Ontario during the seventeenth century and the scattering of the Hurons, some of whose descendants became the Wyandots who eventually populated northwest Ohio.[9]

In 1788, however, it was not the historic tribes like the Wyandots that captured the public's romantic attention but the puzzle of the monumental artifacts left behind by the mound-building groups. The so-called mystery was the presence of the mounds, the living tribes' apparent ignorance about them, and American citizens' belief that the "ignorant savages" were too uncivilized to have constructed such edifices. When the organized vanguard arrived from the eastern United States in 1788 at what is now Marietta, they offered fanciful explanations for the "earthworks" they encountered. Rufus Putnam, a leader of the Ohio Company of Associates who had been a military engineer during the American Revolution, carefully measured the "ancient works," as he called them, speculating how they might have been transformed into defensive breastworks by the use of palisades at strategic points.[10] The militaristic connotation of Putnam's description seems permanently fixed; in a recent essay about the Hopewell peoples, the term "earthworks" is still used.[11] Putnam's creative imagination even led him to reflect on how travelers using canoes could follow the Gulf of Mexico and the Ohio and Mississippi Rivers to reach Middle America, where, the New Englander speculated, the architects of the Marietta mounds became the "ancestors of the Mexicans." (He did not think the modern Indians he knew capable of such sophisticated engineering.)

When Putnam first encountered the "Marietta Works" in their long-undisturbed state, he found exposed human bones on top of the Adena mound. His journal notes that these were reinterred. One of his colleagues in the meantime carried out an early example of dendrochronology in the United States by felling a tree that had grown on the top of one of the Hopewell mounds and counting the growth rings at more than four hundred. This action, in accordance with the instructions of the company that "a number of the largest and oldest trees be cut down, in order to count the rings," archaeologist Wesley Clarke describes "as one of the earliest attempts at absolute dating in the New World."[12] If we follow this lead, the Hopewell settlement at Marietta might be dated at about A.D. 1390.

Although the Ohio Company arrived in a spot at that time unoccupied by the historic peoples, to the north and west lay villages whose founders had sought refuge in Ohio during the previous half century. About ninety miles north of Marietta along the upper Muskingum River lay the villages of the Delawares who had abandoned their eastern ancestral homelands in search of richer, safer hunting, farming, and dwelling sites. Some miles northeast of the new Delaware villages, clusters of western Iroquois longhouses had spilled out of the Seneca country as their builders tried to escape many of the same pressures driving the Delaware westward. Northwest from the Delaware towns the Great Trail led across the lake plains toward the country of the Wyandots, whose Huron ancestors had fled the epidemics and wars of seventeenth-century Huronia to find refuge near the western end of Lake Erie. Present-day northwestern Ohio was also home to Ottawa and Miami peoples living at various points along the Maumee and its tributaries. Southward almost to the Ohio River, a venturesome traveler would have found the fields and towns of the Shawnees, whose movements east of the Mississippi River from the Schuylkill to the Savannah from 1650 to 1750 challenge even the most imaginative historical geographer following their migrations.

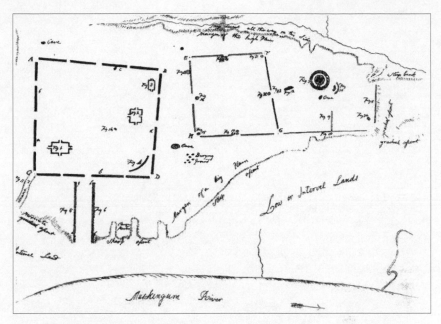

Rufus Putnam's map of the mounds at Marietta, 1788. Courtesy of the Ohio Historical Society.

The story of native peoples in Ohio is both familiar and unfamiliar to the casual and the scholarly reader alike. It is familiar because the nineteenth-century myth of ancient mound-building peoples unrelated to the historic tribes attracted the attention of the public. This intense lay interest generated the production of the first published maps tracing many of the ceremonial complexes across the state. One was the famous Squier and Davis work that recorded the location, dimensions, and topography of these features as they had survived into the early decades of the century.[13] These authors perpetuated the original militaristic interpretation by labeling the features "works." Unfortunately for modern scholarship, their observations of the "ancient monuments" would come too late to record certain aspects of the structures that had stood in the way of developing cities. At Marietta, for example, parallel earthen walls had flanked a pathway from the Muskingum River to an enclosed area in which more low walls delineated a ceremonial center. These low walls and mounds intersected the checkerboard of streets laid out by the builders of early Marietta. The earthen borrow in these structures was primarily relatively soft material

Delaware settlements drifting westward into Ohio. From Clifford A. Weslager, *The Delaware Indian Westward Migration with the Texts of Two Manuscripts (1821–22) Responding to General Lewis Cass's Inquiries about Lenape Culture and Language* (Wallingford, Pennsylvania: The Middle Atlantic Press, 1978), 25.

that could easily be put to other uses. It was no small task—whether for their original builders or for the renovators intent on reconstructing a New England town on the banks of the Ohio and Muskingum Rivers—to relocate the amount of soil (approximately two tons per linear foot) in these two walls that ran the equivalent of three city blocks. Part of the fill went into the making of European-style bricks in an early Marietta brickyard, according to local tradition.

Readers should bear in mind, of course, that what has been written about Adena, Hopewell, and Fort Ancient peoples is based largely on informed conjecture. There are no eyewitnesses to those cultures, so the only evidence we have for analyzing them is what they left behind. We have no contemporary source for the precise usage of any artifact. Think of how will we be judged by our garbage two thousand years from now. If those who uncover our civilization do not comprehend our language, how will they assess us? Picking through the middens of our cultures, they may begin to find scattered bits of a shiny, yellowish material. As they extract more fragments, they may piece them together until they begin to resemble an arch. Clearly these were associated with structures of religious significance, future scientists will conclude, because there seem to have been so many of them, located at important cultural intersections. Though they were not physically enormous, all roads led to them, and large, flat areas striped

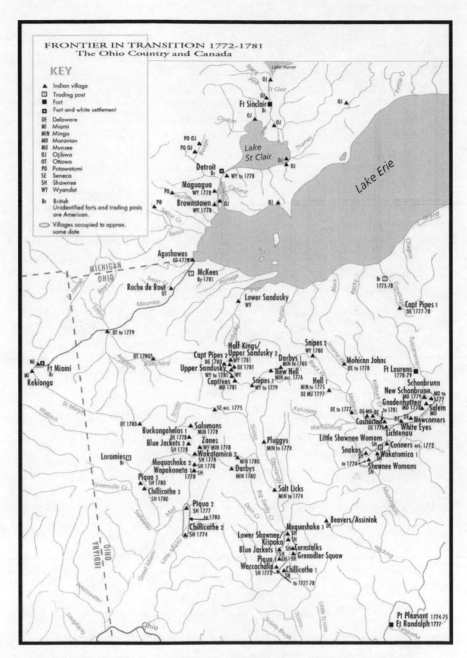

The Ohio frontier, 1772–81. Based on Helen Hornbeck Tanner, ed., *Atlas of Great Lakes Indian History* (Norman: University of Oklahoma Press, 1987), 80.

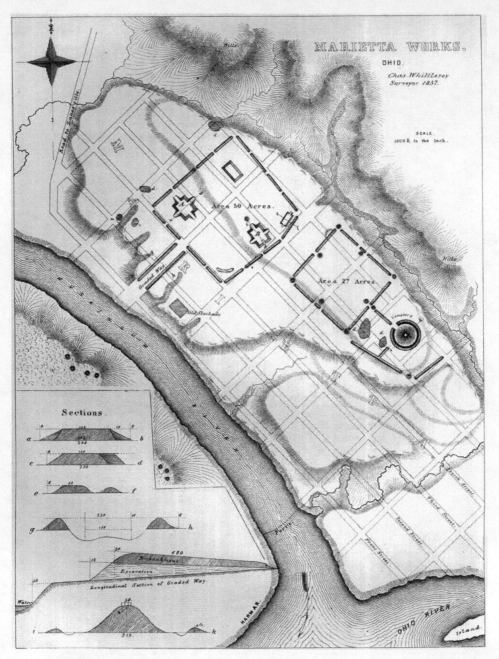

Charles Whittlesey's plan of the Marietta earthworks, 1837. Courtesy of the Ohio Historical Society.

for ceremonies surrounded them. Inside the worship centers there seem to have been ritual fires and altars. No doubt the archaeologists from another galaxy will dub us the "Golden Arches" people!

There is no modern treatment of all the native peoples of Ohio from arrival to removal. Certain groups or periods have received attention. Robert Silverberg's work of 1968 traces what he terms the "archaeology of a myth," in which eighteenth- and nineteenth-century observers concluded that a mysterious race had come to construct the mounds and then had disappeared. The disappearance thesis rested on the assumption that the Native American peoples present at the time Ohio was settled were incapable of such efforts and organization. Worse yet, writes Silverberg, the mythmakers hypothesized that the builders "had been exterminated at some past date by the despicable, treacherous, ignorant red-skinned savages."[14] Randolph Downes, on the other hand, focused his attention on the middle eighteenth century in his 1940 *Council Fires on the Upper Ohio*. Written from the historical perspective of the 1930s, his work is concerned more with the interface of war and less with the culture of the Native Americans. Credit should be given to him, however, simply for writing about the Native Americans at a time when that was not a fashionable research topic. More recently, attention has been given to specific tribes in the works by James Howard on the Shawnees and C. A. Weslager on the Delawares. Two highly romanticized figures who played major roles in Ohio's Indian past were Tecumseh and his brother, the Shawnee Prophet. R. David Edmunds has written the most plausible accounts of their lives in separate works on each. Not to be depended upon for factual accuracy is the romanticized story of Tecumseh by the fiction writer Allan Eckert.[15]

In the twentieth century, archaeologists have generated much of the scholarship about Native Americans in Ohio. Among the more recent works is William F. Romain, *Mysteries of the Hopewell: Astronomers, Geometers, and Magicians of the Eastern Woodlands* (2000). Also published that year was *Cultures before Contact: The Late Prehistory of Ohio and Surrounding Regions,* edited by Robert A. Genheimer. The latter is another of the useful collections published from time to time by the Ohio Archaeological Council. Similarly helpful are *A View from the Core: A Synthesis of Ohio Hopewell Archaeology,* edited by Paul J. Pacheco in 1996, and *Ohio Hopewell Community Organization,* edited by Pacheco and William S. Dancey in 1997.

Although Ohio celebrated two hundred years of statehood within the United States in 2003, it was a home to native peoples far longer than that. Unquestionably the historic tribes have been absent from Ohio for more than 150 years, but they and their predecessors had inhabited its hills and valleys for many centuries. Who were these people who lived across Ohio for so many centuries but are no more? We have called them many names over the years, but as we remember them in our bicentennial celebration we should not forget their basic identity simply as human beings. Perhaps it is not too farfetched to see them as caught up, like us, in a hierarchy of needs. If we borrow the ideas of psychologist Abraham Maslow, we might conclude that native peoples' first needs, like ours, were physical—food, clothing, and shelter.[16] Secondly, Native Americans most likely sought safety and security in order to protect themselves and their families. Also important would be what Maslow termed "Love/Belonging," which would be categorized for Native Americans as the family and clan into which they were born and the village where they lived. The intensity of their grieving, the rituals of condolence, the presence of grave goods, and the extensive mortuary remains reflect this emotion. Esteem and recognition too were matters of concern, as symbols found on clothing and goods indicate. Although it may be harder to document self-actualization among Native Americans, there is evidence that this too was a concern for them. The two speeches incorporated into this book, the first by Logan in 1774 and the second by Captain Pipe in 1781, anticipate many of the concepts we would include in self-actualization.

My purpose in this volume is to remind contemporary Ohioans of those who lived here before. Native peoples' assistance was instrumental to European settlers in finding the high ground for trails that highways still follow, cultivating soils that farmers still plant, and harvesting some of the plants that still feed us. The following chapters will pursue the story of the Native American presence in Ohio from the time of their settlement until their expulsion. Like citizens of the state today, the first Ohioans sought only homes for themselves and their families. We can never in any real sense recover this past, but we can gather the evidence and the stories to acknowledge that there was such a past. If the past is indeed prologue, then we will all be better for knowing that there was an Ohio Indian past.

The chapters tracing this past are organized chronologically, beginning with the pre–European contact Adena, Hopewell, and Fort Ancient peoples, followed by the story of the next wave of inhabitants (Delawares, Shawnees, and Wyandots), who came in the early eighteenth century. The last and longest part of the narrative will focus on the experiences of the historic tribes as they tried to meet their needs in the face of the tsunami of newcomers who would not tolerate their continued presence. Despite the fact that the Native American groups used only a relatively small portion of the land, they were assumed to be in the way of the state's growth. No matter what kind of face one put on it, it was simply a matter of European ethnocentrism. Both Logan (c. 1725–80) and Captain Pipe (c. 1725–94) realized that the difference was about color; as Captain Pipe said, the whites could not "love a People differing in Colour to that of [theirs], more than those . . . who have a white Skin like unto that of [theirs]."[17] Thus much of what unfolds is about war, in a sense one long armed conflict that lasted from the 1750s until the 1790s, followed by a brief intermission, and then the finale with the death of Tecumseh, the last great Native American leader from Ohio, in the War of 1812. The closing chapter of the story will trace the removal of the remaining tribes from Ohio, with the last groups leaving in 1843, forty years after the achievement of statehood. As we celebrate the anniversary of the state's founding, we would be wise also to remember those who walked here before, those whose love and knowledge of this land enriched us then and still does so today.

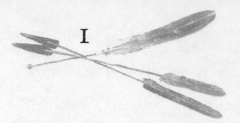

I

PEOPLES OF "INGENUITY, INDUSTRY, AND ELEGANCE"

WHEN THE FIRST PARTY OF SETTLERS FROM THE NEW UNITED STATES arrived at the confluence of the Ohio and Muskingum Rivers in 1788, they entered, to use the late Francis Jennings's metaphor, widowed land.[1] It was evident to Rufus Putnam, one of their leaders and an experienced western traveler, that the lands they had sought had been used before. Lying before them like some ghost city were the large, walled enclosures, encompassing on the one hand the flat-topped mounds built during a period of occupancy that modern archaeologists have labeled Hopewellian (100 B.C. to A.D. 400), and on the other a cone-shaped mound identified with the ceremonial complexes of the Adena (500 B.C. to A.D. 100). Putnam's military mind led him to conclude that these were all part of one complex, remnants of some ancient fortification, which he elaborately mapped and described.[2]

The "ancient works" at Marietta so impressed the self-taught surveyor and engineer that he dubbed their creators people of "ingenuity, industry, and elegance."[3] On September 6, 1788, Putnam and other directors of the Ohio Company measured and examined the elaborate Marietta earthworks. Given Rufus Putnam's relatively recent service under General

Washington during the American Revolution, it is not surprising that he interpreted the expanse of substantial earthen walls as military fortification: "Every person who sees them must be fully convinced" that they were "undoubtedly connected for Defence."[4]

Although he saw the earthworks as defensive in nature, Putnam did not lose his sense of awe at the accomplishments of their builders. The two mounds in the "Great Square," on which no doubt "once stood some spacious public buildings" were "as level on top as a mosaic pavement." In his military imagination, "the Chasms or opening in the walls" may have served at times as gateways, but, Putnam argued, were supplied "with wooden works" for repelling the enemy in time of attack.[5]

Despite his militaristic perspective, Rufus Putnam acknowledged the aesthetic accomplishments of Marietta's ancient citizens. He compared the gradual ascent to the tops of the two largest mounds, designated "Quadranaou" and "Capitolium" by the newcomers, to a beautiful flight of steps in the yard at the governor's house in Massachusetts. "Nor is the gravel walk of the Boston Mall more regular and uniform then [sic] what we call the covered way an [sic] passage from the Muskingum." "Nor is the Bowling Green in New York a more regular ellipsis than the Base of the Great Mound . . . with its Ditch and parapet are regular circles." Putnam's measurements of the "covered way" made it even more impressive.[6] The 231-foot-wide walkway began near the bank of the Muskingum River. An arriving visitor immediately was confronted by the perspective of a great roofless hall or corridor framed by parallel earthen walls rising twenty-six feet high from a forty-two-foot-wide base. Following the hallway uphill, the visitor would gradually ascend from the river toward an exit where the walls were only eight feet high. The "spacious and butifull" passage was so well designed that on the outside it was never more than five feet high. From the end of the passageway the traveler would pass into the Great Square through openings in a wall of earth standing from three to five feet high that was about twenty feet wide at the base. Putnam was aware that the builders had chosen a site well above likely flooding, for, as he noted, the drop from the tableland to either the Ohio or the Muskingum was forty feet.[7] In a sense the Hopewellian engineers had chosen the natural equivalent of a raised platform upon which to construct their own raised platforms. Perhaps credit should be given to their Adena ancestors, who had already used the site for a thirty-foot-tall cone-shaped mound. Some geologists, on the other hand, have argued that the Adena-Hopewell were using the top of an ancient island created and confirmed by the emerging Muskingum River during the period of glacial melting.[8]

What Rufus Putnam described in great detail, and what other travelers noted also, modern scholars have identified as a cluster of "centrally located public works . . . at the intersection of physiographic provinces."[9] At the confluence of the Muskingum and Ohio Rivers generations of Native American inhabitants had left vestiges of multigenerational, multicomponent usage. Although Putnam and succeeding generations of antiquarians speculated about what these structures were and about the identity of the so-called Moundbuilders, these late arrivals actually had encountered a sequentially constructed cluster of ceremonial centers. The first probably was located there by the peoples identified as the Adena, who shaped the thirty-foot-high mound and its adjoining sacred area of perhaps thirty acres. Then, only a short distance to the northwest, Hopewellian celebrants had demarcated the larger tract of about fifty acres enclosing three flat-topped mounds connected to the river by a dramatic earthen cloister.

Putnam and others examined the cone-shaped mound on Saturday, September 6, 1788. When the party reached the top of the artificial hill, they discovered a partly uncovered burial at the top. Putnam indicates that they covered the bones and removed nothing. A later visitor claimed that these were the "bones of an adult in a horizontal position, covered with a flat stone. . . . That this venerable monument might not be defaced, the opening was closed without further search."[10] Since the mound was clearly a place of burial, the city of Marietta reserved a block around it as a local cemetery, thus guaranteeing that it would not be destroyed in the construction of the city.

The Adena legacy thus has been forwarded into the twenty-first century in the continued existence of this tumulus that probably began as a single burial of an Adena citizen, perhaps a village leader, shaman, or beloved child. If the ceremonialism of the Adena mortuary cult was followed, other graves were added later with accompanying layers of earth. The mound's dimensions are drawn from Rufus Putnam's measurements described in his "Plan . . . 1788." The measurements are keyed to an accompanying map. On Putnam's map, "Figure 25 is a mound of Earth whose base forms a regular circle 115 feet diameter and its altitude 30 feet. . . . Figure 26 is a level space of 33 feet between the mound and ditch. . . . Figure 27 a ditch 15 feet wide and 4 feet deep. . . . Figure 28 a wall or bank of earth 4 feet high, whose circumference is 45.9 perch [a surveying unit equal to 16.5 feet, thus 757.35 feet would be the circumference] and its base 15 feet." Rufus Putnam has effectively delineated what archaeologists would term a "sacred enclosure" ringing the mound of earth. Thanks to the surrounding modern cemetery, the "Conus" at Marietta still stands, in its shape resembling nothing so much as an old-fashioned manual juicer, save that the rim would have to be much wider to be in proportion to the measurements left by Putnam.

Other Adena mounds that have been excavated have contained multiple burials—some may have been simple single burials joined to make a larger mound; others were built in layers. Within the individual interments the graves varied, apparently depending on the particular time and practice; some were lined with bark and some with logs. Many had evidence of the use of red ocher, on either the corpse or the bones; sometimes pieces of the ocher were in the grave itself. Other grave goods included articles of flint, copper, and stone. Mica was also a treasured object found in graves; one visitor to Marietta described the unearthing of a burial of a "male figure buried in the extended position, lying east and west with a quantity of isinglas [sic; mica] on his breast."[11] Many of the graves contained effigy pipes of stone, usually resembling animals, birds, and fish; one of the most dramatic was a full figure of a human excavated from the Adena mound in Ross County, Ohio.[12]

The Adena mound at Marietta, like others across the region, is believed to have been a center for the increasingly elaborate mortuary practices of those who built it. The builders of this structure came to the site for a single purpose, to bury their dead according to the dictates of their culture. Their daily lives were lived in scattered hamlets of perhaps twelve families that spent their time hunting and gathering the necessities of life. As their lives became increasingly ritualized, the families of these hamlets co-operated in the construction of the mortuary centers, often located near a stream or at the confluence of streams, such as the Muskingum and the Ohio. Homes were built on bottomland, where of course the soil was better for harvesting the plants these people used, and were at an easy travel distance to the mortuary site but not adjacent to it. The Adena's concepts of life and death may have been changing, as indicated by the more elaborate types of grave goods. This of course was building on some patterns already established by such late Archaic groups as the Red Ocher and Glacial Kame peoples.[13] Because Adena culture tends to be eclipsed by its more elaborate successor, known as Hopewell, Don W. Dragoo reminds us in his basic work that "the Adena Peoples . . . in the Ohio Valley developed the first extensive burial cult, built the first substantial homes, made some of the first ceramics, and practiced agriculture."[14]

Although Dragoo refers to Adena agriculture in his classic study, his attention is devoted mainly to physical artifacts recovered from burials. The most recent investigation of the botanical remains has been carried out by the paleoethnobotanist Dee Anne Wymer. In her examinations of archaeobotanical remains covering a period of some two thousand years, beginning about 600 B.C., she has identified many of the foods used by the Adena. Her research has uncovered the presence of nuts, fruits, berries, and seeds gathered by these people. In addition she has found evidence of the "members of the Eastern Agricultural Complex" at all the sites she examined.[15] These include maygrass (*Phalaris caroliniana*), goosefoot (*Chenopodium sp.*), erect knotweed (*Polygonum erectum*), little barley (*Hordeum pussillum*), sumpweed (*Iva annua* var. *macrocarpa*), and sunflower (*Helianthus annuus*). On the basis of her research, Wymer argues that there was "a complex interaction of the prehistoric population with their environment."[16] She reminds modern observers that "we are dealing with a human-manipulated and dominated ecosystem, an ecosystem that was in some ways independent of the specific environment parameters of each site. In other words, the use of what must have been a complex schedule of in-use, recently abandoned, and older garden plots affected the environment in similar ways, regardless [of where] the community was located."[17] Modern students of the Native American experience should note that maize is absent from the majority of sites, with only a few specimens recovered from the mid–Ohio Valley sites examined by Wymer.[18]

Adena peoples were not bound to their living areas; the nonlocal goods left in the graves clearly indicate extensive trade carried on throughout eastern North America. Trade goods moved throughout a regional network of trading paths that had evolved over many generations, so that northern copper, southern shells and feathers, and even western grizzly bear teeth circulated freely. Some of these goods were carried by tribal diplomats as they journeyed from place to place, while others no doubt were transported by those we might call traders, whose importance allowed them to travel with relative ease, much as the Iroquois diplomats did in later centuries.

TOWARD THE END of the Adena period an even more elaborate mortuary ritual began to emerge, one that built on Adena foundations and extended them. This marked the beginning of the Hopewellian period. Most of the well-known mound sites in Ohio today are Hopewellian, like those at Marietta, Newark, and Mound City. At these and many other sites across Ohio, extensive constructions were completed, resulting in walled enclosures and mounds, often built in, near, or on sites already consecrated by Adena mortuary practices. Again, these are believed to have been ceremonial centers rather than living centers. The structures at Marietta had been abandoned for perhaps fourteen hundred years when Rufus Putnam encountered them in 1788. Their size and obvious importance—it would have taken a huge commitment of time, effort, and materials to build them —led Putnam, former military officer that he was, to conclude that they had a military significance.

Modern scholars, however, have offered other interpretations for the purposes of these earthworks. Influenced by twentieth-century archaeoastronomers, a number of recent interpreters have argued that the earthworks are astronomical observatories. William Romain, for example, has proposed an elaborate system of measuring the mounds to determine whether they were used for this purpose. He hypothesizes that the two remaining large flat-topped mounds in Marietta have axes closely aligned to the position of the sun at the winter solstice. The associated sacred way or covered way, named Sacra Via by the town's settlers, which leads from the Marietta Large Square to the Muskingum River, points toward the sunset at the winter solstice.[19] Twenty years ago the team of astronomer Ray Hively and philosopher Robert Horn examined the Newark works for evidence of Hopewellian astronomy. What they found was that the construction was measured with precise care, so much so that the diameter of the structure called the Observatory Circle became the basis of measurement for building other features of the Newark works. It was also the standard measurement unit for the similar circle and octagon known as the High Bank works at Chillicothe. Archaeoastronomers speculate that both of these structures were used for sightings of moonrise points throughout the 18.6-year lunar cycle. High Banks also can be used for observing sunrise and sunset during the summer and winter solstices.

Also in recent years archaeologist Brad Lepper of the Ohio Historical Society has posited the presence of a Great Hopewell Road running arrowstraight some sixty miles cross-country from Newark to Chillicothe, in Hopewell days from the astronomical observatory at Newark to the similar one at Chillicothe. If these were people for whom the movements of the

heavenly bodies were life-promising, the completion of two similar observatories might have helped confirm their beliefs. The road that Lepper hypothesizes would have been useful not only for astronomer priests traveling
back and forth but also for pilgrims coming from afar to this site of powerful culture. Since one of the great north-south trails followed the course of
the Scioto through south-central Ohio, visitors from the south could easily
reach the Hopewell complex on the Scioto and follow the pilgrim's path
northeastward to the Great Circle and Octagon near the present Newark.[20]
"Based on several interwoven lines of evidence, including . . . paleoenvi-
ronmental reconstructions, archaeoastronomy, and ethnographic as well
as archaeological analogy," Lepper concludes that

> the Great Hopewell Road was a virtually straight set of parallel walls 60 m
> apart and extending a distance of 90 km from the Newark Earthworks to
> the cluster of earthworks in the Scioto Valley centered at modern Chilli-
> cothe. Near its terminus at Newark, the walls were nearly 1 m in height.
> They may have been somewhat reduced in size, and hence more ephemeral,
> at increasing distances from the termini. This roadway was designed and
> laid out with great care and with intimate familiarity of the intervening
> landscape. The function of the Great Hopewell Road is unknown, but
> similar structures built by the Maya were monumental expressions of
> politico-religious connections between centers.[21]

The generally accepted view today is that all these great earthen structures were the creation of a Middle Woodland people who influenced a
wide area of eastern North America between 200 B.C. and A.D. 400. The
two areas of greatest concentration were in Ohio and Illinois. The name
itself, "Hopewell," was taken from the name of a farm in Ross County,
Ohio. The so-called Hopewell culture was marked by large numbers of dis-
tinctive mounds, by elaborate mortuary customs, and by a far-flung exchange network. Because scholars are dependent for information on what
the culture left behind, there are many aspects of Hopewell daily life that
remain a mystery.

The most impressive accomplishment of these peoples still comprehen-
sible in the twenty-first century is their earthworks. The simple physical accomplishment is staggering. In 1875 the state's geologist, Ebenezer Baldwin
Andrews, examined several mounds near Athens, Ohio. Since Andrews
grew up before the age of power equipment, he appreciated manpower.

By his estimate one of the mounds he examined contained approximately 437,742 cubic feet of dirt. His analysis of the mound and of others nearby led him to conclude the fill was dumped in loads of about a peck (eight quarts in dry measure), meaning it would have taken 1,405,152 basketloads of material to build the mound.[22] Even if the borrow pit was nearby, the number of hours required to build this probably would have exceeded 281,000.

The exotic trade goods left behind by the Hopewell reflect a far-flung zone of connectivity that implies an exchange network of both goods and ideas. Such activity seems far more complicated than Europeans who created the mythology of the "Moundbuilders" could have imagined. The South provided shells as well as shark and alligator teeth; the Appalachians yielded mica, chlorite, and quartz crystal; Great Lakes mining produced copper and silver; and the Missouri River country forwarded galena, pipestone, flint, grizzly bear teeth, obsidian, and chalcedony flint. One puzzle in this interchange concerns whether anything was traded for these incoming goods. To date no large caches of Flint Ridge flint have been found at the ends of the routes. It is Brad Lepper's interpretation, derived from his Great Hopewell Road thesis, that pilgrims brought in the exotic goods and took away nothing tangible, perhaps only a deepened spirituality.[23]

The earthworks and exotic goods are impressive, but Hopewell peoples also left traces of the ways in which they reaped a harvest from their natural surroundings. As paleoethnobotanist Dee Anne Wymer explains, the Ohio Hopewell sites have yielded "carbonized seeds and often curcurbit rind . . . in high densities."[24] Also recovered and identified were nut types including hickory, black walnut, butternut, acorn, and hazelnut, along with fruits and berries such as sumac, raspberry, elderberry, honey locust, and grapes. In addition, her investigations found that the largest number of seeds were cultigens such as maygrass, erect knotweed, and goosefoot; present in lesser numbers were marsh elder and sunflower. It is Wymer's thesis that the Hopewell took full advantage of local resources, cultivated others, and managed to provide sufficient materials for their diets. To date the amount of Hopewell maize recovered is relatively small; at this point it seems likely that maize still played a largely ceremonial role. Concluding that the charcoal from any given site reflects the availability of local forests, Wymer has found at the second century A.D. habitation called the Murphy site in the Licking River valley near Newark evidence of an oak-hickory forest, while at the Marietta Capitolium site the remains suggest a beech–sugar maple forest, as well as stands of sycamore, elm, and ash.[25] In drawing comparisons between habitation locales and ceremonial ones like the Capitolium, Wymer is impressed by the apparently extensive variety of wood types found during the excavation of the latter. It was quite striking to her that there was evidence from the forests of the river terrace (beech and sugar maple) where the mound stands as well as from species native to the lower topography (sycamore, elm, and ash) along the nearby river, not to mention samples from upland natives like oak, hickory, and chestnut. To complete this unique assemblage was the evidence of southern yellow pine. Wymer concludes: "It seems likely, therefore, that . . . species from a wide variety of environments had been deliberately collected and utilized during as yet unspecified ceremonial activities associated with construction and utilization of the Capitolium Mound."[26] As Wymer has analyzed life among the Hopewell, whether they were engaged in the routine of daily survival or constructing ceremonial centers, she envisions them living within the environment of a series of relatively dense forests, with their dwellings part of "dispersed hamlets" ancillary to ceremonial centers; within this larger framework of forest also would be found the Hopewell garden patches, their "abandoned plots" from earlier cultivation, and "secondary forest regrowth in older cleared areas" abandoned generations earlier.[27]

Still a matter of debate among archaeologists is the nature of Ohio Hopewell settlement patterns. The current discussion goes back to the 1960s, when Olaf Prufer borrowed the so-called vacant center model from Meso-American archaeology to describe Hopewell.[28] He did so because ongoing work at the large earthwork and mortuary complexes, some of which stretched back into the nineteenth century, indicated an absence of habitation sites within the immediate environs of the earthworks. It was thought that the ceremonial centers were "vacant," that is, they were used by large gatherings of individuals who then returned to their homes in outlying areas. Although there has been much discussion of this idea during the last four decades, it still seems to hold a degree of validity. In a slight modification suggested by Paul Pacheco, Ohio Hopewell settlements are commonly referred to as hamlets, defined as sedentary, identifiable locales where a cluster of individuals lived and worked. The inhabitants practiced gathering, gardening, and hunting; provided themselves shelter, food,

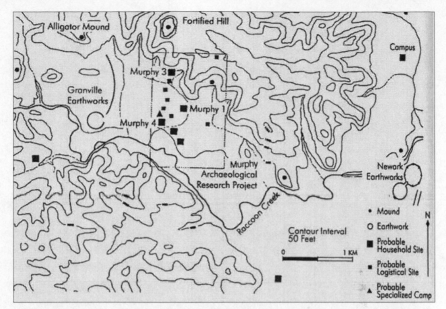

Granville subregion, showing known Hopewell sites and all known mounds and earthworks. From Paul J. Pacheco, ed., *A View from the Core: A Synthesis of Ohio Hopewell Archaeology* (Columbus: The Ohio Archaeological Council, 1996), 24. Reprinted by permission of the Ohio Archaeological Council. Copyright © 1996.

and clothing; and participated in ritual activity. The kind of dispersed hamlets adjacent to a ritual center are well illustrated in Pacheco's map of the Upper Licking River drainage, putting the habitations relatively close to the great ceremonial earthwork at present-day Newark.[29]

LIFE FOR THE peoples of Ohio has always depended in large part on the sources and abundance of food supply, whether mastodons, mayflower, or maize. Populations at any given point in time rose and fell in connection with the availability of dietary mainstays. A dramatic shift occurred at some point early in the tenth century, when the number of domesticated cultigens was expanded by the emergence of maize. Small garden patches, perhaps within still relatively dense forest, gave way to what scholars define as "field agriculture," in which numbers of villagers plant and harvest maize. Because this foodstuff was much more dependable and nutritious than were items like maygrass and chenopodium, villages had better dietary resources and eventually could support more people in residence. It may also have improved health and increased life expectancy. Given the apparent abandonment of Hopewellian ceremonial centers, the new form of agriculture may also have accompanied a shift in beliefs and practices. Archaeological scholars working on sites from this evolving culture in southwestern Ohio have called it Fort Ancient. From about the eleventh to the late seventeenth century, concludes a 2001 synthesis of archaeological scholarship, "Fort Ancient people developed and sustained a way of life characterized by maize horticulture, nucleated villages, nonhierarchical settlement patterns, a social organization with a single level of achieved authority, and significant interregional interaction."[30]

The introduction of maize had several results, the most important being its dominance as a dietary staple and its ultimate displacement of all earlier plants except the sunflower.[31] According to students of paleoethnobotany, this eastern eight-row maize, or northern flint, became widespread not only because of its caloric importance but also because of its hardiness as a plant, its ability to provide seed for the next season, and the possibility of storing the grain for use months after harvest. Still open to question is whether this more cold-tolerant variety was introduced from outside or whether Hopewellian maize was hybridized into a more tolerant successor.

As important as maize was, Fort Ancient peoples also cultivated beans, squash, tobacco, and sunflower and gathered fruits and nuts according to the season. The increasing dependence of these peoples on planted foodstuffs—maize in particular—meant that villages tended to be located in the rich bottomlands beside streams, where centuries of rising and falling water during periodic flooding had deposited rich layers of fertile sediment. Today's farmers, whose bottomland fields of modern corn are the successors of the Fort Ancient's, still reap the rewards of these flooding patterns. Thus the Ohio and its tributary streams would have been most inviting to Fort Ancient settlers. Penelope Drooker and Wesley Cowan point out, by the way, that there was an expansion of Fort Ancient settlements almost to the "hydrological divides" of the Ohio system in the fourteenth century, but an apparent climatic cooling in the fifteenth century caused a withdrawal to areas within twenty kilometers of the Ohio.[32]

Animal resources for these settlements included deer, elk, bear, and turkey. Late in the Fort Ancient period the villages on Blennerhassett Island

Ohio's First Peoples

in the Ohio River, near present-day Belpre, Ohio, relied so heavily on the island's resident herd that more than 80 percent of the faunal remains were from deer.[33] For the larger Fort Ancient area, however, deer was not the dominant faunal resource. On the western edge of the Fort Ancient development area, at the Madisonville site, there is evidence of bison usage.[34] Other small game was used at each locale according to availability and season.

The nucleated Fort Ancient villages were organized around central plazas where ceremonial activities were carried out. As the settlements developed, the dwellings tended to be single-family structures, often accompanied by maize storage pits—clear evidence of the way food supply procurement patterns had changed as northern flint corn flourished. One carefully examined site yielded a storage feature with every household. At the most completely excavated of the Early-Middle Fort Ancient sites, the Incinerator or SunWatch site near Dayton, archaeologists have speculated that the posthole patterns suggest the possible existence of observatories for tracking solar occurrences. That same locale also has indications of sweathouse constructions located adjacent to dwellings.[35]

If the communal ceremonialism of the Hopewell peoples (and perhaps the Adena) changed into the village-specific activities of the Fort Ancient settlements, so, too, did mortuary practices. Burials in Fort Ancient villages varied, with some interments in mounds near the plaza and others in graves either at the edge of the plaza or near houses. Grave goods included ornaments, tools, and pipes. Ornamentation on pipe bowls incorporated peering lizards perched on the edge; a particularly striking grave object from Neale's Landing is a roosting vulture pipe left among the grave goods in the burial of a three-year-old child.[36] The presence of exotic grave goods in the graves of children and infants, such as the "engraved deer tibia" found in one child's grave, may "have correlations with wealth indicators."[37] Some scholars have concluded that the introduction across the Fort Ancient culture of certain types of ornamentation, like the perching lizards and other creatures, reflects the possibility of relatively widespread visiting or intermarriage by women, since they are believed to have been the settlements' potters.[38] Similarly, the frequency in occurrence of pipe bowls could mark the prevalence of "intergroup greeting ceremonies."[39] At Madisonville, Drooker found that certain adult males "were buried with pipes of foreign materials and styles"; it is possible that these individuals "might well have been directly involved in external interaction, functioning in a capacity of secular leadership."[40]

Of similar nature are the so-called medicine bags identified with "teenagers and adult males . . . [who have been] interpreted as ritual specialists."[41] As Drooker's tables of "Gravegoods with Recognizable Representational Aspects" and "Mortuary Associations of People with Pipes and/or 'Medicine Bags'" indicate, there were no actual physical bags left, because they had deteriorated, but the goods were those items associated with shamanistic activity, such as bird and animal skulls, claws, beads, pipes, worked horn items, and a "whistle made from a bird bone."[42] The whistle was found interred with "three long-billed bird skulls [and] copper-stained animal or bird bones" in the grave of an older adult.[43] Other adult males were interred not only with "medicine bags" but also with such items as pots, pipes, "copper covered wooden objects," and "a large, double barred copper pendant, an emblem badge with supralocal associations."[44] One particularly powerful person was buried not only with a medicine bag and pipe but also with "carefully arranged human bones."[45] The concentration of these items suggests the individual was involved in some kind of leadership activity. Such items also may have indicated status, as reflected by the worked section of a pelican's bill found in a grave on Blennerhassett Island.[46] At the same time, however, Drooker found "virtually no indicators of wealth or high status."[47] The spatial distribution of structures around a plaza in the Fort Ancient villages seems to indicate a lack of hierarchy.

Coeval with the more familiar Fort Ancient settlements (eleventh century to late seventeenth century) were the locales in northeastern Ohio (from Lakewood to Painesville on a modern Ohio map) that have come to be designated Whittlesey tradition, after Charles Whittlesey, the first surveyor general of the state of Ohio. In the tradition of his contemporaries in the early statehood of Ohio, Whittlesey described some of these sites as "fortified villages."[48] Twentieth-century archaeologists working with these locations have found them to be year-round agricultural villages with alluvial bottomland fields of maize, beans, squash, and tobacco. Faunal resources included whitetail deer, elk, and black bear, but apparently no bison. Nearby streams added a variety of fish. Dwellings at the South Park site included elongated houses with from one to three hearths, accompanied by nearby smudge pits, cache pits, large storage pits, and sweat

Ohio's First Peoples

lodges.[49] It is striking to modern researchers that to date investigators have found no "direct or indirect evidence of European contact," even at the South Park site on the Cuyahoga River, which was in relatively close proximity to Lake Erie and, one would think, early European explorers and traders.[50] The decline of the Whittlesey tradition apparently resulted from changes in the length of the growing season—perhaps due to a period of environmental cooling in that area of Ohio—that made agriculture less dependable. David Brose has hypothesized that the Whittlesey may have engaged in a "cultural debouchment to the lower Muskingum and the Upper Ohio."[51]

In the thirteenth century, development was marked in the central Muskingum Valley by a number of Fort Ancient "agriculturalists living in nucleated villages along the central portion of the Muskingum Valley."[52] Specifically, these peoples are identified by Carskadden and Morton as the "Fort Ancient Philo Phase."[53] From the banks of the Tuscarawas and Walhonding streams that join to form the Muskingum River, downstream to the confluence with the Ohio, there are twenty-three known Late Prehistoric and Protohistoric sites in the valley. It is the opinion of Carskadden and Morton that the Fort Ancient populations in the Muskingum Valley had moved upstream from the Ohio River as a result of population pressure in the second half of the thirteenth century. During their residence in the valley, these Fort Ancient villagers often relocated their villages, probably along lineage lines because of increasing numbers, but they never moved more than two kilometers. Over time there was a small amount of exchange with the outside world, indicated by the presence of a Madisonville vessel with a salamander motif, a Mississippian water bottle, a Monongahela vessel, and some marine shell beads and gorgets.[54] Eventually, for reasons still unclear, all the Fort Ancient sites in the Muskingum Valley were abandoned, leaving the area vacant until the Delawares arrived from the East in about 1743.

2

OHIO SANCTUARY

By the end of the seventeenth century the lands once occupied by the Fort Ancient peoples and their ancestors were largely free of Native American occupancy. To the east and north, however, the ripple effects of colonial expansion, imperial warfare involving the French and the English, and the accompanying rivalry for control of the fur trade were beginning to dislocate native peoples far to the west. Tribes uprooted in these struggles often moved several times as they sought advantageous sites.

Among these migrants were the Wyandots, originally Hurons (from present-day Ontario), driven west by fighting with the Iroquois and lured in the same direction by the hope of finding a location where they could rebuild their villages and agricultural fields and gain a chance of profit from the fur trade. During the latter half of the seventeenth century they had moved frequently in the Upper Great Lakes region, but after the founding of Detroit in 1701, they relocated there in the vicinity of Potawatomi and Ottawa villages near Fort Pontchartrain.[1] From that location they had access to the French nearby for fur trading purposes, proximity to other native peoples, and a convenient location from which to hunt southward into the Ohio country. The primary target of the Indian hunters in Ohio was the Virginia white-tailed deer, game that would provide meat for their diets and a skin that could be traded with the Europeans because of its utility as a soft leather. For a time at least some of the Wyandots actually lived in a village surrounded by a European-style fortification near Detroit; that expedient was abandoned when many moved southward into Ohio.[2] There they built their multifamily longhouses in more normal clusters near streams.

Some decades later the possibility of increasing their portion of the fur trade and weakening the French monopoly precipitated a British venture into the Ohio country that resulted in the construction of a post at Sandusky Bay in 1745. That opportunity for trade, along with some friction with their Ottawa neighbors, would bring the movement of Wyandot peoples into the Sandusky area. The Wyandots hoped to play the rival European traders against each other to receive higher prices for their animal skins and perhaps also to obtain larger portions of the royal largess when the monarchs of England and France contributed their annual presents to the tribes.[3]

On the southern perimeter of modern Ohio, a Delaware leader named Wendocalla had led his followers in 1749 to found a town on the south bank of the Ohio River near the mouth of the Scioto River.[4] When that site directly on the Ohio proved too exposed, Wendocalla's villagers crossed the Ohio and relocated a short distance up the Scioto. Delaware movements westward had been going on even prior to that, as groups of Delawares and associated peoples sought escape from the pressures of dealing with the Europeans. Constant demand for land, treaties concluded through fraud or at least what the Delawares perceived as fraud, dishonest trading practices, recurrent outbreaks of European-introduced diseases, and the basic hatred displayed by the majority of white settlers toward the Native Americans had finally convinced the Delawares that they would have to relocate.

The classic land deal that illustrates Delaware disgust with all such transactions is the infamous Walking Purchase of 1737. In this episode, the representatives of Pennsylvania doubly manipulated the Delawares. First, they browbeat them into confirming an altered version of a treaty with William Penn from 1688; then they engaged in chicanery to extend how far a person could "walk" in a day and a half. They used trained woodsmen walking over a previously cleared path who were backed by a support team with horse loads of provisions. One Indian observer quit in protest,

Gustavus Hesselius's portrait of the Delaware named Lapowinsa [Lappawinzo], showing tattoos, fetish bag, and blanket, 1735. Courtesy of The Historical Society of Pennsylvania Collection, Atwater Kent Museum of Philadelphia.

proclaiming that the whites ran rather than walked. As Lappawinzo, one of the chiefs present at the treaty, described the walk, the whites "no sit down to smoke, no shoot a squirrel, but *lun, lun, lun* all day long."[5] By this device the "walkers" covered sixty miles rather than the twenty-five or thirty it was expected an ordinary person could cover in a day and a half.[6]

Also drifting westward away from their traditional homelands in New York were Seneca and Cayuga peoples from the Iroquois confederacy. By the early 1740s their village at Cuyahoga had attracted the attention of the well-known trader George Croghan, who established a trading post there. The movement of the Iroquoians into Ohio brought the assumption of power on the part of the Iroquois council, but it was largely devoid of any real control.[7] The settlement at Logstown near Pittsburgh became a focal point for trade and diplomacy where there were so-called half kings designated by the Anglo-Iroquois alliance for the sake of convenience. During the middle of the eighteenth century, it was much easier for colonial representatives to negotiate with Tanaghrisson as the Seneca spokesman, Shingas for the Delawares, and Scaroyady for the Shawnees.[8]

Ohio's First Peoples

The Shawnees also were moving or returning to the Ohio country in the eighteenth century. Although some scholars have suggested that their ancestors were the Ohio Fort Ancient peoples, no definitive proof of that has been established. At the beginning of the eighteenth century, Shawnee bands lived with or near the Delawares in Pennsylvania, with or near the Creeks in Alabama, and also in Maryland; one band had lived for a time in Kentucky. As other groups moved into the Ohio country, so did they, some at Logstown for a time, and then, by the late 1730s, others had established Lower Shawnee Town at the mouth of the Scioto River. During the decades from 1740 to 1774, the settlements along the Scioto became the center of Shawnee life, giving rise to the diplomats and warriors who established the tribe as a presence to be reckoned with, certainly until 1795, and to the personages of Tenskwatawa and Tecumseh, who led the tribe until the War of 1812.[9]

By the time the Shawnee people arrived in Ohio, their towns had evolved so that their dwellings were variations on some form of log hut with a bark roof. Since at one time or another during their movements they had been neighbors of the Delawares and the Creeks, their building styles had been somewhat influenced by both. Central to most settlements of any size was a council house constructed of wood. Observers have described these as square in shape with dimensions of sixty feet by sixty feet and even ninety feet by ninety feet, indicating a floor space of thirty-six hundred and eighty-one hundred square feet. The Shawnees' preference for holding meetings within such structures may explain why a twenty-by-sixty-foot council house was constructed at Fort Finney when it was built.[10]

As the Kentucky raiders found during their numerous attacks on the Shawnee towns in the period from 1775 to 1790, fields of corn and other crops surrounded the villages. The attackers usually spent some time cutting or burning the crops in order to deprive the villages of food for the ensuing winter and seed corn for the next year's planting. Once the maize was harvested in late August, those villagers able to travel engaged in the winter hunt to gain meat for subsistence and pelts for trade. Much of a town's ritual and economic activity was disturbed during periods of intense warfare.

About a dozen years after the establishment of Wendocalla's village, the Delawares also established French Margaret's Town and Maguck in south-central Ohio.[11] Also in the 1750s, Shingas left Pennsylvania to begin a village on the Tuscarawas River near the present-day Bolivar, Ohio, that would come to be known as Beaver's Town, named after Shingas's brother, once authority passed to him.[12]

Even though all those who now peopled Ohio were emigrants fleeing European expansion, they could not, perhaps would not, exist without the manufactured goods that had become daily necessities of life. A visitor to one of these new villages in Ohio immediately would be struck by the presence of trade goods. Clothing, weapons, tools, jewelry, horses, tobacco, and most pernicious of all, rum clearly indicated that trade was the engine of life. Leaders like Netawatwees had adopted nearly European housing forms; his house at Newcomer's Town had "a shingled roof, wood floors, staircase, and stone chimney."[13]

Although the plush carpet of fur from the beaver was the prize pelt in the profitable business of the frontier, deerskins too were a prized commodity in the exchange with the traders. In areas where the beaver was not plentiful, the harvesting and trading of deerskins fueled the trading economy.[14] The buttery soft leather tanned from deerskins was highly desirable for making luxury items such as gloves and hats for wealthy Europeans. The native migrants from the East found this resource far more plentiful in the relatively unoccupied lands beyond the Ohio River than in the overhunted areas of Pennsylvania from which the Delawares and Shawnees had come. Also present in many of these communities were traders, who often married into the tribes with which they lived. They gained power in the tribe through their wives' relations and became useful as intermediaries. A number of multiethnic individuals who resulted from these marriages became influential on both sides of the frontier. Another presence in many villages would be captives who had not returned to the settlements because they found life hospitable in the societies that had adopted them.[15]

Village life in the eighteenth century focused largely on procuring the necessities of life, protecting the family, and defending the settlement itself. Physically the dwellings had evolved from the prehistoric oblong lodges of saplings, bark, and skins (sometimes called wigwams), into a cabinlike structure modified from the log dwelling techniques the Delawares observed during the Swedes' brief sojourn in the New World. Doorways were covered with loosely hanging deerskins or other pelts, fires tended to be more smoky than the Europeans', and the structure generally had a more temporary appearance than the typical European frontier cabin, especially given the inclination of the Delawares to relocate towns as time and circumstance dictated.[16] Dress, too, had been modified by the encounter with the Europeans, so much so that Delaware clothing in the eighteenth century was a potpourri of trade cloth and deerskins. Moccasins were the universal footwear on the trail. Food came from game hunted by the men and boys and from the fields (largely tended by the women) of corn, beans, and squash (plus tobacco grown for ceremonial purposes) that lay close to the clusters of dwellings; the center of these settlements often was a council house or "big house" used for political and religious purposes. The scene in any of the Ohio Indian villages was a noisy one, enlivened by the daily sounds of men, women, children, traders, visitors, horses, and dogs.[17] By the third quarter of the eighteenth century the presence of Moravian mission towns (three were located in east-central Ohio in the 1770s) and visiting preachers from other denominations had undermined traditional Delaware beliefs. Political and military leadership still tended to be held in families where possible, and leaders often courted the European powers in order to gain preferential treatment for the tribe. Captain White Eyes, for example, had adopted European-style housing and farming by the time of the Delaware relocation to Ohio. So convinced was he of where the future lay for his people that until the time of his death he hoped to obtain special recognition by the United States for the Delaware, perhaps in the creation of an additional state in the union for the tribe.[18]

Once they had begun their resettlement in the Ohio country, the villagers also discovered that the wars that had plagued them for so long had not disappeared. The two longtime imperial adversaries, Great Britain and France (who had been fighting one another in North America off and on since 1610), went to battle again in 1754 in a war the American colonials called the French and Indian War, with control of the western country as the prize. While the tribes might choose their allies on the basis of which gave them the most support, the Europeans saw these forest auxiliaries as means to an end. No concerns over native land claims were of importance. The Delaware leader Shingas discovered this in conversation with the British General Edward Braddock, who would lead the expedition westward to reclaim the Ohio Valley for the English king. When Shingas sought affirmation that the Indians would be free to use the land after the French were defeated, the English officer replied "that No Savage Should Inherit the Land."[19]

This statement would be a powerful incentive for the Ohio peoples to help the French or, at the least, not to help the British, especially since the war really was about the lands on which the tribes were living. The military contest also was telling in revealing the disdain with which many British military men regarded the Native Americans. General Braddock, who had been given command of a British expedition commissioned to drive the French from Fort Duquesne at the confluence of the Monongahela and Allegheny Rivers, was unwilling to acknowledge the possibility of help from forest soldiers. Braddock, unfortunately, either insulted or dismissed those warriors who might have been his eyes and ears on that fateful day in 1755. In an engagement in many ways similar to Arthur St. Clair's later defeat farther west, General Braddock's command found itself surrounded by a deadly fire in which two-thirds of the enlisted men fell as well as three-quarters of the officers.[20] The commander himself was one of those killed.

With the defeat of this major British army in 1755 and its retreat all the way to Albany, New York, the French held the field in the west. As Shingas explained: "But after the French had ruined Braddock's Army they immediately compelld the Indians To join them and let them know that if they refused they wou'd Immediately cut them off, On which the Indians Joind the French for their Own Safety."[21] According to Shingas's interpretation, as reported in Charles Stuart's captivity narrative, there were some fourteen hundred French and Indians organized into parties to attack the British frontiers.[22] Stuart identified the warriors who captured him as "a Company of Delaware Mingo & Shawnese Indians who were about 90 in Number."[23] The Ohio native peoples clearly had chosen the French because they had become so dependent on European trade goods that they were unable to do without.[24] Having the French as their suppliers of manufactured goods certainly was better than having no one, but it had its down side. As one Native American commented, the days of the French trade were lean ones, "when the best of them would run for any White Man by Day, or by Night, whether Hot or Cold, wet or dry, any distance for a Small Flap [breech-cloth]."[25]

The captivity narrative left by Pennsylvanian Charles Stuart reveals the nature of the attacks and the fate of the prisoners taken in large part by forest soldiers from Ohio. Braddock's defeat in the summer had left the frontier exposed to raiders such as the substantial band of Delawares, Western Senecas, and Shawnees, who moved without molestation into the Pennsylvania frontier. Consequently, on October 29, 1755, Charles Stuart of

Cumberland County, Pennsylvania, was taken captive along with his wife and their two children, Mary, aged six, and William, aged four. Sweeping up the captives, the party advanced to a home about a mile and a half away, where Mrs. John Martin and four children were captured. Other captives brought in the next day included Elizabeth Galloway and her two children, David McCleland's wife and two children, and a servant girl. David McCleland had surrendered himself to Captain John Peter of the Lower Shawnee Town but he was killed. Within two days Stuart's captors had collected some nineteen prisoners and about eighteen head of cattle that they drove along as they began the return journey toward Ohio. Along the way they were joined by small bands of raiders and their prisoners and plunder. After two frontiersmen killed their guard and escaped, the Indians held a council and determined to kill Stuart and another captive. Shingas, however, intervened, and spared Stuart because the Englishman had been hospitable to traveling parties of Indians when they stopped at his house. Since the raiders had accumulated more than one hundred horses, they divided, with one party led by Captain John Peter going in one direction, while Shingas took another party, including Stuart, in a different direction, traveling for three days before camping for a few days' rest. It was at this juncture that Shingas decided to give his prisoners an explanation for his actions. After leaving this rest stop they proceeded to several small Delaware towns, where they left two or three children and some cattle, but the rest of the prisoners and livestock were carried to Shingas's town (his village in western Pennsylvania, not the later one in Ohio). There Stuart was wounded when forced to run the gauntlet between two lines of armed captors seeking to injure him; afterward, he and his wife were sent as a present to the Wyandots, escorted by a pair of warriors, a Delaware and a Western Seneca. En route they camped near Fort Duquesne at the confluence of the three rivers in modern Pittsburgh, Pennsylvania. Stuart actually was taken into the fort for questioning and his wife was sent some loaves of bread, but no effort seems to have been made to ransom them. From Duquesne the party traveled west into Ohio, being overtaken en route by the party under Captain John Peter, which included Stuart's son and two other prisoners; his daughter had been left at a small Shawnee town through which the party had passed. On one night during their travels, Stuart's young son was permitted to sleep with him, but then John Peter took him toward his Shawnee town on the Scioto, while the Stuarts were taken toward the Wyandot village of Sandusky. In his narrative Stuart goes to great pains to advance the idea that even in the midst of war the Indians with whom he spoke professed a preference for English traders; the French, however, had cut the Indians off from trade with the English. Stuart and his wife reached Sandusky village on December 21, 1755, and stayed until April 27, 1756; they were then taken to the Wyandot village near Detroit, living there until June 25, when they were sold to two priests for whom they worked out their ransom money until March 1, 1757. They then served the priests another month for thirty French livres. On April 13, 1757, the Stuarts and five other prisoners were taken to Quebec, where they were imprisoned until July 23, when they were put on board a French exchange vessel bound from Plymouth, England, from which they were returned to New York.[26]

The raid in which the Stuarts and others were captured was only one of many strikes against the settlements by native raiders acting with the backing of the French. These assaults certainly terrorized the frontiers of Pennsylvania and Virginia, but the final determination of the war was not in the western forests but on the Plains of Abraham, near modern-day Montreal, Quebec, Canada. An English invading force had penetrated deep into Canada and defeated a crack French army outside Montreal. With this loss came not only the end of the war but also the finale of France's century and a half of imperial presence in North America.

In the peace that followed the English victory, the former allies of the French were of no consequence. To the dismay of the Ohio peoples who had backed the French—which was certainly to be expected, given the presence of the French at Duquesne and Detroit—the French were leaving America forever, abandoning not only their former military outposts but also their allies. Since one of the major points in France's anti-British propaganda had been that the French did not want the lands of the Indians, but the British did, the Native Americans in Ohio were in a predicament indeed.

The postwar policy of the British toward the Native Americans was nothing short of breathtaking. Gone were the days of royal largess, favorable trade, and recognition of native people's desires. The new military establishment was headed by General Jeffrey Amherst, one of the architects of the British victory over the French. He had little or no use for the Indians (or, for that matter, North America). His basic philosophy was that if

Ohio's First Peoples

the Native Americans did not cooperate, they would be crushed by British power. While in the interest of economy the newly formed Northern Indian Department headed by William Johnson might reduce the number of "gifts" distributed, in reality cutting the supplies of powder and lead was destructive to the villagers' way of life. Without manufactured guns along with powder, lead, and flints, the hunters had no way of keeping a supply of deerskins, which were fundamental to the trade. The tribesmen were placed in a vicious downward cycle of no weapons, no skins; no skins, no weapons ad infinitum. Almost as if to rub salt in their wounds, territory was granted for settlements that the chiefs had asked to be exempt from such actions.

Among the most infuriated were the Senecas, who lost crucial lands at the Niagara carrying place that they had believed never would be taken from them. They were among the earliest to circulate the idea of war with the British that would allow the return of their French "fathers," better trade, and the restoration of the lands that had been taken from them. Although the reaction of the other tribal councils was to reject their belts of dark wampum sent calling for war in 1761, the parsimony of British policy began to take its toll.

By early 1763 an Ottawa warrior named Pontiac had begun to circulate the idea of an attack against the British fort at Detroit. This plan was in part driven by the circumstances of British policy—that is, Amherst's policy—and in part inspired by the teachings of a Delaware prophet known as Neolin. Whether Neolin's message was central, supportive, or tangential, his ideas about rejecting the presence of the Europeans and gradually their goods was typical of the revitalization movements that emerged within the villages in the latter half of the eighteenth century.[27] The message of purification by ridding themselves of the Europeans, their trade goods, and rum in particular was appealing to those who needed a spiritual justification for war.

Early in May 1763 a combined band of Ottawa, Chippewa, Potawatomi, Wyandot, Shawnee, and Delaware warriors laid siege to the British post at Detroit. Despite internal dissension within the Native American camp over leadership issues and disinclination to stay the course, the besiegers held on from May until September, much longer than most would have imagined forest soldiers could. The combination of a relief force from Fort Niagara and confirmation that the French "father" was not coming back because the king had given Canada to the British sapped the last ounce of will among the warriors.

Across the Ohio country and lakes the associated tribes had carried out assaults with greater success. An attack overwhelmed the outpost of Michilimackinac, while farther to the south and east Seneca warriors took the forts at Venango, LeBoeuf, and Presque Isle (the present-day Pennsylvania towns of Franklin, Watertown, and Erie) and laid siege to Niagara. On the Ohio, when the Delaware encircled Fort Pitt, formerly Fort Duquesne, the British commandant asked the leaders of the opposing force for a parley, which, according to the protocol of forest diplomacy, was granted. Had the Delaware known that the British had no intention of playing by the rules, they might not have been so willing to agree to the truce. The officers at the fort took blankets from the patients in the smallpox hospital within the fort and gave them to the chiefs.[28] The outbreak in the fort turned into an epidemic among the Delawares, who inherited no genetic antibodies and were unfamiliar with the process of inoculation.

This "resistance of 1763," as Jennings styles it, seeing the conflict "as integral to the series of wars waged by the tribes of the Old Northwest from 1755 to 1795 against Britain and then the United States," had been designed "to force the aliens to withdraw."[29] Instead two British punitive expeditions marched into the Ohio country. One, led by Colonel Henry Bouquet, penetrated to the heart of the Delaware homeland and the other, led by General John Bradstreet, took a much longer route from Niagara to Presque Isle to Sandusky Bay to Detroit. Bouquet made camp at the forks of the Muskingum near the site of present-day Coshocton, Ohio, and called for tribal representatives to come in and agree to a peace. If they did not he would put all their villages and fields to the torch. Bouquet wrote on November 15, 1764:

> I have the pleasure to inform you that the Mingoes, the Delawares and the Shawonese, after a long Struggle, have at last submitted to the Terms prescribed to them, vizt:
>
> 1st. To Deliver up all the Prisoners without Exception
>
> 2nd. To give fourteen Hostages to remain in our Hands as a Security for the strict performance of the 1st Article, and that they shall commit no Hostilities against His Majesty's Subjects.
>
> Upon these Conditions they are permitted to send Deputies from each Nation to Sr. William Johnson to make their Peace.[30]

Bouquet's immediate logistical problem was that once he reached the heart of the Delaware country, he found himself confronted with the support of 206 liberated captives.[31] If the Charles Stuart captivity narrative is in any way representative of the whole, they would range in age from children aged four to adults. Stuart's children, for example, if still alive, would have been thirteen and fifteen years old, having lived as Indians longer than they were in the Stuart household. What a trauma this must have been for many of these captives! Some of this may be glimpsed in Benjamin West's engraving depicting the return of the captives. In the crowd of figures standing before the British officers who are to receive the redeemed, one can see a sea of human emotion. West uses light and shadow dramatically, enhancing the poignancy of the moment. A European military figure sits on the right, his arm outstretched toward a tearful white child who is literally being pushed by his Indian parents toward the soldier. In the center of the scene an Indian father's grim visage peers protectively over the head of his white child. To the right of this father stands a warrior covering his tearful face with his hand, while behind them an obviously European woman with an Indian child in her arms hesitates to move forward. In the left background a mother and two children are locked in an emotional embrace, dreading the moment when they must part. The artist uses the bower overhead to suggest the comfort of leaves and forest, but in the background, rifles and bayonets make it ominously clear that the captives must be returned.[32] The chronicler of Bouquet's expedition commented that "they delivered up their beloved captives with the utmost reluctance; shed torrents of tears over them, recommending them to the care and protection of the commanding officer."[33] The touching scenes continued, as a young Mingo warrior insisted on shadowing the troops and returnees in the hope of glimpsing his beloved wife; and, too, "some women, who had been delivered up, afterwards found means to escape and run back to the Indian towns."[34]

By November 18 Colonel Bouquet had led his troops and the redeemed captives back toward Fort Pitt, along with some hostages he had demanded against the springtime return of the rest of the captives and the future peace. His penetration of and presence in the heart of the Delaware lands had made it clear that their Ohio sanctuary was no longer a place of safety. Perhaps if they could get the British authorities to agree to the Ohio River as a permanent boundary between European settlements and native villages they might still live unmolested in their towns.

Engraving after Benjamin West. The return of English captives to Colonel Henry Bouquet at the end of Pontiac's uprising, 1764. Courtesy of the Ohio Historical Society.

The driving force behind diplomacy and war between the British and the Native Americans between 1760 and 1768 was the Europeans' desire for Indian land. Speculators, settlers, and statesmen wanted more land, while tribal peoples wanted their homelands confirmed. British officials in London, aware that these issues needed resolution, took a step toward a solution in issuing the Proclamation of 1763. Its primary purpose was establishing the principle of a boundary between the territory of the colonials and that of the tribes. Although there were other imperial political issues involved, so far as the frontiers were concerned, the boundary was the issue. Spun off from this directive were a series of treaties drawn up between numerous tribes from the Great Lakes to the Gulf, aiming at giving specific delineation to a boundary line. The implementation of this proclamation on the ground was laborious and expensive. Between November 1763 and June 1767 eighteen completed negotiations took place! These do not include any temporary agreements during wartime, or the 1768 treaties of Hard Labor, South Carolina, or Fort Stanwix, New York.[35]

For the tribal peoples of the Ohio country there was a sticking point in all the negotiations, which was the Iroquois presumption of hegemony. Because of the longtime power and influence of the Iroquois League, they continued to assert that they had conquered the Ohio territory, that the tribes who lived there did so at the pleasure of the Six Nations, and, most ominously, that the Iroquois could sell the area if they were so inclined.[36] Indeed, at Fort Stanwix as well as the lands south of the Ohio that became Kentucky, that is exactly what the Iroquois did.

Where the two societies came into the most intimate contact and conflict, however, was not at official treaty negotiations but in the fields and forests of the Ohio Valley. The frontier farmer was obsessed with land. Even a captive such as Charles Stuart noted the kinds of lands and forests through which he passed on his long journey from McConnellsburg, Pennsylvania, to Detroit, Michigan. He took care to note that the streams could be crossed by travelers, even by the animals—horses, cattle, dogs, and even pigs had no difficulty swimming across.[37] The desire for new lands kept driving the settlers into the next valley in search of better soil and more land. Royal proclamations and colonial legislation to the contrary notwithstanding, they kept moving. Even when burned out by soldiers under orders to evict them, the settlers kept coming back.

All along the great sweep of Virginia's frontier, from the birthplace of the Ohio River at Fort Pitt (which Virginia claimed) south and west through the Kentucky country, there was little love between the two sides. Native Americans called their adversaries Long Knives, or the Big Knife, referring to the short saber many of the mounted troops used, while the frontier folk tended to blame their troubles on either the hated Shawnees or dreaded Mingoes. If a Native American speaker in a council wished to express disbelief of some statement made by the Europeans, it became a "Virginia lie"! The pent-up hostility between the two sides helps illuminate the intensity of the gratuitous violence that occurred between them. The spirit of this violence on the Native American side is vividly described in Charles Stuart's account of how his captors threatened to put him to death.

> The Deaths we were to suffer were as follows. First our fingers were to be cut off and we were to be forced to eat them, then our eyes pulled out which we were also to eat, after which we were to be put on a scaffold and burnt, the manner of scaffolding is first to tie them to a post or tree with so much length of rope as will allow them about 3 foot to move about the tree, then they raise them a little from the ground on a log or what else happens to be most convenient to set them on and then puts wood about them and burns them up.[38]

The unprovoked and premeditated attacks on several parties of Indians (including family members of a well-known western Seneca leader named Logan) along the Ohio in 1774 as well as the wartime activities of George Rogers Clark are merely the tip of the iceberg on the frontier side of this violence.[39]

By the early 1770s the Ohio Indians were increasingly worried about the ever-closer line of settlements stretching south and west along the Ohio River like a sickle blade poised to mow. It is clear that the presence of white settlers on the east bank of the Ohio was commonplace. In April of 1773, the Reverend Mr. John Heckewelder, with twenty-two canoe loads of Moravian Delawares, was headed down the Ohio and up the Muskingum to join the party of converts under the Reverend Mr. David Zeisberger, who had gone out the year before. North and south of Mingo Junction Heckewelder noted the presence of "plantations of the white people," a number of whom hailed the convoy and wanted to talk.[40] Indeed, one group "came across the river and looked at all our people and our whole outfit.

Ohio's First Peoples

They pitied the old people, because of the hardships of traveling; they fondled the children, and wished to all of us a happy journey. Now I learned that they were Baptists; one of them was a gentleman from Philadelphia. They sat down on the riverbank and were astonished at the general quietude of our people."[41]

Contrast this peaceful exchange with the paroxysm of anti-Indian violence along the same stretch of river one year later. There are at least nine accounts of the episode at Yellow Creek in which a party of whites invited five Indian men, a woman, and an infant over to the east side of the river. Once the plotters enticed three of the men into drunkenness, they invited the others to a target match, thereby getting the Indians to empty their rifles. Immediately they shot the two men and the woman as she fled; they then tomahawked the inebriated. Those Indians who had remained on the west bank tried to flee but were pursued, and at least one of their number was killed.[42] Later these events were politicized because Thomas Jefferson included them in his *Notes on the State of Virginia,* blaming the wrong individual for the death of the woman, who was the sister of Logan, a well-known Western Seneca leader in the Ohio country.[43]

Tensions along the Virginia frontier already were high in the spring of 1774, as these attacks indicate, but the murder of Logan's relatives and his response led to the conflict labeled by historians as Lord Dunmore's War. As frustrated as the Ohio peoples were they would have been well advised to heed the warning from Lieutenant Governor John Penn of Pennsylvania. Although he thanked them for keeping traders from his colony safe in the early days of the war, he wrote: "Consider, Brethren, that the People of Virginia are like the Leaves upon the Trees, very numerous, and you are but few, and although you should kill ten of their People for one that they kill of yours, they will at last wear you out, and destroy you."[44] British General Thomas Gage had put it another way, assessing the frontier settlers as "a Sett of People . . . near as wild as the country they go in, or the People they deal with, & by far more vicious and wicked . . . too Numerous, too Lawless and Licentious ever to be restrained."[45]

What neither Penn nor Gage addressed was the role of Virginia's elite in promoting the movement westward through land speculation. If the "lawless" frontiersmen were simply carving themselves homesteads wherever they pleased, the movers and shakers had long sought approval at home and in the colonies for various land schemes. George Washington, whose military activities had helped plunge the Ohio country into war in the 1750s, was also an avid land speculator. His interest in the Ohio country was so intense that he not only had a western land agent, William Crawford, but had descended partway down the Ohio in search of prime lands in 1770.[46] In confidence he let Crawford know that the Proclamation of 1763 was only "a temporary expedient to quiet the minds of the Indians. It must fall, of course, in a few years, especially when those Indians consent to our occupying the lands."[47] Clearly, Washington regarded more cessions of Ohio Indian lands as inevitable.

Although major leaders within Shawnee, Delaware, and Iroquois communities wished to avoid war, the nature of tribal society was such that individuals bent on conflict always could find someone to listen. Logan found his audience at Wakatomika, where he recruited enough warriors for a strike across the Ohio. In accordance with Newton's third law, that raid called for a counterraid by frontier militia against Wakatomica. The most ominous response in the eyes of the Ohio native peoples, however, was the plan of the governor of Virginia, Lord Dunmore. If an army of Virginian frontiersmen could advance into the Ohio Valley, the power of the Shawnees might be broken, leaving the legions of settlers moving westward free of the fear of Shawnee attack. In August of 1774 the militia force from Virginia's southwestern counties was attacked near Point Pleasant on the south bank of the Ohio River by a well-organized force of Shawnees, including not only the well-known leader Cornstalk but also the father of Tecumseh, who died in the fighting. Applying their practiced style of the enveloping half-moon, the warriors fought brilliantly throughout the day, but toward the end the Virginians began to turn the tide. Using their knowledge of the terrain and the mastery of their tactics, the forest army withdrew safely across the Ohio, taking their casualties with them. Dunmore, however, was not to be denied. Coming south from Fort Pitt with the militia from his colony's northwestern counties, the governor's combined army pursued the enemy deep into Shawnee territory. There at a temporary camp, the governor signed a preliminary agreement with the Shawnees, bringing the war to an end, forcing the Shawnees to give hostages as a guarantee of peace, and securing Virginia control of what is present-day Kentucky. Traditional accounts indicate that near this camp in the Ohio heartland, a saddened Logan met quietly with a frontiersman named John Gibson and delivered his famous oration.[48] Like many other Native Americans along this frontier, Logan had tried to live in peace, but had found his intentions overturned by the killings along the Ohio; now he faced the possibility that the Iroquois condolence ritual would be denied because he feared his losses would leave no relatives to mourn for him. For Logan, as for the tribal peoples across Ohio to whom he was Everyman, the worst was yet to come. The tragedy of 1774 would pale in comparison to the next twenty years, when the noise and miseries of war erupted and blood and murder stained the land.

THE NOISE AND
MISERIES OF WAR

The political turbulence and war between the colonies and Great Britain increased the anxiety of the tribes. How could the tribes deal with either party without offending the other? During 1775 the tribal peoples wanted to stay out of the war, protect their lands, and display neutrality to all. At the same time, and where it was possible and relatively safe, leaders attempted to inform the belligerents of their intended status. Accordingly, Delaware leaders risked death by undertaking diplomatic missions to Fort Pitt, where Shawnee messages also arrived; to the west the Wyandots, Ottawas, and Miamis journeyed to Detroit for discussions.

Perhaps the most exposed villages in the Ohio country were those of the Delawares. Their location lay astride the Great Trail running from Detroit to Fort Pitt. Messengers or attackers from either post could not avoid passing through the heart of Delaware country. If those coming through were other tribal peoples, Delaware hospitality demanded that all be welcomed and entertained. Such groups often tried to recruit Delaware warriors to join them, increasing the internal pressure on a people already severely divided. On the other hand, if the visitors were non-Indian, the potential dangers increased. British parties from Detroit would look to the pro-British Delawares for shelter. That being given would then encourage passing American parties to confiscate supplies from the supporters of Great Britain and kill any Delaware who lacked the good sense to hide while the parties were present. Since most frontier dwellers operated on the premise that the only good Indians were dead ones, they showed no mercy to any Delaware who crossed into their gun sights. Battle wise as well as weary, a number of Delaware parties went to both Fort Pitt and Detroit in 1775 on diplomatic missions aimed at maintaining peace.

In the summer of 1775 Delaware and some western Iroquois deputies traveled on a peace mission to Fort Pitt.[1] On this occasion progress was blocked because the colonials were disputing "who should rule at home," as the historian Carl Becker once put it. Fort Pitt technically was controlled by the Earl of Dunmore's alter ego in the West, John Connolly, but pro-American forces were at work trying to topple Connolly and seize control of Fort Pitt. Consequently there was talk of peace but little peace. Coquethagechton (Captain White Eyes) received assurances from Dunmore that the Virginians wanted only peace, not the Delaware lands, but the chieftain was not so naïve.[2] Nor, moreover, were his fellow Delaware chiefs; while he talked with the Americans at Fort Pitt, others went to Detroit in hopes of some word of assurance there, not to mention their hope of securing some trade goods.[3]

During the gathering at Fort Pitt, John Connolly presented belts to the Delaware party led by Captain White Eyes, urging them to pass the word of peace westward to the Shawnees, Wyandots, and other western nations. On July 6 White Eyes responded in a speech advocating peace. White Eyes purported to represent the Shawnees, Delawares, and Mingoes, who wanted Connolly to know that they still held fast to the peace made by both sides long ago. The Delaware leader, Captain Killbuck, seconded this address. Then Kayashota, the Seneca diplomat who often acted on behalf of the Iroquois council at Onondaga, responded for the Six Nations delegates present, thanking the Delawares for their peaceful speeches. Reflective of the general frontier hope for peace was the presence of a delegation from "Augusta County on the West Side of Laurel Hill," which also gave assurances of a desire for peace and hope that the native peoples could be protected in their lands. That spirit of peace was likewise echoed in Virginia's revolutionary legislature, which voted on July 25 to reimburse the cost of the treaty and the presents to the Indians to the county for acting "with propriety and prudence."[4] Even the royal governor acted in the interest of peace, assuring Captain White Eyes that his lands would be protected and asking him to forward those assurances to the Mingoes and other Six Nations peoples in Ohio.[5]

Peace efforts continued in the fall of 1775 at Fort Pitt, which by then had been taken over by the revolutionary leaders, thus eliminating Connolly from the scene. Again the primary Native American spokesman was Captain White Eyes, who led a delegation of Delawares, Six Nations, Wyandots, and Shawnees. At this meeting the Ohio peoples were conferring both with the Virginians who had called for the meeting and the commissioners of the Continental Congress who were sent out to preach peace and neutrality to the tribes. The Virginians focused their efforts on persuading the tribes to return the captives, both white and black, as well as the stolen horses that the warriors had captured during the most recent hostilities. They also urged the tribes to maintain neutrality, directing specific remarks to the Wyandots by urging them to ignore the pleas of the British commandant at Detroit.[6] If the tribes demonstrated their good intentions by returning white prisoners, captured slaves, and stolen horses, the Virginians promised, they would dispense trade goods in addition to those that the Continental commissioners had brought west.

Despite the ongoing negotiations aimed at bringing peace for the Ohio frontier in 1775, the native peoples in Ohio feared that a new surge of frontier farmers was poised to cross the Ohio in search of fresh lands. This worry was intensified by the British governor at Detroit, who circulated the accusation that the Americans were ready to undertake a campaign to conquer the Ohio country. From the swirl of rumors ever present on the frontier also came the report that alarmed tribes had posted sentinels at the mouths of the Great and Little Kanawha, Hockhocking, and Muskingum Rivers. At the same time bands of Wyandots and Shawnees had gone to scout the Kentucky country in order to report on the expansion of settlements there.[7] The Shawnees understood without seeing a modern map that they were being flanked by the settlements in Kentucky. They were only too happy to join the watch parties along the Ohio and burn the abandoned colonial post at the mouth of the Great Kanawha left there after the withdrawal of the Virginia expedition sent out by Governor Dunmore. In the northwestern corner of Ohio the Wyandots too were apprehensive about the speculations concerning the advance of the Virginia frontier. They sought assurances from the British officials at nearby Detroit that they would not be drawn into the war. In messages to the Delawares they expressed their concern about negotiating with the Big Knives, as the native peoples called the hated Virginians.[8] Despite the misgivings and fears of his Shawnee and Wyandot friends, the Delaware leader White Eyes persisted in his efforts to realize peace with the fledging United States. He demonstrated his intent by journeying east to appear before the Continental Congress, assuring the delegates of his nation's peaceful intentions as well as its desire to have a schoolmaster and minister live among them.[9]

Despite the apparent determination of White Eyes to engage in diplomacy with the representatives of the United States, others grew increasingly fearful even of leaving the Ohio country's relative safety to journey to the outpost at Fort Pitt. As a leader named Conessaway explained, "It was hard to expect them to go to the council fire with the Tomhock [tomahawk] sticking in their heads."[10] Conessaway and his fellow leaders knew only too well that even if they were not "tomhocked" before they reached Pittsburgh, the same thing could happen on the way home. Others feared that an invitation to a treaty was only a ruse, designed to draw the warriors away from home, so that in their absence the Big Knives could attack the women, children, and old people.[11] Some leaders believed that those who went to Pittsburgh would be killed and their bodies hung up on poles like the dogs used in the Iroquois White Dog Ceremony (in which a white dog was killed and hung on a pole in the village).[12] Even if they were not killed, they might be jailed and held for months on some pretext.[13]

Because of this zone of hatred on the western frontier, few Native American leaders went to Pittsburgh without a bit of cold fear along their spines; no one knew when groups of trigger-happy frontiersmen might start shooting at them. White Eyes seems the exception to this rule, never missing an opportunity to speak for peace right up until his treacherous murder in 1778 while he tried to guide an American army through Ohio toward Detroit. In 1775 alone he traveled to Pittsburgh in June and July and again in October.[14] Within a few weeks of the October meeting he rode far east of Pittsburgh to plead the Delaware case before the Continental Congress.

What made life difficult for the Ohio country peoples in 1775 was the growing confusion resulting from the dispute between Great Britain and her colonies. When, for example, White Eyes and others went to Pittsburgh in the early summer of 1775, the person seemingly in charge was John

Connolly, acting on behalf of Governor Dunmore of Virginia. Present were certain members of the British Indian Department whose loyalties appeared to favor the crown, but there also were persons of the opposite persuasion, most notably a group from western Augusta County, Virginia, led by a justice of the peace named John Gibson. Shortly after this meeting the provisional government of Virginia seized Fort Pitt and Connolly was asked to explain his actions to the new authorities.[15] Accordingly, when the delegates met at Pittsburgh once more in October, the problems of the frontier remained unsolved and there was a new power structure to confront.

On this occasion the peoples of the western tribes found the Big Knives more intractable, since there was no longer a British Indian Department to act as a buffer. Accordingly, Virginia interests took precedence over those of the Continental Congress. There were four representatives of Virginia (James Wood, Andrew Lewis, John Walker, and Adam Stephen), three Indian commissioners from the Continental Congress (Lewis Morris, James Wilson, and Dr. Thomas Walker—who was also from Virginia), and a Pennsylvanian named William Trent who was there to protect the Indian trading interests of merchants in Philadelphia.[16] The primary demands heard by the Ohio Indians at this conference were that all prisoners taken, slaves seized, horses captured, and property confiscated during Lord Dunmore's War and its aftermath be returned to the commandant at Fort Pitt before there could be a final peace.[17]

Once the Ohio peoples began to negotiate with the representatives of the new government they found that business was done in the same old ways. Fear that they might lose their lands did not diminish, especially when the Congress raised the question of the lands occupied by the Delawares in Ohio. The Delawares were warned to obtain a public declaration from the Wyandots that they had granted the Delawares the lands bounded by the Ohio River, Lake Erie, the west branch of the Muskingum, and the Sandusky, and Presque Isle.[18]

Even while the American government questioned the right of the Delawares to their lands, the Continental Congress began trying to influence Delaware society. In early 1776 the Congress reiterated its hope of supporting a minister, a schoolmaster, and a blacksmith among the Delawares and of establishing European customs among them as well.[19] In order to smooth the way for additional influence Congress rather patently curried favor with White Eyes by appropriating $100 to buy two horses and tack

Ohio's First Peoples

for him and by appointing a committee to settle a financial dispute between the Delaware leader and the Pennsylvania trading concern owned by the Gratz family.[20]

Despite the overtures to White Eyes and the Delawares, many of the other people in Ohio as well as groups living farther west did not trust the Big Knives. They feared that if the Americans established themselves in the area inhabited by the Delawares it was only a matter of time before they would move westward. Hoping to secure support in defense of their homes, numerous western delegations trekked to Detroit in the summer of 1776. About seven hundred went in the spring, including Wyandots, Kickapoos, Tewas, Miamis, Potawatomies, and Ouiatenons who feared the collapse of the tribes in the Ohio valley.[21] In August another two hundred visited Detroit, this time including Shawnees, Ottawas, Chippewas, Wyandots, Senecas, Delawares, Cherokees, and Potawatomies.[22] Among the Delawares were Captain White Eyes and John Montour, a Delaware mixed blood who had attended the College of William and Mary at one time. Their mission was to deliver belts inviting all the western tribes to attend a great council at Pittsburgh in the fall of 1776. They also brought with them a copy of the *Pennsylvania Gazette* of July 25, 1776, which contained a copy of the newly approved Declaration of Independence. In his capacity as host, Detroit's British lieutenant governor, Henry Hamilton, responded to the invitations by cutting up the belts and tearing up the written messages before the assembled western delegations. White Eyes and Montour enjoyed the protection of their diplomatic immunity and thus were allowed to return unharmed.

After their departure the lieutenant governor denounced the plans of the Americans and asked for the assistance of the tribes in a British assault against the colonies. Hamilton urged that these be controlled attacks, not simply scattered raids, although he professed to his superiors in London that the latter would be more likely. It was, he wrote Dartmouth, "a deplorable sort of war, but which the arrogance, disloyalty, and imprudence of the Virginians had justly drawn upon them."[23]

Despite the attitude of Hamilton and his adherents toward the Virginians, the Big Knives still hoped to draw representatives of the western tribes to Pittsburgh for a conference in the summer of 1776. The Continental Congress, which already had approved personal gifts to White Eyes, voted that presents, including some silver trinkets, be used as inducements to bring the delegates to Pittsburgh.[24] Despite such overtures, the western tribesmen were wary of exposing themselves to danger posed by the hostile intentions of frontier settlers. The journey seemed hardly worth the risk, given the possibility that there were few if any supplies stored at Fort Pitt and little in the way of "physick" in case they were injured. The uneasiness over the frontier tension in the Fort Pitt area was so great that no one could be sure whether visiting Native American delegates had greater need for provisions or protection.[25]

Indicative of the western people's desire for peace was the action of some Shawnees who followed Cornstalk in the summer of 1776: they surrendered themselves to the Virginia authorities as guarantors of peace![26] Because the Shawnees wanted to end Lord Dunmore's War officially, not only did some give themselves up as hostages, others made the dangerous journey to Fort Pitt late in the summer of 1776 and then followed that with a longer trip eastward to visit the Continental Congress. The parley at Pittsburgh was not held until November.[27] After that gathering a number of western Senecas, Delawares, and Shawnees also were taken to the Congress in an attempt to impress the visitors with the greatness of that legislative body. Some of the luster must have faded rather quickly when the Congress failed to appreciate the symbolic significance of the journey. "The Indians, being introduced, spoke to Congress, but having said nothing relative to the matters between them and the United States, no notice was taken of it, and they withdrew."[28]

The insensitivity of the Congress to the metaphors and practices of native diplomacy makes one wonder about the abilities of the Indian commissioners appointed by the Continental Congress and their capacity for giving advice. No Native American diplomat ever laid his cards on the table in the opening speech of a conference. In their opening speeches, experienced forest diplomats always used metaphors of condolence to gauge the temper and reaction of the audience.[29] The Congress's rather blunt attitude did not augur well for diplomacy with the western peoples. It also reveals a great deal about the congressional leaders' perception of Native American peoples and cultures.

Despite the relative indifference of the Congress, Ohio peoples continued to seek assurances of peace from the representatives. Early in 1777 John Heckewelder and Shebosh conferred with the president of the Congress before traveling westward to the Delaware villages. Learning that British-inspired rumors about American negativism toward the Delawares had dispirited Captain White Eyes, they assured him that the American leaders still remained friendly toward the tribe. In order to confirm that diplomatic tie, the Delawares sent a delegation under John Killbuck eastward to visit not only the Congress but also the headquarters of the army.[30] The peaceful overtures of the Delawares in early 1777 were seconded by those of the Shawnees, who assured the Continental Congress that their foremost desire was peace on the Ohio frontier.[31]

Unfortunately for the Ohio peoples the officials in Virginia were unconvinced that the trans-Ohio Indians wanted peace. The Virginians specifically blamed the Shawnees of Pluggy's Town for raids on the state's western frontier and maintained a spirited discussion of the best ways to break the power of the Shawnees.[32] Virginia legislators and leaders debated a punitive raid on the village throughout the early weeks of 1777; Governor Henry finally called it off in April, but was still debating its merits as late as July.[33]

Other Ohio peoples in the meantime sought assurances of support from the British at Detroit. In June of 1777 Wyandots, Shawnees, and Delawares were joined by other western peoples in conferring with Lieutenant Governor Henry Hamilton.[34] The histrionic Hamilton addressed the assembly and dramatically delivered eight strings of black wampum, urging the assembled delegates to embrace the British cause. His invitation was backed by the Wyandot leader Tseendattong, who brought forward a belt of wampum from the Six Nations that measured six feet long, contained thirty grains, and was marked at one end by a interwoven black beaver totem. The Iroquois urged the tribes of the West to support the British. On the following day Hamilton spoke again, bearing a sharpened axe and a red belt while singing the song of war.[35]

For strongly pro-American peoples like the followers of Captain White Eyes, the activities of those who accepted Hamilton's invitation spelled disaster. The initial difficulty for them would be the hospitality expected of them as the raiding parties passed eastward. Afterward they would be regarded as enemies by the Americans, whose vengeance might mean retaliatory raids. Given the numbers of raiding parties in the summer of 1777 this was a major concern to Delaware leaders like Captain White Eyes, who on more than one occasion tried to persuade the raiders to drop their plans.[36] Despite the pleadings of White Eyes, at least thirty-two parties were organized in the summer of 1777, with the support of the British authorities at Detroit.[37] Suspicion of the Ohio tribal peoples was intensified not only by the numerous frontier raids but also by the distribution through

Henry Hamilton's sketches of chiefs, 1778. *Clockwise from top left:* Pepiquenne of the Nipissins; Tzenoritze, a Huron noble; Otcheek, a Mohawk warrior; and Quooquandarong of the Huron nation. By permission of the Houghton Library, Harvard University.

Sketch of Pacane by Henry Hamilton. This 1778 sketch of the Miami leader known as Pacane/Pacan/Paccane illustrates the gifts received by a high-status chief. Pacane wears an elaborate trade shirt decorated with cowry shells; both sleeves are held in place by silver armbands. His hair is twisted around the copper worm screws usually designed for cleaning rifle barrels, and his pierced ears and nose septum carry trade silver decorations. He appears relatively healthy, without the sunken cheeks usually associated with alcoholism and accompanying malnutrition. By permission of the Houghton Library, Harvard University.

those raids of Hamilton's proclamation offering equal rank and pay as well as a military land bounty to anyone who would join the British side.[38] While the Delawares might have been the most nervous about the raids, it was the Wyandots from northeastern Ohio who were actively involved in carrying them out. During July alone at least three such bands passed through the Delaware towns. The first came through on July 7, followed two weeks later by another, this one led by the Wyandot chief known as the Half King. That leader actually came before the Delaware Council with a war belt while singing his war song, but the Delawares, led by White Eyes and influenced by the Moravian missionary David Zeisberger, refused to accept his offer.[39] The next two parties of Wyandots did not stop in the Delaware towns, but their passages were observed.[40]

Despite the repeated attempts by the Delawares to promote peace, the frontiersmen who "liked chastising Indians" gave them no consideration; several tribesmen were murdered at Fort Pitt in the fall of 1777 even while they tried to further diplomacy.[41] Given the animosity of the frontier settlers, the Delawares became increasingly convinced that it was only a matter of time before they were driven from their new homeland in Ohio.[42] The ever-loyal White Eyes also was concerned that this hatred might explode if an expedition against Detroit came marching through the Delaware towns. He urged the Congress and the military planners of the proposed assault to plan the route away from the Delaware towns, lest careless soldiers kill tribal members. White Eyes was worried, too, that visiting frontier soldiers might covet the fertile Delaware farmlands.[43] There may also have been some self-interest here, since White Eyes had made extensive improvements on the numerous acres of bottomland that he farmed. Indeed, asserted his friend George Morgan, cattle, horses, plows, and occasional hired hands from the settlements were as much a part of White Eyes' frontier farm as of any cultivated east of the Ohio.[44]

Among the Shawnees there also was a faction led by Cornstalk that clung to the hope of peace, even through the most trying of times.[45] The severest test for this group came late in the year. Cornstalk, his son, the Red Hawk's son, and another warrior visited Fort Randolph on a mission of diplomacy. On November 10, 1777, while inside the fort, these literal hostages for peace were killed by a band of frontiersmen angered by the recent death of a soldier who was shot while hunting outside the fort.[46] Even though the names of the murderers were known and rewards of $100, $150, and $200 placed on the men for the sake of placating the Shawnees and other Native Americans in Ohio, no jury of their peers would have convicted them.[47] So died one of the most determined and outspoken advocates of peace among the Native Americans in the Ohio country. It is perhaps reflective of the intense hatred for the tribal peoples in Ohio that within a year of Cornstalk's death, Captain White Eyes also would be dead at the hands of the people he tried so loyally to assist.

With the death of Cornstalk the Shawnee peace faction weakened, making it difficult for anyone else in the tribe to advocate the same policy. Circumstances of war also affected the Shawnees, as did the growing number of settlements cast westward into the Kentucky country. The cabins and stockades of Daniel Boone, the noted frontiersman, and his compatriots lay almost directly south of the Shawnee villages. Although the Shawnees tried to blame frontier unrest on the so-called dreaded Mingoes, it was Shawnee raiding parties that harassed the increasing number of Kentucky settlers.[48] During one of these raids south of the Ohio the Shawnees under Blackfish captured Daniel Boone and twenty-six other westerners.[49] The British at Detroit tried to capitalize on the Shawnee distaste for the American settlements, urging them to attend a conference at Detroit.[50]

Ohio's First Peoples

Among the native peoples in Ohio, moreover, fear of attacks by bands of militia was ever present. Yet in early 1778 the official Virginia policy was peace with the Shawnees. Governor Patrick Henry promised to pay all the expenses of a treaty with the Shawnees and, as an indication of how far the state was willing to go in its search for peace, posted the names of and rewards for those accused of Cornstalk's murder.[51] Henry's primary motive in these concessions to the Shawnees was to pacify the Ohio frontier while George Rogers Clark organized, recruited, supplied, and fulfilled his dramatic expedition to the Illinois country.[52] Despite the peaceful intentions of Governor Henry, however motivated, the entire Ohio country was too easily penetrated by vengeance-seeking frontier militia and too filled with separate groups of Native Americans regarded as enemies. In early 1778, for example, an American force of more than three hundred struck out from Fort Pitt, intent on capturing Cuyahoga Village and its substantial cache of British supplies. When streams swollen by the spring runoff prevented them from reaching Cuyahoga Village they fell on and killed a group of "straggling women and children."[53] Most of these victims were Delawares, a number of whom were relatives of the tribal leader known as Captain Pipe. This merciless treatment may have been instrumental in persuading Pipe to swing to the British side, a move he later came to regret.[54] Such incidents, moreover, undermined any larger vision of frontier peace held by the national government.[55]

The Ohio frontier also was a matter of concern to George Washington and the Continental command. As long as the British officials at Detroit supported raiders against the Pennsylvania and Virginia frontiers, the leaders of those two states could not be single-minded in their support of the war in the East. The only answer seemed an expedition into the Ohio country that would neutralize or destroy the native peoples and capture the British post at Detroit. General Edward Hand even warned the Delawares, with whom he had had some experience in negotiation, that they should complete a peace with the Continental officials lest their towns be razed.[56]

By May 1778 General Washington had begun to indicate the seriousness of his intentions. Because of the interstate jealousies between Pennsylvania and Virginia, in which Hand was regarded as being involved, Washington transferred the experienced westerner to Albany, New York, and assigned General Lachlan McIntosh to Fort Pitt.[57] To support this trans-Ohio operation, General Washington ordered some Continental troops to Fort Pitt, hoping that they could be the core of a new operation and that their discipline might help prevent incidents like the 1778 "Squaw campaign," in which soldiers from Fort Pitt killed women and children when they found no warriors.[58]

For the Delawares and their leaders the summer of 1778 was a time of tension. They were being both wooed and warned by the Americans, wooed to carry out reconnaissance missions to Detroit and negotiate a treaty at Fort Pitt, and warned of the impending expedition through their settlements.[59] The tribal leaders let the missionary David Zeisberger know of their reluctance about journeying to the fort because they feared embittered frontier militia would kill them.[60] Within the tribe itself there was also distress because of divided allegiances. Some who favored the British were critical of Captain White Eyes and David Zeisberger, because they clearly acted as informants for the Americans at Fort Pitt.[61] These activities proved troublesome for Delaware leaders who did go to Detroit that summer, since they were looked on with suspicion by other tribal delegates, who feared anything said at Detroit would ultimately be reported back to the Americans at Fort Pitt.[62] Even the well-known mixed-blood John Montour fell victim and was imprisoned at Detroit for a time under accusation of double-dealing; only the intervention of his Mingo and Wyandot friends secured his release.[63]

The Delawares finally succumbed to the entreaties of the Americans and gathered at Fort Pitt early in September. When deliberations began on September 12, the tribe was represented by Captain White Eyes, Captain Pipe, and John Killbuck. General Lachlan McIntosh wasted no time on diplomatic niceties: the Americans wanted only the guarantee of a safe passage through the Delaware country toward Detroit, nothing more. White Eyes in turn asked for guarantees of safety of their women, children, and elderly, plus the construction of a stockade post where noncombatants could take refuge when the warriors were away. The Delaware leaders also promised help from some of the young Delaware warriors if Colonel John Gibson could command them.[64] The articles of the treaty smoothed out some of McIntosh's bluntness by forgiving former offenses, pledging perpetual friendship, and arranging not only for the safe passage and the purchase of supplies from the Delawares but also the construction of a fort in the Delaware country. After stipulating extradition arrangements for criminals and the return of fugitive slaves in Article IV and promising a "well-regulated trade" in Article V, the signers included the most surprising article of all, the creation of an Indian state.

Ohio's First Peoples

Certainly in the realm of what might have been, and perhaps never seriously intended by the Continental representatives, Article VI sought to counter the British disinformation campaign aimed at convincing the Indians that the Americans wanted to "extirpate the Indians and take possession of their country."[65] Instead, promised the agreement, the Delawares would be guaranteed their territory. In the bicentennial of Ohio statehood, and again in the realm of what might have been, it is interesting that the document proposed that "other tribes who have been friends to the interest of the United States" might be invited "to join the present confederation, and *to form a state whereof the Delaware nation shall be head, and have a representation in Congress.*"[66]

Despite the "good words" of the treaty, it was not a prelude to better days for the Delawares or the Ohio frontier. It did not bring peace to the Delawares but resulted in the death of White Eyes and the attachment of Captain Pipe and his followers to the British.

The door was now open for the long-discussed western expedition, backed by the Congress and supported in on-again, off-again fashion by the Virginians.[67] Because troops, horses, and supplies were so slow in coming, the army did not cross Big Beaver Creek until September 24, building Fort McIntosh there and not leaving until November 4. When they departed west from Big Beaver Creek they were guided by the trusting Captain White Eyes, who came to look out for the safety of the army and of his people as the army passed through the Delaware country. Unfortunately no guardian protected the chief; at some time between November 4 and November 20 he was murdered, as George Morgan later revealed, by an American assailant never identified.[68] Worried American officials scrambled to cover up this tragedy lest all their diplomatic accomplishments be lost. Smallpox became the scapegoat since it was a disease still dreaded by the native peoples and still usually contracted through contact with Europeans.[69] There was no indication of Delaware suspicion of foul play, especially given that other Delaware warriors came to the army with gifts of venison, expressions of grief over their leader's death, and professions of willingness to join the army once a fort had been built to protect their families.[70] A fort would indeed be built, although not precisely in the Delaware country; indeed, succeeding events brought no protection to the Delaware, only more anguish.[71]

The presence of a new American outpost at Fort Laurens (near the present Zoar, Ohio) may have offered some comfort to the Delawares, but it also represented a deeper intrusion into the Ohio Indian country. The thrill of alarm was raised to an even higher pitch for the Delawares, the Shawnees, and the Wyandots by the news of Colonel George Rogers Clark's successful mission from Virginia to the Illinois country. Under orders from Governor Patrick Henry, Colonel Clark had led his men west to erase the threat of Indian attack by occupying Detroit. Once the confident Clark had seized Vincennes and captured Henry Hamilton, the British commander who had left Detroit to defeat Clark, he believed he could not only capture Detroit but also crush all the hostile nations. The native peoples of Ohio knew this because a letter from Clark to officials in Virginia was taken from a slain express near the falls of the Ohio by a band of Wyandots, who then transported the letter to Detroit.[72] Word of Clark's savagery toward native peoples also was communicated throughout Ohio by eyewitnesses who saw Clark and his men butcher five captive Ottawas before the siege of Vincennes was completed.[73] Clark's presence in the West represented the Native Americans' worst fears, an unchecked American military expedition that had flanked all of Ohio and seemed poised to eradicate British support at Detroit. Those Shawnees and Delawares who had put themselves at the mercy of the British garrison at Detroit for supplies seemed particularly vulnerable, since they had abandoned their villages in the hope of protection.[74]

To some of the western peoples, like Captain Pipe's Delawares, along with the pro-British Shawnees, Wyandots, and Miamis, it appeared that the friendship for the Americans displayed by Captain White Eyes had brought only more grief. The noble words of the Fort Pitt treaty meant nothing, White Eyes was dead, the British establishment was shaken, and the American troops roamed freely across the western peoples' lands. As if these conditions were not worrisome enough, the frontier settlers were ignoring both the treaty and the threat of Indian attack to cross the Ohio and build cabins in a number of places from the mouth of the Muskingum River to Beaver Creek. Some had even rowed as far as thirty miles up some of the Ohio tributaries in search of prime locations for their cabins and fields.[75] Although Daniel Brodhead, the American commander at Fort Pitt, sent a detachment of troops to evict the trespassers under the terms of the 1778 treaty at Fort Pitt, he, the soldiers, the Indians, and the squatters knew that they would be back. He did take the precaution of sending a messenger to the Delaware towns asking them not to attack the settlers before his detachment of troops had time to drive them away and burn their cabins.[76]

Given the pressure on the Delawares both from the expectations of American officials and from the approaching settlers, it should be no surprise that the group led by Captain Pipe had relocated near the Wyandots at Upper Sandusky. Here there were allies led by the Wyandot chief known as the Half King.[77] Clark's threatened attack against Detroit did not materialize, and the post once again became a center for Native American conferences with the British. Because of its reputation and location, Chippewas, Ottawas, and Potawatomies from the West could meet Miamis, Shawnees, Wyandots, Mingoes, and Delawares from the Ohio country as well as visiting diplomats from the east and south.

In the spring of 1780, for example, the Wyandot chief Sasterasszee returned from a council at Niagara, bringing word that the Iroquois urged against peace with the Americans, despite the torching of the Mohawk Valley in 1779 by a United States military expedition. Sasterasszee brought with him message belts not only for the Ohio and western tribes but also for the southern tribes he was commissioned to visit, using his diplomatic status to travel in safety.[78] A few weeks later another messenger, the widely traveled Iroquois known as Kayashota also visited the Niagara council fire (where there reportedly were three thousand Indians present in early April) and came west bearing four belts containing twenty-four thousand wampum beads, woven into a message of support for the king and opposition to his enemies.[79] An invitation also came to Detroit requesting the selection of delegates to attend a major intertribal meeting on the St. John's River near Fort Howe.[80] The ease and safety with which diplomats such as Sasterasszee and Kyashota moved from meeting to meeting reflects the structure of forest diplomacy, which made communication possible among the tribes.

Detroit was also the organizing center for bands of raiders who struck the frontiers of Pennsylvania and Virginia, despite the snow and cold. Three bands of Wyandots—one led by the Half King—totaling 126 warriors, along with a group of Delaware warriors, were among those active against the settlements in the early spring of 1780.[81] After the vernal equinox brought more moderate weather, others sallied forth. One such party captured a Quaker family and four blacks who were on their way to Canada. The captors took their prizes to Detroit, whence they were transported to Montreal, where the Quakers were ransomed and the blacks were freed.[82]

The Shawnees, however, planned the most ambitious counterattack by

Ohio peoples against the pressures of the settlers' encroachments, with the assistance of their allies at Detroit. Virginia was the nemesis of the Shawnees, particularly the enormous county known as Kentucky that stretched west to the Mississippi River. Every cabin and stockade not only reduced the available hunting in the lush bluegrass but also housed potential attackers against the tribal towns along the Scioto River. In an effort to remove this threat the Shawnees laid plans for a summer campaign to eradicate the Kentucky settlements, an expedition that would involve not only warriors but also some British partisans, along with a small cannon that would be operated by an officer and some men familiar with it.[83] Since this was no ordinary expedition the participants were instructed carefully when they were recruited; the warriors, for example, were admonished when they volunteered that they must "act with spirit" from the beginning to the end of the campaign; otherwise, Captain Bird and his men would return to Detroit immediately.[84] The British commandant at Detroit was emphatic that the forest soldiers understood "that taking a few scalps is not the object of the present enterprize."[85] The party of regulars, partisans, and Indians moved southward by the Maumee-Auglaize-Miami water route to the Kentucky country, where both Ruddell's and Martin's Stations were taken.[86] By August 5 the raiding party had returned to Detroit, but many of the regulars and partisans had feet so badly blistered they could hardly walk.[87]

Although the frontier leaders had some inkling of the military operation, they could do nothing to prevent it.[88] Given the mutual antipathy between the Shawnees and the Virginians it should be no surprise that the Virginians planned not only retaliation but also the elimination of the Shawnees. Governor Thomas Jefferson urged Colonel Clark to establish a settlement at the mouth of the Ohio from which peace could be cultivated with all the southern and western tribes except the Shawnees.[89] Likewise the governor advocated an Indian policy of divide and conquer according to which all other tribes would be encouraged to engage in warfare with the Shawnees, thus forcing them to abandon their villages. Tribes who enlisted in this campaign of harassment would be given free ammunition for the purpose. Additional pressure would be placed on the Shawnees by granting 560 acres of land to any settler who would move to the proposed town at the Ohio's mouth.[90] In the meantime Jefferson was only too pleased when he learned that Clark had followed his suggestions by raiding the

Shawnee towns at Pickaway and Chillicothe.[91] The frenzied frontiersmen not only destroyed the towns and burned the corn during their summer raid but also killed an Indian woman by slashing open her stomach, and then desecrated Shawnee burials by digging up the corpses and scalping them.[92] Clark and his men were congratulated by Governor Jefferson, who regretted only that Clark did not have men and supplies sufficient to destroy all the Shawnee towns and the British post at Detroit. Destruction was the only policy applicable to the Shawnees, thought Jefferson, who concluded that since the Shawnees could not be taught to keep the faith, they would have to be taught fear.[93]

The heightened tensions in the Ohio country were not restricted to the Shawnees. The badly divided Delawares were affected too, especially those who clung to their homes in the Muskingum-Tuscarawas valleys. Exposed to the demands of raiders passing to and from the frontier and endangered if they traveled to Pittsburgh, they were in a predicament. Since Captain Pipe's band had moved within the orbit of Detroit, the rest of the Delawares were urged by their fellow tribesmen and by their friends among the Wyandots, Chippewas, and Potawatomies to relocate to the relative safety of Upper Sandusky.[94]

According to Captain Pipe and the Half-King of the Wyandots, the loyalty of the Delawares still living in the old towns would always be undermined because of the presence of Moravian missionaries like John Heckewelder and David Zeisberger. Complaints about them even reached the Iroquois council at Niagara, which suggested that the Chippewas and Potawatomies step in and make a broth of the Moravians. Those two tribes, however, did not want to jeopardize the peace they had with the Delawares by interfering.[95] In the meantime Captain Pipe and the Half King decided to cut the knot by leading some of their warriors eastward, taking the missionaries prisoner, and removing them to the vicinity of Sandusky and Detroit.[96]

Clearing the Muskingum-Tuscarawas area of the Moravians was a defensive step for the British-inclined villages in central and northwestern Ohio. Those American eyes in the old villages saw and reported everything that passed. In the summer of 1780, for example, when a party of Wyandots crossed Yellow Creek on rafts, their ambush and the death of eight of their number at the hands of a band of frontiersmen was immediately reported to Daniel Brodhead by John Heckewelder.[97] Given the rapidity with which news could travel on the frontier, it is possible that warnings were given about the Wyandot party by either Heckewelder or Zeisberger. Indeed, news of an American advance against the Shawnee towns, for example, was known by Heckewelder on 14 August, a day before the attacks were reported by an eyewitness![98] News could move along trails and streams with amazing celerity. The Iroquois diplomat Kayashota traveled from west to east and back over the Upper Allegheny–Lake Erie routes with regularity and frequency.[99]

Withdrawal of these Delaware villages in eastern Ohio also meant the pro-American villages no longer could screen unauthorized frontier militia attacks. The severity of this problem was illustrated in the fall of 1780 when a party of forty pro-American Delawares reached Fort Pitt and volunteered their services against the hostile tribes. Colonel Brodhead would have used them, but before he could, a militia force of about forty men from the Hannahstown area led by Captains Irwin and Jack, Lieutenant Brownlee, and Ensign Guthrie reached the fort and attempted to kill the natives. Only the use of Brodhead's regulars prevented the Delaware men, women, and children from being murdered inside Fort Pitt.[100]

The Delawares' neighbors, the Shawnees, also were facing their share of pressures. Since Virginia still regarded the Shawnees as their Native American nemesis, Governor Jefferson sought all possible means to punish them. Because of Clark's victory in the Illinois country, the commonwealth's territorial ambitions stretched westward to Wabash. Accordingly, the governor sent Godefrey de Linctot to Vincennes as a state Indian agent. Jefferson's logic was that because of his connections, de Linctot might not only communicate well with the Creoles (the French-Canadian inhabitants of the former French colonies) of the area but also negotiate effectively with the Native Americans. One specific objective expected of the new Indian agent was to obtain supplies and use them to bribe the Piankashaws and Ottawas to attack the Shawnees.[101]

Within the Shawnee towns proper there was a shortage of provisions brought on by poor crops, repeated raids, and the frequent absences of the warriors. In the Clark raid against Chillicothe and Pickaway in the summer of 1780, for example, the raiders had spent two days burning the corn. The repeated American raids into the heart of Shawnee country had even driven the Shawnees to consider building four blockhouses at Logan's Town, four miles beyond Pickaway. Their plight was not aided by loss of leadership; Blackfish reportedly had died in 1780.[102]

Pressure on the loyal Delawares also was unrelenting. Daniel Brodhead, the American commander at Fort Pitt, seemed unembarrassed about putting his Delaware friends in difficulty. In addition to his expectation that they hunt game and supply the garrison of his post, he urged Killbuck to plot the assassination of a Wyandot leader named Baubee. Killbuck promised to try, but he could carry out this task only at the appropriate opportunity.[103] Although Killbuck was also motivated by threats against his life from Baubee, he knew that care would be necessary, since the Delaware country was now so empty that he had little chance of sanctuary there from the wrath of Baubee's followers. The emptying of the Delaware lands was not helped by Brodhead's insistence that the people of Coshocking move their village to the vicinity of Fort Pitt so they would be protected.[104] Daniel Brodhead's demands for Delaware sacrifices are all the more ironic in light of what the tribe already had given up by signing a treaty, exposing themselves to open hostility from other tribes, evacuating villages, and losing their well-known leader White Eyes at the hand of an American assassin. The pressure on the native peoples was so great that Daniel Brodhead wanted Zeisberger to journey to Philadelphia, where he might depict the plight of the Delawares to the Continental Congress. Of course Brodhead's appeals to and expectations of Zeisberger were so open that even the Moravian might have feared for his own life![105]

By 1781 the Ohio frontier was in a state of flux, with more changes in the offing. The personalities there briefly included the well-known Mohawk leader Joseph Brant, who apparently tired of the politics at Niagara and took a sabbatical in the West. During the course of his Ohio respite he joined the partisan leader Simon Girty and a band of warriors to raid the Pennsylvania frontier.[106] Also present in the Ohio country was a detachment of Virginians under Colonel Archibald Lochry bound west to reinforce George Rogers Clark. The detachment was defeated badly when it fell into a trap at the mouth of the Great Miami River; its adversary was a band of some thirty warriors led by Brant. The skirmish left the colonel and thirty-seven others dead, while the remainder of the 101-man detachment was taken prisoner.[107] Although such a victory would ordinarily have called for a victory celebration in Detroit, Colonel Arents DePeyster asked potential revelers to stay away from Detroit and refused to distribute rum to those already there. There would be no partying until he was certain that the madman Clark was not descending on Detroit.[108]

The Delawares also sustained significant changes in their lives during

1781. DePeyster approved the removal of the Moravians from their villages in the Muskingum-Tuscarawas area. David Zeisberger, John Heckewelder, their Moravian followers, and any Delawares still in eastern Ohio were escorted westward by Captain Pipe and the Half King of the Wyandots. The missionaries tried to stall until after the harvest in the fall but finally lost out and had to move.

The realities of the conflict's impact on the Delaware peoples registered profoundly with Captain Pipe. Despite his realignment with the British interests in northwestern Ohio, he was no fool. To him it seemed clear by late 1781 that the British used the Indians for their own purposes and would quickly abandon them if necessity demanded it. During a council at Detroit early in November he delivered a bitterly sarcastic speech, denouncing the British as mere pretenders to the term "father" in relation to the Indians. John Heckewelder witnessed this "bold, sensible, and satirical speech" and left a record of it.[109]

> *Father!* I have said *Father,* tho indeed I am ignorant of the cause for so calling him having never known of any other Father than the French, and considering the English as Brothers. But as *this* Name is now also imposed upon us, I therefore make us of it and say:
>
> *Father!* Some time ago You put a War hatchet into my hands, saying: take this Weapon, and try it on the heads of my Enemies, the Long Knives (the American People) and let me afterwards know if it was sharp and good.
>
> *Father!* Altho at the time You gave me this Weapon, I had neither cause nor inclination to go to War against a People who had done me no injury: yet out of obedience to You, who *say* You are my Father, and call me your child, I received the Hatchet, well knowing, that if I did *not* obey, he would withhold from me the necessaries of life, without which I could not subsist, and which were not elsewhere to be procured and had, but at the House of my Fathers!
>
> *Father!* Withal You may perhaps think me a fool, in risking my life at your call! And in a cause too, by which I have no prospect of gaining anything; for it is *your* cause, and *not* mine to fight the Long Knives (the Virginians or the American People). You both have raised the quarrel within yourselves; and by right, you ought to fight it out *Yourselves* and *not* compel Your Children, the Indians, to expose themselves to Danger for *Your* sake!
>
> *Father!* Many lives have already been lost on *your* account. Nations

have suffered and been weakened! Children have lost Parents, brothers, and relatives! Wifes have lost Husbands! It is not known how many more *may* perish before *Your* war will be at an end!

Father! I have said: that You may perhaps think me a fool, rushing thoughtless on Your Enemy! Do *not* believe this Father! Think not that I lack sense *sufficient to convince me,* that altho You *now* pretend to keep up a perpetual enmity to the Long Knives; (American People) you may, e'er long, conclude a Peace with them!

Father! You say you love your children the Indians! This You have often told them; and indeed it is your interest to say so to them, in order to have them at your service!

But *Father!* who of us can believe, that you could love a People differing in Colour to that of Yours, more than those (of such) who have a white Skin like unto that of Yours!

Father! Pay attention to what I now shall say! While *You! Father!* are setting me on Your Enemy, much in the same manner as a hunter sets on his Dogs at the game—while *I* be in the act of rushing *on* this Enemy of Yours, with the bloody destructive Weapon You gave me: I May *perchance* happen to look back, from whence you started me: and *what may I see!* I shall probably see my Father shaking hands with the Long Knives. *Yes!* With *those very People* he now calls his Enemys! *and* while doing this: he may be laughing at *my* folly, and having *obeyed* him and am *now* risking *my* life at his command. *Father!* keep what I have said in remembrance.

Now *Father!* here is what hath been done with the Hatchet you gave! (The Pipe hands Depeyster the stick with the one scalp attached) I have done what you bid me to do with the Hatchet and found it sharp. Nevertheless I did *not* do all what I might have done! *No!* I did *not!* My *heart* failed me! I felt compassion for *Your* Enemy! Innocence has *no* share in *Your* quarrels; therefore I distinguished! I *spared!* I took some live flesh (prisoners) which, while bringing on to You, I espied one of Your large Canoes on which I put the same for You! In a few days You will receive this flesh, and find, that the Skin is of the same colour as Yours!

Father! I hope you will not destroy what I have *saved! You! Father!* have the means of keeping *alive* what with me would have to *starve for want!* The Warriors Cabin is generally empty! *Your House is always full.*[110]

According to Heckewelder and other eyewitnesses this was one of the most powerful speeches ever delivered by a native leader to a white officer in the presence of other white witnesses. Captain Pipe became so agitated in the course of his peroration that twice he stepped within arm's length of the British commander and had to be warned to keep his distance. John Heckewelder observed, moreover, that he much doubted "whether the interpreter [Bawbee] ever informed the commandant of all that Pipe said and what the true meaning of his words were. I was astonished to hear an Indian chief deliver himself after this bold manner to a British officer."[111]

The greatest wartime tragedy to befall the Delawares, however, was not the eventual peacemaking between the British and the Americans, although that did come; it was the unfortunate massacre of a number of Moravian Indians. When they were forced westward in the fall of 1781 these Moravian Indians were left to build a new town in an area where they were without support. There was little extra food at Detroit, their kinspeople had none, and bitter winter weather intensified their hunger. Knowing that they had left crops in the fields in their old villages, a group of Moravian Delawares returned the 140 miles in a desperate effort to cut some of the corn still standing. As they did so a band of Pennsylvania militia approached, but there was no alarm since the harvesters regarded them as fellow Christians who meant them no harm. When one young man hailed them as friends, he was murdered. The troops then took approximately ninety prisoners and locked them in one of the houses in the abandoned town of Gnadenhutten. A debate raged over the fate of the prisoners, with some arguing to return them to Fort Pitt as prisoners and others demanding that they be killed so the troops could continue on their way without the bother of captives. A unanimous vote for execution was followed by taking the victims one by one into the schoolhouse, where they were killed by a blow to the head. When the Americans thought all had been slain, they set fire to the building in order to wipe out all traces of this heinous deed. At least one victim, however, had only been stunned, so he lay quietly among the bodies until the Americans had gone; he then slipped away into the forest. Within a matter of days the story would be known in Sandusky and Detroit and soon throughout the Ohio villages and then across the Six Nations country.[112] This catastrophe so alarmed the remaining Moravian Indians and their missionaries that they began to negotiate with the Chippewas for permission to settle along the Huron River near Lake St. Clair.[113]

The death of the Moravian Delawares put the Ohio peoples on guard more than ever and prompted a few to seek an opportunity for revenge, which came in the summer of 1782. Inhabitants of the western Pennsylva-

Modern reconstruction of the Moravian Delaware village of Schoenbrunn ("beautiful spring"). Schoenbrunn was founded in 1772 as a mission to the Delawares. The settlement eventually included sixty dwellings and more than three hundred inhabitants, who created Ohio's first civil code and built its first Christian church and schoolhouse. Courtesy of the Ohio Historical Society.

nia frontiers were convinced that the harassing raids on their settlements were originating in the Delaware and Wyandot settlements in the vicinity of Upper Sandusky.[114] Since most of the Pennsylvania militia (not to mention those of other frontier states) believed the best defense was an offensive strike against the heartland of the enemy, plans were laid for an expedition into northwest Ohio in the summer of 1782. The commander was to be George Washington's friend, confidant, land agent, and fellow speculator Colonel William Crawford, who was an experienced militia officer highly regarded for his leadership. After ten days of marching, the troops reached Upper Sandusky, which was deserted, but they encountered the well-prepared Delawares and allies from Detroit on June 3. After a day of fighting the Native Americans were joined by reinforcements who prolonged the battle yet another day. Crawford elected to withdraw under the cover of darkness, a tactic that allowed a number of the Pennsylvanians to escape, but not Crawford and a surgeon's mate. In retaliation for the

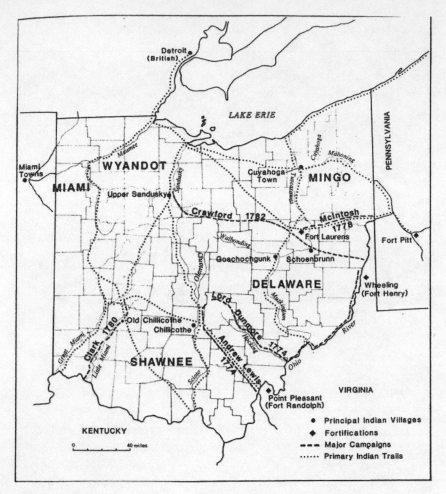

Invasions of Ohio Indian country, 1774–82. From George W. Knepper, *Ohio and Its People* (Kent, Ohio: Kent State University Press, 1997), 39. Map by Margaret Geib and the University of Akron Cartographic Laboratory from *Ohio and Its People,* copyright 1989 by The Kent State University Press, Kent, Ohio. Reprinted with permission of The Kent State University Press.

Moravian villagers the two were marked for death, but the surgeon's mate escaped to tell of their ordeal; Crawford unfortunately was tortured and burned to death.[115]

It is perhaps cruelly ironic that while military operations would end with the British defeat at Yorktown, fighting continued in the Ohio Valley. In addition to the usual raiding, including a party of western Iroquois

Ohio's First Peoples

The infamous death of Colonel William Crawford, 1782, by James Boroff. Courtesy of the Seneca County Museum, Tiffin, Ohio.

assaulting the Virginia frontier near the present Wheeling, West Virginia, a substantial number of Ohio forest soldiers chose once more to attempt rolling back the Kentucky frontier of the hated Virginians. Descending the Ohio tributaries, this expedition laid siege to Bryan's Station in Kentucky for more than thirty hours in mid-August, fooled the inhabitants by pretending to withdraw, and then badly defeated the settlers at the Battle of the Blue Licks. Daniel Boone used the word "rout" in describing the conflict; seventy-five Virginians (including two officers) died fighting a larger party of native warriors from north of the Ohio.[116] Given the nature of the conflict in the Ohio country, it should be no surprise that the quid pro quo for the defeat of Boone and his men was a raid led by George Rogers Clark against the Shawnee villages of Chillicothe and Standing Stone in early November. Since the townspeople were forewarned, they withdrew; the troops killed only ten, captured ten, and destroyed the cornfields of the villages.[117]

At the end of 1782 the native peoples of the Ohio country were still struggling for peace and their homelands. Although the tribes had been drawn into the war for independence that the former colonials called the

American Revolution, that era of warfare was really only a continuation of the preceding decades. Perhaps the most troubling aspect of this change for the native peoples was the possibility that their patrons of the previous twenty years were leaving, opening the way for the tribal leaders to face the new dilemma of holding the Americans at the Ohio. Their war would go on for more than four decades, ending in yet more military defeats and, eventually, the total loss of their homelands.

4

THE WAR FOR OHIO

IF THE YEARS BETWEEN 1775 AND 1783 HAD BEEN A STRUGGLE FOR
survival by Native Americans in Ohio, the next three decades were marked
by continued efforts to maintain their tribal integrity.[1] No matter how many
wars were fought and won, treaties negotiated and boundaries agreed on,
the issue remained the same. As one tribal leader framed it to the Virginians
in 1777: "Brothers . . . the difference is about our land."[2]

What the Ohio peoples had wanted, and thought they had confirmed
in 1768 at the Fort Stanwix conference, was that the Ohio River would remain the western boundary for the European settlements.[3] Unfortunately
for the Native Americans, the rich bottomlands of the river and its tributaries were too tempting to the pioneer farmer for this agreement to stay
in effect. Even before the Revolutionary War was over, cabins began to dot
the alluvial terraces. When federal army units burned them out in the late
1780s, officers reported that the determined frontierspeople were back before the ashes were cold. Hoping to define space for themselves in the face
of this rising tide, the Wyandots, Delawares, Chippewas, and Ottawas met

representatives of the new government at Fort McIntosh on January 21, 1785.

It must have been somewhat bothersome to the dozen Native American delegates that the language of the treaty was condescending toward them. The United States agreed to "give peace," demanded five chiefs as hostages against the return of captives held by the Native Americans, and required that the tribes acknowledge the sovereignty of the United States.[4]

Clearly, the new nation regarded itself as the victor claiming the spoils of war and the native groups as the losers, regardless of previous alliances or devoted service.[5] This guilt-by-association approach meant that even those factions that had remained loyal to the Americans were subject to the same treatment as those that had supported the British. Thus the Ohio tribal peoples had no bargaining position. They could either accept what the United States offered or engage in a resistance that would bring further defeat and humiliation. The chiefs conceded the territory delineated in the treaty's third article.

The larger, long-term threat from the United States to a Native American land of peace and safety was not long in emerging. Indeed, the vision of an Indianless West was already clear in the fertile mind of Thomas Jefferson, whose Ordinance of 1784 envisioned a Northwest scribed like a giant game of tic-tac-toe, with the winner controlling all the squares, that is, the several states he envisioned lying beyond the Ohio River. Although admittedly these new entities within the federal republic would be crafted from lands "purchased of the Indian inhabitants," there were no other references to the presence or rights of Native Americans.[6] Four months after the Fort McIntosh agreement ceded most Indian lands south of the present Dover, Ohio, another step fraught with the potential for conflict was taken when the Congress passed the Ordinance of 1785 on May 20, 1785.[7] Again the Native Americans were mentioned only as sellers of the lands, not dwellers in the lands. The only exception was the land reserved in the towns of Gnadenhutten, Schoenbrunn, and Salem for the Christian Indians "who were formerly settled there, or the remains of that society."[8] Stamping out squares like a giant waffle iron left little space for tribal homelands. Selling acreage to eager farmers meant money for the federal coffers, land to satisfy the citizens, and farmers-cum-militia who could defend the West. Little wonder then that the Ohio country would witness another long period of armed struggle, in effect lasting until the death of Tecumseh at the Battle of the Thames, which took place *after* Ohio gained statehood.[9]

Ohio's First Peoples

Another factor that complicated forest diplomacy during the same period was the Indian policy still practiced by the British officials in the Northwest. Although the Peace of Paris granted independence to the United States, established international boundaries for the new country, and provided for the withdrawal of the British from their posts, the latter were reluctant to evacuate for both economic and strategic reasons. The fur trade was still a lucrative source of income, and the forest soldiers were potentially valuable to the defense of the British Empire in Canada. So long as the royal officials hinted at support for any of the tribes, that gave hope to all that the king had not abandoned them and substance to the American accusations that the British were still behind the scalping and raiding parties in the Old Northwest. If they quietly backed Native American opposition to the United States, the British hoped thus to thwart the expansionism of the fledgling nation. Some scholars even suggest that by the 1790s John Graves Simcoe's approach as lieutenant governor of Upper Canada (now Ontario) was to regain the territory ceded to the United States in 1783 by enlisting the Ohio tribes as allies in that effort.[10]

The least manageable, but in some ways most expected, scene in this tableau was the day-to-day conflict between frontier settlers (desirous of land and the extermination of the tribespeople) and their equally eager Native American adversaries, who were determined to have a safe homeland or exact revenge for some of the destructive raids they had suffered at the hands of the Americans. Among the most fractious of the opposing groups were the Kentuckians and the Shawnees, whose enmity toward each other was painted in blood. The Kentucky settlements of Virginia were so far west as to be beyond practical control by the authorities in Richmond and equally isolated from military assistance. For the most part, then, the settlements were on their own. In the minds of the frontier militia, moreover, there seems to have been no greater sport than going on an Indian raid.[11]

Despite the intention of the United States government to treat the Northwest as conquered territory and its Native American inhabitants accordingly, federal officials were aware that the Ohio River boundary was a sensitive issue. As a result, a series of posts were constructed at key points as a temporary means of keeping the ever-pressing settlers east of the river. In 1785 a small detachment of army regulars built at the mouth of the Muskingum (present-day Marietta) a five-pointed wooden stockade fort that was named Fort Harmar. Also that year the army built a post at the

Computer recreation of Fort Harmar. Courtesy of David Shelburne of Shelburne Films, Athens, Ohio.

mouth of the Great Miami that was named Fort Finney. The following year Fort Steuben was constructed on the site of modern Steubenville.[12]

Many of the Native Americans saw these posts in a different light, looking on them as footholds beyond the Ohio River that would serve only as points of departure for the next onslaught of settlers. These stockades were convenient locations for conversations between the U.S. government and the Native Americans. At Finney, for example, the construction crew also built a twenty-by-sixty-foot council house, outside the fort's walls "but within gunshot."[13] There the Indian commissioners appointed by the Continental Congress intended to negotiate with the Shawnees for lands north of the Ohio River. Within three weeks of the completion of the outpost, several chiefs arrived for a conference, including the Shawnee leader Captain Johnny, the well-known Wyandot chiefs Half King and Tarhe, and the experienced Delaware diplomat known as Captain Pipe, along with his equally influential colleague Wingenund and the son of the fallen Captain White Eyes. Basically this was a courtesy call in which the forest diplomats expressed their delight in seeing the American representatives as "brothers."[14] Two weeks later a group of Indian women assembled in the council house, asking for the attendance of the commandant. Captain Finney and his men were then treated to an oration by one of the older women, who concluded by asking for something to "warm their hearts," that is, alcohol. Indeed two weeks later, when the Indians put on dancing parties in the afternoon, they wanted something to warm their hearts and help them dance, which led them to "break up pretty merry."[15] When no other Shawnees had arrived by the end of December, Captain Pipe suggested that messengers be sent urging them to hasten. Finally, on January 14, 1786, a party of Wapatomica Shawnees reached the fort, and a week later Buckongahelas and twenty more Delawares came.[16] From the day of their arrival the Shawnees held dances every day, including the day that one of their visiting chiefs died![17]

After many weeks of waiting, the conference finally convened at Fort Finney on January 26, 1786, with a speech of welcome by the Americans. No doubt the commissioner giving the speech struck something of a raw nerve when he commented on the American victory in the recent revolution. After a day of reflection, the Shawnee leader Captain Johnny denied the land rights claimed by the United States on the basis of the late war. He "asked if the Great Spirit had given it to them to cut and portion the country in the manner proposed. The Ohio River they would agree to, nothing short."[18] He then hushed the assembly by offering a "mixed belt," indicating neither peace nor war. One of the American commissioners pushed the belt to the floor and put his foot on it while the Indians looked on sullenly. In the afternoon a Shawnee leader named Molunthy tried to soothe ruffled feelings by softening the chief warrior's words. In offering a white belt, he "prayed [the Americans] would have pity on their women and children."[19] Three days later, on February 1, 1786, after the treaty was signed, the American commissioners delivered presents as well as provisions for six days to the Indian leaders. The Half King meanwhile apparently had urged the Delawares not to sign so there would be more goods for the Americans to give to the Wyandots. The usually outspoken Captain Pipe had been sitting listening, but he finally stood up and said: "Brothers, the Delawares are perfectly contented, they have land enough."[20] Pipe promised, furthermore, that he and the Delawares would escort the surveyors when they ran the boundary line. As he made this commitment, he turned to the Half King and stunned him by telling him that he would go too! As a guarantee of this agreement, five hostages were left at the post, which was finally free of all its visitors (more than 150 from December onward) by February 13, 82 days after the first guests arrived.[21]

In the fall of 1786 another episode in the ongoing feud between the Shawnees and the Kentuckians took place, when militia led by George Rogers Clark and Benjamin Logan headed a two-pronged invasion across the Ohio.[22] Clark and his troops were to advance toward the Miami towns while Logan and his followers, including Daniel Boone and Simon Kenton, targeted the Shawnee villages on the Mad River. In the passion of the attack, no distinction was made between Shawnees who had been willing to accept peace and those unwilling to do so. Molunthy, the leader of a village hoping for peace who had promoted agreement at Fort Finney, was killed by an officer named Hugh McGary still burning with vengeance for earlier defeats by the Shawnees during their raids into Kentucky.[23] With this raid the door to negotiation seemed to close, opening the portal onto another long period of attack and retaliation.

In the face of the conquest mentality of the United States and the burning antipathy of the Kentuckians, many of the western tribes talked of renewing their long-desired confederacy. At Brownstown, near Detroit, in November and December of 1786, representatives of numerous tribes gathered in an effort to present a united front. The well-known Mohawk leader Joseph Brant urged the council to accept the position that "the interests of any one nation should be the welfare of all the others." After several days of consideration the Five Nations, Wyandots, Delawares, Shawnees, Ottawas, Chippewas, Potawatomies, Miamis, Cherokees, Weas, and Piankeshaws addressed the Congress of the United States. They indicated a desire for all negotiations to be carried out between the United States on the one hand and the "whole confederacy" on the other. The confederated tribes were unhappy with the divide-and-conquer approach of the Congress, blaming the unrest of the early 1780s on the policy of the United States.[24] Despite the call for unity, there were many divisions among the tribes. The Wyandots, Delawares, and Six Nations already had signed treaties with the United States in 1784 and 1785, thus placing their interest in peace, not resistance. These treaties drew the scorn of the Shawnees, whose constant defense of their villages against raiders from south of the Ohio had honed both their defensive skills and their resentment to a fine edge. Despite the tribal bickering, the tribes all agreed to ask the United States for an inclusive new treaty that would confirm the Ohio River as the boundary and settle all outstanding differences.[25]

Mohawk chief Thayendanegea, or Joseph Brant. During Brant's visit to England in 1786, the renowned artist Gilbert Stuart captured the charisma of this powerful Iroquois leader who influenced the Ohio frontier during the last two decades of the eighteenth century. Courtesy of the Fenimore Art Museum, Cooperstown, New York.

There were so many competing agendas on the Ohio frontier in the postwar period that distilling a clear policy on either side was nearly impossible. Native peoples wanted guarantees of lands protected from aggrandizement; settlers wanted ever-more lands plus an absence of raids; American governmental officials wanted peace but also the opportunity to acquire land from the Native Americans that was already considered in the national domain by virtue of the Peace of Paris; the British wanted a continuation of the fur trade and a check on the westward push of the Americans; and easterners were looking to this new west as a land of opportunity where they might relocate to establish themselves and their children's children.[26]

Whatever frontier emissaries may have said about the recognition of tribal rights or land, the Northwest Ordinance of 1787 cast the American die. The Northwest was to be surveyed, sold, settled, and shaped into new states. A territory led by a governor and judges, followed in due course by a general assembly elected by the free male inhabitants, provided no place for Native Americans. Article III spoke of "good faith" toward the Indians, who would not lose their property "without their consent" or be "invaded or disturbed, unless in just and lawful wars authorized by Congress." There was, too, the provision that "laws founded in justice and humanity, shall from time to time be made for preventing wrongs being done to them, and for preserving peace and friendship with them."[27] Perhaps most ominous to the tribes was the role specified for the Ohio River. It was not to be a dividing line keeping the settlements and native villages apart, but, as Article V of the Ordinance explained, the Ohio would be a part of the boundary for each of three new states formed from the Northwest Territory.[28]

Even as this ordinance was being passed on July 13, 1787, plans already were under way for the first organized assault by settlers. While there had been earlier scattered attempts by small groups and individuals, these technically violated existing treaties, so small detachments of troops like those stationed at Fort Harmar and Fort Steuben repeatedly attempted to drive back the settlers. The new plan, however, would have the blessing of the federal government and would be led by well-connected companies intent on staying. One of these was the Ohio Company of Associates, organized in 1786, which managed to buy more than 1,700,000 acres from the Congress for $1,000,000.[29] By late 1787 the first group sponsored by the company was ready to move west under the leadership of the experienced

Computer recreation of Campus Martius and mounds. Courtesy of David Shelburne of Shelburne Films, Athens, Ohio.

Revolutionary War officer Rufus Putnam.[30] Putnam had been dreaming of western land since the 1770s, when he and other New Englanders in the Company of Military Adventurers explored the possibility of founding a settlement in west Florida on the banks of the Mississippi River.[31] Given Putnam's background and the constant threat of Indian attack in the Ohio country, each man in the party was to be armed for war; clearly, one did not use bayonets for hunting![32] So great was the fear of assault by forest soldiers in 1788 that the Ohio Company settlers determined to build a fort for a retreat in time of attack. No simple stockade, this four-sided bastion christened Campus Martius had overhanging corner blockhouses, an outer defensive abatis of sharpened trees, a palisade, and posts driven at an angle into the base of the fort's main wall. Despite the fear driving the labor involved in such a construction, the fort was never assaulted and was eventually dismantled.

Even as the builders of Campus Martius erected the square timbers carefully marked to match along the fort's main wall, there were plans underway for a major conference with the western tribes at the falls of the Muskingum River about thirty miles from the new settlements. Supplies had been stored at the falls by territorial governor Arthur St. Clair in preparation for the conference, but when roving Ojibwa raiders struck the guard detail and killed two soldiers, St. Clair cancelled the meeting. The governor blamed the cancellation on the tribes, thus poisoning the possibility of communications and increasing the likelihood of renewed raiding. Since neither Arthur St. Clair nor Josiah Harmar trusted negotiations with the Indians, they assumed war was in the offing. On the other side only the Shawnees and Miamis refused to confer, so Joseph Brant informed the Americans that the majority of the tribes did want a conference. Since St. Clair refused to meet outside the shadow of a fortified post, the delegates gathered at Fort Harmar, just down the Muskingum River from the new Campus Martius.

One can only speculate about the delegates' feelings as they rode down the Muskingum River trail. The high bluff along which the trail ran on the west side of the Muskingum afforded a striking panorama of the lower-lying east bank of the Muskingum and its confluence with the Ohio River. The absence of tree cover in January would have allowed riders to see both American forts (Campus Martius and Fort Harmar), the buildings going up outside Campus Martius (the new settlement of Marietta), and in the background, almost as a reminder from the past left behind by the Adena and Hopewellian builders, the sacred grounds marked by earthen walls and ceremonial mounds.

On January 9, 1789, St. Clair and the delegates signed the Treaty of Fort Harmar, which had been agreed to by representatives of the Wyandots, Delawares, Ottawas, Chippewas, Potawatomies, and Sacs. Among the witnesses were Lieutenant Colonel Josiah Harmar of the First U.S. Regiment, Ebenezer Denny and three other ensigns from the regiment, and several interested civilians. Conspicuously absent from the proceedings was Joseph Brant, who had carried on some diplomatic correspondence with St. Clair and who had been one of the motivating forces behind the renewed attempts to energize the confederacy. Since neither Brant nor delegates from the Wabash and Miami were present, the treaty could hardly be called a united effort. Also absent were the Shawnees, who were among the most adamant critics of St. Clair and his attempts to negotiate the Ohio peoples out of their lands.

From the first article of the agreement, it was clearly a reiteration of earlier ones made at Fort Stanwix and Fort McIntosh. The Fort McIntosh agreement about the return of prisoners was repeated, again with two Wyandots being specified as hostages until the "prisoners are restored."[33] The boundary stipulated at Fort McIntosh, not the Ohio River, was re-affirmed. To render this more palatable, the Wyandot, Delaware, Ottawa, and Chippewa received $6,000 worth of goods "to the end that the same may remain as a division line between the lands of the United States of America, and the lands of said nations, **forever**."[34] The ultimate power of the United States over the territory granted to the tribes "forever" is clear in the third article, which states that the tribes may not dispose of the lands to any other "sovereign power" other than the United States.[35] Articles IV and V were likely to prove problematic. Ohio's first peoples were given permission in the first to hunt on the lands ceded to the United States, "so long as they demean themselves peaceably, and offer no injury or annoyance to any of the subjects or citizens of the said United States."[36] In Article V, an Indian accused of murder or robbery would have to be surrendered to the authority of the United States, but a citizen of the United States accused of similar crimes against an Indian would not be turned over to Native American law but to the authorities of the United States. Interestingly, however, any citizen who tried to settle on Indian lands could be punished by the nations "in such manner as they see fit."[37] Horse stealing merited the complete attention of Article VI, because "the practice of stealing horses has prevailed very much." Anyone continuing to steal horses was "to be punished with the utmost severity."[38] The newly allied nations were asked to warn the United States of any impending attacks in Article VIII, while Articles VII and X attempted to lay the basis for an organized trade. The remaining articles reserved the posts of Detroit and Michilimackinac for the United States, confirmed the peace, welcomed the Sacs and Potawatomies into the fold, and clarified the Miami River section of the boundary line specified at Fort McIntosh.[39]

Arthur St. Clair signed for the United States, while twenty-eight tribal representatives did likewise for their respective nations. Captain Pipe, the Delaware leader who had predicted that the English and the Americans would make peace behind the backs of the Native Americans, decided to take the path of least resistance and sign this agreement as he had the treaty of Fort Pitt, eleven years earlier.[40] Since Captain White Eyes was dead and John Killbuck Jr. had fallen from leadership, Pipe was the only repeat signee. His agreement, however, was all the more important since he had led his followers away from the Delaware villages along the Muskingum-Tuscarawas, had directed attacks against the Americans during the Revolution, and then, with British backing, had persuaded the Moravian ministers and their followers to move closer to the Wyandot-Delaware nexus near Upper Sandusky.[41] He and the leader known as Wingenund, who also signed this document at Fort Harmar, had witnessed the brutal death of Colonel William Crawford in retaliation for the massacre of the Moravians at Gnadenhutten.[42] If two of the strongest anti-American Delawares were willing to agree to peace, apparently their realism had led them to understand the necessity of compromise.

In order to divide the tribes who might have cooperated in the worrisome Indian Confederacy of the Northwest, a separate article gave the Wyandots permission to take away lands being used by the Shawnees, because "the Shawanese have been so restless, and caused so much trouble, both to them and to the United States. . . . [I]f they will not now be at peace, [the Wyandots] will dispossess them, and take the country into their own hands."[43] Also to placate the Wyandots the United States allowed them to continue living in two small villages that otherwise would have fallen out of the territory granted the Indians.[44]

This agreement was in some ways a compromise for both sides, largely because neither wanted war. Secretary of War Henry Knox, a longtime confidant of President Washington, perceived the issue in terms of money to recruit, arm, and garrison troops. The new nation did not have the funds to expand the military presence in the Northwest and carry out protracted wars in order to conquer the tribes. Negotiation and concession were far less costly both in terms of money and soldiers.[45] The tribes, on the other hand, had gone through decades of warfare, death, destruction, loss of villages, and forced relocation of entire populations. The westward trek of the Delawares and Shawnees across the Ohio country between 1775 and 1782 is well illustrated by the maps in Helen Tanner's *Atlas of Great Lakes Indian History.*

Given the divided nature of the several tribes in Ohio, the absence of major delegations, the less-than-representative nature of the parties present, and the almost daily warfare throughout the region, it is no wonder that the Treaty of Fort Harmar resolved nothing. The Shawnees clamored for more pressure on the western settlers, while the frontiersmen repeatedly pled with the government to break the power of the Indians. The federal

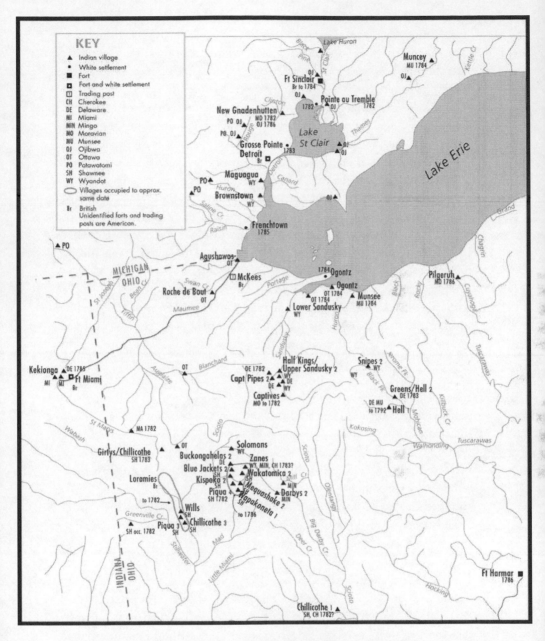

KEY

▲ Indian village
● White settlement
■ Fort
⊡ Fort and white settlement
⊡ Trading post
CH Cherokee
DE Delaware
MI Miami
MIN Mingo
MO Moravian
MU Munsee
OJ Ojibwa
OT Ottawa
PO Patawatomi
SH Shawnee
WY Wyandot
⬭ Villages occupied to approx. same date
Br British
Unidentified forts and trading posts are American.

Lake Huron

Muncey
MU 1784

Ft Sinclair
Br to 1784

OJ

OJ

Pointe au Tremble
1782   1782   OJ   1782

New Gnadenhutten
PO OJ   MD 1782   OJ 1786
PO OJ

Lake St Clair

Grosse Pointe   1783
Detroit   Br

OJ

Maguagua
WY

OJ

Lake Erie

Brownstown
WY

Frenchtown
1785

MICHIGAN
OHIO

Agushawos
OT

McKees
Br

Roche de Bout
OT

1784 Ogontz

Ogontz
OT 1784   Munsee
OT 1784   MU 1784

Lower Sandusky
WY

Pilgeruh
MD 1786

Kekionga   DE 1785
MI   MI   Ft Miami
Br

OT

Blanchard

DE 1782
Capt Pipes 2   WY
DE   WY
DE

Captives
MO to 1782

Half Kings/
Upper Sandusky 2

Snipes 2
WY

WY

Greens/Hell 2
DE 1783

DE MU
to 1792   Hell 1

MA 1782

Girtys/Chillicothe
SH 1783

Buckongahelas 2
OT   DE

Solomons
WY

Blue Jackets 2   SH
SH

Kispoko 2   SH

Piqua 4   SH 1782

Loramies
Br

to 1782

Greenville Cr.

Wills
SH

Piqua 3   Chillicothe
SH   SH

Zanes
WY, MIN, CH 1783?

Wakatomica 2
MIN

Mequashake 2

Tapakaneta 1
to 1786

Darbys 2
MIN

INDIANA
OHIO

Ft Harmar
1786

Chillicothe 1
SH, CH 1782?

Westward movement of tribes after 1782. Based on Helen Hornbeck Tanner, ed., *Atlas of Great Lakes Indian History* (Norman: University of Oklahoma Press, 1987), 85.

government had neither the troops nor the money to carry out a punitive war against the Indians of the Ohio country. There was also the larger issue of international diplomacy, no small matter for a fledgling country that did not want nor could afford for a frontier incident to blossom into renewed warfare with the British. By 1790, however, the government could no longer postpone an operation. General Josiah Harmar was to lead his troops into western Ohio, where they were expected to destroy the villages and punish the warriors of the tribes.

Unfortunately for Harmar, he was ill equipped to carry out his mission. While he had wanted an army of regulars, his force was largely composed of militia. Even his regulars were not in peak condition, given the parsimony of the government. The pay of the regular army had been cut, a step that had led at least some of the soldiers at Fort Harmar to sell their shoes in Marietta in order to raise some ready money. A poorly supplied force of more than 1,100 militia and only some 300 regulars was ill starred at best. If there ever were sunshine soldiers that certainly was the case with the frontier militia. Most of these individuals were inexperienced in warfare and expected no resistance from much-maligned "savages." Militia also weren't accustomed to following orders, especially from someone not one of them.[46] Those without experience, moreover, were often impetuous and rash, attributes that had cost the Kentuckians dearly at the Battle of the Blue Licks. What few, if any, of the militia would admit was that the sylvan soldiers were skilled in the art of forest warfare. As Leroy Eid has pointed out, many of the Indian victories resulted from superior tactics on familiar ground.[47]

Despite the low opinion of the Shawnees held by the frontiersmen, the Shawnees were no mere "banditti," as they often were characterized. By the summer of 1789 the leader known as Blue Jacket had emerged as a powerful advocate of reviving the much-desired confederacy of western tribes that individuals like Joseph Brant had preached for some years.[48] An insightful diplomat, Blue Jacket sought to cultivate the support of the western tribes, the Indian traders, and the British officials. Warriors were necessary, but guns, powder, lead, and other supplies were fundamental. The pipeline to European manufacturing had to be kept open. His own Shawnee followers and their western Seneca allies who lived among them were firmly behind him, as were some of the Delawares who had not gone to Fort Harmar for the treaty in January and would not negotiate with the

Artist's depiction of Little Turtle. Reproduced by permission of the Smithsonian Institution. B.A.E. negative no. 794.

Americans. Among the Miamis the leaders known as Le Gris and Little Turtle supported Blue Jacket.

It was not until September 1790 that Harmar and his troops left Fort Washington at the present Cincinatti. The general's goal was to advance northward toward present-day Fort Wayne, Indiana, where Miami, Shawnee, and Delaware villages were to be destroyed, their inhabitants dispersed, and their warriors killed or captured. The villages' advance scouts, who knew the troops were coming, carefully watched the movement of the expedition. In an effort to allay the fears of the British and of nonhostile Native American groups that might believe themselves the target of the invasion, the Americans actually had sent out messages warning of the expedition. Progress on the march was slow because of the size of the columns and the large numbers of livestock being driven along as meals on the hoof, or MOH.[49] John Armstrong reported in his diary of the expedition that in three days they had advanced only thirty miles.[50] In advance of the invading army, Native American leaders took steps to protect themselves. At the site the invaders called Miami Village, which was Kekionga, at the site of modern Fort Wayne, Indiana, the defenders burned the village and abandoned others nearby. The absence of Native Americans led the militia to begin looting what was left of the dwellings for souvenirs. After several days of sacking in the area, the frontier forces entered an apparently empty village that they proceeded to plunder. When the allied natives under Little Turtle sprang their trap the militia panicked; more than 90 percent of them fled the field, leaving Captain John Armstrong, thirty of his regulars, and nine militia to hold off the assault. As Armstrong described it, "from the dastardly conduct of the militia, the troops were obliged to retreat. I lost one sergeant and 21 of the 30 men of my command. . . . Many of the militia threw away their arms without firing a shot, ran through the federal troops and threw them in disorder."[51] When it was apparent that no rally was coming, Captain Armstrong and his surviving troops ran for their lives. Armstrong first hid between a stump and a log until it was dark, and then waded into a pond, where he stayed for seven hours. Despite the ice forming on his clothes, he remained in the freezing water, because he could hear the Indians scouring the woods for stragglers. When he finally came out he found a deep ravine, where he built a fire and dried his clothes before continuing his attempt to rejoin the army.[52] Armstrong and the other survivors returned to Harmar's camp near the burned town of Chillicothe, from which the general allowed raids against other nearby villages to be undertaken. By October 20, 1790, he had decided to withdraw to Fort Washington, but he warned his troops that the artillery would fire at anyone who broke ranks.[53] Before leaving he allowed another raid toward a previously abandoned Miami town that reportedly had been reoccupied. This proved to be another military disaster; the commander divided his troops to flank the village and they were themselves decimated. Harmar then commanded the withdrawal to Fort Washington. The combined Native American forces might have fallen upon the retreating columns, but a lunar eclipse so worried the Ottawas (as a bad spiritual omen) that they refused to continue. Once Harmar reached safety, he claimed victory in light of the villages destroyed and corn burned, but he was forced to return east for a court martial to clear his name. Subordinates like Major David Zeigler testified in the general's defense that the failures of the militia and its lack of organization had scuttled the expedition.[54] Zeigler even reported that when he planned to discipline a militia sergeant, he could not because the militiaman's brother was a captain who would have used his influence to "bid defiance."[55]

While the Shawnees and Miamis might celebrate their defeat of the 1790

Ohio's First Peoples

expedition, it would be only a matter of time before yet another attempt would be made to crush them. The new nation could not tolerate a loss of face, despite Harmar's exoneration and the assertions that the Indians had been punished. Governor St. Clair was ordered by the secretary of war to begin laying plans for renewed operations along the western borders of Ohio. Despite the hope of recruiting more regulars, St. Clair found himself also dependent on militia and six-months recruits, little better than the militia. Captain Armstrong, who certainly had experience judging such troops, described them as "the worst and most dissatisfied troops I ever served with."[56] St. Clair's plan was to move slowly into the Indian country, cutting roads and establishing a series of posts to support the army. Nothing went quickly or swimmingly, so the train was still moving slowly two months after it started, by early October advancing at about five miles a day. In late October another fort was built near present-day Greenville to serve as a supply depot. Because of construction delays, it was early November before the expedition reached the Wabash River.

As St. Clair's fatigued men pitched their tents, their exhaustion was so extreme that the commander did not order any defenses built around the camp. The general was confident that there was no danger, since he believed the forest army was nowhere near them—nor was it likely the Native Americans would confront such a powerful force. In fact his opponents were much closer than the American commander thought. Almost weekly since the defeat of Harmar, Blue Jacket, Little Turtle, and their allies had been preparing themselves to confront any new American expedition. The allies had two principal goals. The first was to gather as many warriors from the several tribes as possible; the second, which was far more problematic than the first, was to secure the assistance of the British. Try as they might, the Native American diplomats could not shake the British from their determination to avoid direct military assistance. Sympathy they would give, supplies the Indian Department provided, and the officials even offered to mediate the dispute by suggesting to the United States government the boundary proposed by the tribes, but there would be no British combatants.

Still inspired by the victory the previous year and assisted in part by gifts of supplies from the British, more than a thousand warriors had gathered near Miamitown. It was truly a pan-Indian force, composed of Shawnees, Miamis, Delawares, Mingoes, Cherokees, Wyandots, Ojibwas, Ottawas, and Potawatomies. The events of the preceding year had so emboldened them that Simon Girty believed that "the Indians were never in greater heart to meet their enemy, nor more sure of success. They are determined to drive them to the Ohio, and starve their little posts by taking all their horses and cattle."[57]

The warriors were convinced that they need not wait for a defensive battle but that they could carry the attack to the enemy. Their plans seem similar to the attack at Point Pleasant some years before, when the forces under Lord Dunmore were attacked at dawn by the Shawnees and their allies. Although Blue Jacket may have remembered that failed attack, he believed his force of allies was equal to the task. The camp would be enveloped much as the lines of Braddock had been swallowed up in 1755. As James Smith observed (based on his captivity during the 1750s), Native American fighting forces "can perform various necessary maneuvers, either slowly, or as fast as they can run; they can form a circle, or semi-circle: the circle they make use of, in order to surround the enemy, and the semi-circle if the enemy has a river on one side of them."[58] At sunset on November 3 the two armies probably were barely a mile apart, but it seems the American pickets were unaware that more than a thousand warriors were preparing to assault them. Before dawn the attackers silently formed the semi-circle that would soon grip the American camp like a fiery pincer. Although the soldiers were awake and preparing breakfast, they were unsuspecting until the woods echoed the Indian yell. One of the American officers said "it was not terrible . . . but more resembling an infinitude of horse bells suddenly opening to you."[59]

The first to feel the brunt of the attack was the advance guard of three hundred Kentucky militia camped across the Wabash. Terrified into what Adjutant General (and territorial secretary) Winthrop Sargent called "ignominious flight," they plunged across the river, broke through two rows of tents (spaced seventy yards apart) and bolted for the rear, only to find that the circle had enclosed the entire camp.[60] Once the fluid stream of warriors had encircled the desperate troops, the warriors seemed to disappear, using the cover of trees and brush as camouflage, even as they poured a hail of fire into St. Clair's camp. The American commander described the Native American tactic: "The weight of the fire, which was always a deadly one, and generally delivered from the ground, few of the enemy showing themselves afoot except when charged, and that, in a few minutes, our whole camp, which extended above three hundred and fifty yards in length, was entirely surrounded and attacked on all quarters."[61] One fortunate surviving officer perceived the enfilade as it formed: "The enemy from the front filed off to the right and left, and completely surrounded the camp, killed and cut off nearly all the guards, and approached close to the lines. They advanced from one tree, log, or stump to another, under cover of the smoke of our fire."[62]

When Sargent visited the battlefield four months later, he described a scene comparable to a later shattered wood. Like those who chronicled the aftermath of Antietam, he was astonished at the "amazing effect of the enemy's fire; particularly from the artillery of the front line, on, to, and around the left flank, and beyond the artillery to the rear. *Every twig and bush seems to be cut down, and the saplings and larger trees marked with the utmost profusion of their shot.* Our own fire seems very loose, and, even the artillery, to have been directed with very little judgment."[63] An attempted bayonet charge briefly pushed back the attackers, but the heavy brush slowed the charge sufficiently to allow the warriors once again to direct a punishing fusillade, targeting especially the officers (56 percent of them were wounded or killed) and the artillerymen. One of the experienced regular army officers, Lieutenant Ebenezer Denny, grudgingly admitted that his foes "seemed not to fear anything we could do. They could skip out of reach of the bayonet and return as they pleased. They were visible only when raised by a charge."[64]

After three hours "the ground was literally covered with the dead."[65] General St. Clair decided the only way to end the slaughter was to break through the ring of death in retreat toward Fort Jefferson. Anyone unable to flee would fall victim to the mercy of the conquerors. When the surviving Americans penetrated the circle, they fled almost unpursued as the victors pounced on the spoils left behind, not only prisoners but also weapons (including twelve hundred muskets), supplies, and horses. The allied tribes had succeeded beyond their wildest dreams by defeating a second army more overwhelmingly than they had the first. It was estimated that the Americans had lost a total of 918 men—killed, captured, or wounded— plus thirty women killed out of the thirty-three still in camp when the attack came.[66] For the Americans who lost that day, two things seemed certain: that Arthur St. Clair's military career was over and that the new nation would not let this defeat go unavenged. The Native Americans, on the other hand, could bask momentarily in the glow of their victory dances, but they would have to maintain a steady resolve of determined alliance if they were to confront the retaliatory expedition that they knew would come.

By early 1792 Native American leaders could back their appeals for unity with a catalog of accomplishment against the Big Knives. Two victories in two years gave rise to renewed belief that the Ohio River could be secured as a permanent boundary that would restrict the line of settlements. Councils throughout the West preached defiance and persuaded the uncommitted to join in support of the confederated position so long espoused by leaders like Joseph Brant, Blue Jacket, and Little Turtle. Overtures once again were made to the British. Supplies were essential but rum was not welcome. What seemed certain was that the British would listen sympathetically but would stop short of providing actual manpower. Also on the list of Native American goals during 1792 was keeping pressure on the settlements that had been constructed beyond the Ohio.

In June of that year a party of soldiers harvesting hay near Fort Jefferson was attacked, with the loss of fifteen men.[67] Sporadic raids continued throughout the next two years, largely because there was no effective force present in the West to stop them. In the meantime the center of renewed Native American activity in the Ohio country was a rapidly growing settlement at the confluence of the Maumee and Auglaize Rivers, where a multiethnic population lived in a community commonly referred to as the Glaize.[68] Blue Jacket, for example, had decided Miamitown was no longer safe, so he and his followers had relocated to a new village on the Maumee about a mile from the junction of the two streams. Within a few miles were Miami and Delaware villages as well as smaller towns inhabited by Nanticokes, Cherokees, and Mingoes, as the western Senecas often were called during this period.[69]

From this location, parties determined to pressure the frontiers of the United States were able to attack southwestern Ohio, striking twice in October of 1793, once near Fort St. Clair and again only miles from Cincinnati. Seventeen soldiers plus one civilian and his two children were killed in these raids designed to intimidate those who had crossed the Ohio. Early in 1794 the warriors struck again, ambushing wagons driven by army contractors near both Fort Jefferson and Fort Hamilton.[70]

In the meantime, President Washington had turned to another former officer from the Revolution, General Anthony Wayne. He had been successful in the South and, late in the war, had even encountered Native Americans in battle when the Creek leader Emistisiguo attempted to penetrate the American lines near Savannah, Georgia. Momentarily stunned by the Creek attack, the Patriots had rallied, killing seventeen Creeks, including their leader, whom Wayne described as "our greatest enemy and principal warrior of the Creek Nations."[71] Wayne now would face far more Native Americans than he had in 1782, but he had been given congressional approval to reorganize the army. With increased funding and manpower, he hoped to accomplish what neither Harmar nor St. Clair had been able to do. His intention was to recruit well, train hard, and defeat the enemy, even if that took longer than the public wanted. From November 1792 to April 1793 Wayne drilled his new legion near Pittsburgh, attempting to instill pride and practice in the troops before relocating them for more training near Cincinnati in May 1793.

In the meantime the Native Americans of northwest Ohio had not been idle. Led by Shawnee orators like Blue Jacket and Red Pole, missions had traveled extensively throughout the Northwest and South preaching the idea of unified resistance. The impassioned recounting of success against Harmar and St. Clair was stirring and emotionally persuasive, but in the cold light of morning's reality would not bring bands of warriors streaming northward from the Gulf South. The other goal in 1792 was a great intertribal congress to be held on the Maumee, at which the advocates of resistance hoped to consolidate their position.

The staunchest advocates of continuing opposition to the United States were the Shawnees, emboldened by victory in warfare. Their primary point was the Ohio River boundary; that was nonnegotiable, along with the demand that the agreements signed at Fort Harmar be rescinded. Small bands from several tribes agreed, but what the Shawnee war leaders wanted was a broad, intertribal agreement that would provide thousands of warriors for the effort. There were of course those who opposed war, like the pro-American Senecas, the Moravian Delawares, and the Ottawas influenced by Egushaway, not to mention individual leaders who simply wanted peace for their villages.

One of the most influential voices on the frontier was Thayendanegea, the Mohawk war leader most commonly referred to as Joseph Brant. Since he was well known both in Canada and the United States, some groups would listen to him. Because the hard-liners demanded the Ohio River boundary or war, they were not persuaded by the brokered peace terms advanced either by Brant or by Red Jacket, the Seneca orator. Both these Iroquois had conferred with the Americans and were trying to mediate a settlement. Although the Shawnees did not budge from their terms, they did indicate that they would meet with negotiators from the United States.

As the two sides prepared for the meeting, in the spring of 1793, their positions had not changed appreciably. The United States held to the validity of the Fort Harmar decisions, but the Continental Congress's Indian commissioners had been promised $50,000 in goods and $10,000 a year in annuities if they were needed to smooth the way. One sop thrown to the tribal leaders was the destruction of the military posts built north of Fort Washington. Whatever the commissioners' positive intentions, however, all goodwill was lost when they revealed their desire to purchase an additional 150,000 acres that would be used to reward the followers of George Rogers Clark. Clark's name was not one that would have inspired generosity in the hearts of the Native Americans, given his record of destroying villages and killing Indians. Outside Vincennes, witnesses had observed him personally tomahawk several Indian prisoners.[72]

Because the British had volunteered to act as hosts for this meeting in the spring of 1793, it was clear that they, too, had an interest in the outcome of negotiations between the United States and the assembled Native American delegates. Officially the British position was to avoid being drawn into war over Indian affairs, so they tried to escape the appearance of supplying the native peoples. Unofficially, on the other hand, Lieutenant Governor Simcoe of Upper Canada hoped Indian successes would force the United States to give ground in the Northwest, thus ensuring homelands for tribes whose assistance was invaluable in time of war. Some scholars have even argued that his larger goal was sufficient Native American victories to force United States abandonment of the territory beyond the Ohio, which could then be returned to the British. The bottom line, however, was whatever served British interests, which for the moment was acceptance of the Shawnee position in the interest of unity. This position reaffirming the Ohio River boundary line was repeatedly upheld by British Indian agent Alexander McKee in numerous conferences throughout the summer of 1793 as the several parties tried to negotiate. It was this rock

Ohio's First Peoples

upon which the ship of compromise would founder in 1793, leaving an eventual war as the only alternative. The American army was growing stronger every day, even as settlements were inching up the rivers; the bottom line was that the United States would not retreat to a Muskingum River and Ohio River boundary, while the Shawnees and their allies were immovable on the issue of the line as fixed in 1768 by the British and Native American delegations at Fort Stanwix. War seemed unavoidable.[73]

While the negotiators had danced this *pas de toutes sortes* throughout the spring and summer of 1793, the methodical Wayne was moving northward. Despite disease (including his own gout and the usual camp contagions), desertions (five hundred Kentucky volunteers had gone home), and despicable contractors, he cut a road six miles beyond Fort Jefferson and built a post named in honor of his friend Nathanael Greene, under whom he had fought in the South during the American Revolution. Then he decided to symbolize the return of American arms by building a post on the site of St. Clair's defeat. There, on Christmas Day 1793, American troops ignored the still visible skeletal parts of their own kind to begin construction of Fort Recovery. Unlike with Pershing and MacArthur in later times, there were no immortal words, but the message of retaliation was just as clear.

Likewise clear was General Wayne's determination not to deviate from his goal. This became evident in January of 1794 when a small delegation of Delaware diplomats came to Fort Greenville. Their immediate purpose was to secure the release of two prisoners held by Wayne, but the peace faction used the diplomatic opportunity to raise again the question of a general frontier settlement. The general was firm; there would be no discussion of peace unless all prisoners were returned, all war parties were recalled, and there was a general conference attended by all the chiefs or their delegates. When this report was taken to a general council, the minority who had carried the mission to Wayne was overwhelmed.

Even as it was obvious that the United States intended military action against the Native Americans living in northwestern Ohio, the forest diplomats were certain that they not only had a just cause but had the advantage. They were strengthened in their attitude by renewed backing from the British. Sir Guy Carleton, now Lord Dorchester, had returned to Canada as governor, a post he had held during the late war. In early 1794 his interpretation of world affairs led him to believe that there would renewed warfare between the United States and Great Britain, a situation exacerbated in part by the ongoing Anglo-French war and the common threat that the British and the Spanish allies saw in United States expansionism on the frontier. Although Dorchester may have overstated the case, he certainly found eager listeners among the Shawnees and their allies. The Native Americans were even more elated by the construction of the British Fort Miamis at the rapids of the Maumee River, where it would be in easy reach of the towns comprising the Glaize; it also was close enough to Detroit to receive supplies from that post by water. More than one hundred British troops along with some small cannon might discourage any commander from an assault. Whatever else could be said, building the fort was risky business, since it was clearly a violation of the 1783 peace agreement.

One of the most pressing military issues facing the leaders of the Indian confederation during the summer of 1794 was keeping the warriors motivated so they would not drift homeward. Emboldened by their own past successes, the large numbers of warriors who had gathered, and the apparently changed attitude of the British military, several hundred warriors attacked a pack train outside the new Fort Recovery. When rescuers rushed out to protect the pack train they were ambushed by this large force of warriors. The survivors who fled to the fort found themselves well protected by the accurate fire of the well-trained troops inside.

If the defense of Fort Recovery was a pretest of the expedition's abilities, the final examination was about to come. On July 28, 1794, Wayne headed a column of troops made up of his legion plus Kentucky volunteers; the total was more than thirty-five hundred men, clearly more than either Harmar or St. Clair had commanded, and probably 75 percent more armed soldiers than native warriors. Learning from the mistakes of his predecessors, General Wayne had each night's bivouac carefully defended with breastworks and reveille sounded each morning an hour before sunrise. Early in August his troops built Fort Adams on the St. Mary's River to maintain his communication and supply line southward and to provide a fallback position. By August 8 Wayne and his army had reached the rich fields of the bottomlands where the Auglaize and the Miami meet. There he set his men the task of building Fort Defiance, which one officer believed was meant to challenge "the English, Indians, and all the devils in hell."[74]

From scouts and prisoners General Wayne learned that all the prosperous villages of the Glaize had been abandoned to him; the defensive stand was to come downriver near the new British Fort Miamis. Wayne tried one last peace overture, offering lasting peace and informing the Indians that the British probably would turn their backs on them. The American commander's offer was debated in council on August 14, with the war party carrying the day. The next step of the American force was to move farther along the Maumee and build Camp Deposit as a supply depot. This delay frustrated the waiting warriors, many of whom had gone without food for several days in anticipation of the battle. Thus by the time Wayne's legion encountered the forest soldiers on August 20 many had been without food for three days, while others had left the field to find sustenance.

As Wayne's legion moved into a tangled area called the Wilderness (now called Fallen Timbers) the remainder of the awaiting warriors attacked, rolling back a group of mounted Kentucky volunteers. In the confusion the early moments of battle may have resembled St. Clair's disaster, but the officers and regular troops re-formed and charged with fixed bayonets. Outnumbered by men bearing cold steel and assaulted by actual Big Knives in the form of saber-wielding dragoons, the forest army gave way, headed downstream toward Fort Miamis. True to Captain Pipe's 1781 prophecy about peoples of the same skin color working against the Indians, the British locked their gates and gave succor to no one.[75] Although General Anthony Wayne and the British commander of the post exchanged terse communications, neither wanted to be the one to fire the first shot in a new war. Consequently the American force withdrew to strengthen Fort Defiance, from which the troops scorched the earth for miles along both sides of the Maumee, leaving the Indians homeless and bereft of supplies for the winter. At Kekionga, where Harmar had met defeat, another post was built, named after the commander of the legion, General Wayne. Thus the losses of Harmar and St. Clair had been avenged and the first phase of the War for Ohio completed. Thanks to Anthony Wayne, the United States now held all the cards in the Northwest. The general would spend the next twelve months in preparation for a general treaty, receiving delegations and watching for unrest, all the while holding firm to the demands of the United States.

Since Wayne was the dealer in this game, the players had to come to his table. He let them know this in one instance by sending his terms in a message carried by a captive Shawnee woman who was released.[76] Among the first to ask for a hand from the new deck was Tarhe, now leader of the

Wyandots at Sandusky, who sent spokesmen to confer with the victorious general in September. Wayne explained the game carefully, letting the Wyandots know what the terms would be and that there would be no punishment for those who brought in prisoners. Then in October he permitted the release of an influential French-Canadian trader named Antoine Lasselle, who had been captured during the battle, dressed as an Indian and fighting side by side with his customers. The opportunistic Lasselle saw the way the cards were running and quietly began to shift toward the American game. On New Year's Day, 1795, General Wayne issued an invitation to a general peace to be held in the summer. Then, late in January, Blue Jacket ventured in, bringing along four captives to give the appearance of having practical business with the Americans.

As a backdrop to the scene being dominated by Wayne was the activity by the British, themselves now about to deal a completely new game. Although the gates of Fort Miamis had been locked to keep the fleeing warriors out, British spokesmen like Alexander McKee, John Simcoe, and Guy Carleton had continued to maintain some semblance of influence with the tribes. Throughout the fall and winter of 1794–95, thousands of rations had been issued to homeless villagers who had gathered at Swan Creek near the mouth of the Maumee River. However grateful they might be for this support, their doubts about future British commitments were grave indeed. Then came news of Jay's Treaty, signed in November of 1794, which stipulated that all British posts had to be evacuated by January 1, 1796. Clearly there was no longer a need for pretense; whether they liked it or not, they had to make peace with the Big Knife.

Anthony Wayne signed the Treaty of Greenville on August 3, 1795, almost a year after the Battle of Fallen Timbers. As sole Indian commissioner of the United States, Wayne agreed to peace with ninety-two representatives from fifteen tribal groups.[77] Although the preamble lists only twelve tribes, the signatures or marks reflect distinctions identifying fifteen.[78] In addition to establishing "perpetual" peace, the agreement specified the giving of hostages by the tribes, the mutual release of prisoners, the delineation of boundaries and specification of parcels to be transferred to the United States, the promise of a lump sum to be given to the tribes immediately and of annuities "every year forever," the restriction that future tribal land sales had to be to the United States, the procedures for the punishment of trespassers on either side as well as for the redress of larger

Ohio's First Peoples

Benjamin Lossing's portrayal of Tecumseh, taken from a
sketch made by French fur trader Pierre Le Dru in 1808.

grievances, the allowance for hunting by Indians on the ceded lands if they
"demean themselves peaceably," the establishment of a regulated trade,
and the understanding that all previous treaties were void.

Among those not signing the 1795 treaty was an individual who would
lead the last phase of the Indian war for Ohio. Tecumseh, who would
emerge into leadership a decade later, was by 1795 an experienced, capable
young warrior who had been among those in the fight at Fallen Timbers.[79]
He, along with two of his brothers, Sauwauseekau and Lalawethika, had
fought the Long Knives until they had had to retreat past the closed gates
of the British fort. Unfortunately for Tecumseh, another of his brothers fell
in that battle, bringing to three the number of members of his family who

had since 1774 died fighting to defend their country. Tecumseh's father had fallen at Point Pleasant; a fourth brother died in an assault on a frontier outpost. Embittered by their deaths and the treachery of the British, who failed to offer shelter to the Indians, Tecumseh did not enter any communication with either side. His goal was to continue following the Shawnee way, with the usual routines of hunting for food and pelts, trading for manufactured goods, farming for subsistence, and practicing traditional religion—but that was going to prove exceedingly difficult.

The option that the newly triumphant United States would push was for all the tribes to adopt the settled life of the farmer. That idea was implicit in the provisions of the Treaty of Greenville. Within Article II was a proviso concerning the $1,000 annuity promised to the Shawnees and other tribes.

> *Provided,* That if either of said tribes shall hereafter at an annual delivery of their share of the goods aforesaid, desire that a part of their annuity should be furnished in domestic animals, implements of husbandry, and other utensils convenient for them, and in compensation to useful artificers who may reside with or near them, and be employed for their benefit, the same shall at subsequent annual deliveries be furnished accordingly.[80]

The path of the plough, not the forest trail, was urged by the Americans on the Shawnees and their neighbors. For those like Tecumseh, who wished to maintain the traditional ways, such a change seemed impossible, but the older patterns too were exceedingly difficult to follow. Hunting and gathering pelts for the trade was less productive not only because of hunting lands lost in land cessions but also because white hunters were killing game without regard to need. Deer and bears in particular were becoming scarcer, as was some of the smaller game traditionally harvested by the native hunters. Those who did manage to harvest enough pelts to trade were victimized by unscrupulous merchants who played on their desire for rum.[81] Alcohol was ever present in all the villages. It afflicted many, including Tecumseh's brother Lalawethika. Some tribespeople even took advantage of their own by hoarding small amounts to sell to the highest bidder when the communal barrel was dry. Adding to the tribespeople's sense of victimization were the recurrent bouts of infectious diseases contracted from the whites. These outbreaks further reduced the population and weakened the survivors. Even those who tried to go their own way in

peace were targets of opportunity for whites who believed random violence against Indian property or the Indians themselves was justified. The
years after Fallen Timbers were a disappointing departure from the heady
days after the victories over Harmar and St. Clair, when native communities prospered and life seemed full of promise.

Where to turn for the future of their people was a disquieting question.
Some, like those in Black Hoof's band, decided to undertake walking the
white man's path. Black Hoof was so determined that he led a delegation
to Washington in search of support and guidance from the secretary of
war. If the Shawnees wished to become successful imitators of white farmers, they needed cabins, fences, and livestock. More importantly, the old
statesman asked for some legal guarantee to the title for the lands where
he and his people were living. This request was the opening many Jeffersonian philanthropists had wanted, an excuse to change the native peoples
into yeoman farmers.[82]

No federal official was likely to give deeds for land to a Native American chief, but helping identify model farmers might be possible. In this case
the decision was made to send a Quaker missionary named William Kirk
who had some experience working in a similar setting near Fort Wayne.
Relocating eastward, Kirk set up his model farm at Black Hoof's village
of Wapakoneta on the Auglaize River. The issue of course was not that
the Shawnees had never farmed. They had raised crops quite successfully
in the bottomlands of the Auglaize and the Maumee, but not in the European manner of tilled and fenced fields with meadows reserved for livestock. Especially difficult would be persuading determined Shawnee men
that success in farming was an admirable and manly trait. Although
William Kirk's efforts were successful, his mission was closed after only
seventeen months because he failed to maintain the proper records to satisfy officials in Washington.[83] Blue Jacket, in the meantime, had made himself useful to the American officials and managed to have a house built for
his family by the Americans during the winter of 1796.[84] In the interim he
and his comrade in arms Red Pole made frequent trips to the American
post at Fort Greenville, where they obtained rations. His biographer reports that Blue Jacket received "115 pounds of beef and bread, 15 pounds
of pork, 165 pounds of flour, 6 pounds of soap, 3 quarts of salt, and 3
quarts of whiskey between April 24 and May 19, 1796."[85] Shawnees still
drawn to the British were making similar pilgrimages to Swan Creek in

order to secure comparable support there. When United States forces assumed control of the posts at Detroit and Fort Miamis in 1796 as part of the Jay's Treaty arrangement, those who had been receiving the king's largess found the hand of the United States also was open.

Indeed the upturned palm was so widespread that General Wayne had approved an official junket for Blue Jacket and Red Pole to visit their new "father" in Philadelphia. Along with three other representative chiefs from the tribes who had signed the Greenville treaty, the two sailed from Detroit to Presque Isle and then journeyed overland through Pittsburgh to Philadelphia for a meeting with President Washington. Since the president was no stranger to frontier diplomacy, he was familiar with the rhetorical devices practiced by the chiefs as they reviewed the story of past relations and asked not only for redress of their tribal grievances but also for specific presents for themselves. Then it was time for sightseeing in the city, including C. W. Peale's recently organized museum of natural curiosity. There by chance they encountered a visiting delegation of southern Indians; several were known to the northern group and at least two had fought with the Americans at St. Clair's defeat.[86] After momentarily bristling at the sight of each other, they decided discretion was the better part of valor and let the past be the past. The delegation of Blue Jacket and Red Pole received no satisfaction from President Washington in changing the terms of the Greenville Treaty, but they did receive a substantial number of gifts. Blue Jacket, moreover, received a certain level of recognition in a speech made by George Washington to the western nations. He assured them of the friendship of the United States and urged them to be alert for those who would violate the peace. In addition, the president let the chiefs know the secretary of war would furnish them with a "testimonial" similar to that given to Blue Jacket as an indication of Washington's "Esteem and friendship."[87] Unfortunately, not all returned home safely. Red Pole fell ill in Pittsburgh and died, robbing Blue Jacket of a longtime ally.[88] While Red Pole no doubt succumbed to pneumonia, another tribal ally of Blue Jacket's who died about the same time was rumored to have been poisoned. The resulting intratribal tensions set off a ripple of revenge killings that left a total of five dead. As if it were not enough that some of his Shawnee allies were dead, Blue Jacket also lost a respected American adversary when Anthony Wayne died.

Among the more conservative bands of Shawnees, like those who fol-

lowed Tecumseh, the decade after the Treaty of Greenville was increasingly
frustrating. Unwilling to become settled farmers or opportunistic political
entrepreneurs, they found life unsettling. The precariousness of this position often was intensified by problems in supporting themselves and widespread difficulties with alcoholism. Included in the latter dilemma was the
inept Lalawethika, who had attached himself to his brother Tecumseh's
band largely for purposes of survival. Given to depression and bouts of
alcoholism, he tried to find a place for himself by apprenticing with an
older shaman.[89] According to his biographer in April 1805 he fell into a
deep trance, from which he awoke with a vision of personal and tribal
deliverance.

Although many naysayers regarded this occasion as simply another of
the Noisemaker's drunken stupors, he seemed a changed man. In accordance with his experience of rebirth he condemned the evil practices of
many Shawnees, in particular the widespread drunkenness that was cor-
rupting village after village. Also reflective of his conversion was an appropriate name to accompany a new identity. Lalawetika (the "Noisemaker")
became Tenskwatawa, or the "Open Door" through which he could lead
his followers to a better life. The Open Door's new system emphasized
personal holiness and avoidance of evils such as fighting, dishonesty, and
sexual promiscuity. Tenskwatawa preached a doctrine designed to purify
his followers and deliver the Shawnees and any other Native American converts from what appeared to be certain doom. One theme was the avoidance of white men's ways, whether their bread or their flint and steel. The
Master of Life wished for the Shawnees to be Shawnee; avoid the Americans, those "scum of the Great Water" at all costs. On the negative side, his
condemnation of the traditional shamans with their medicine bundles and
those alleged to be witches established a deadly tension within the villages
that took up the way of the "Prophet," as Tenskwatawa was called. The
consequences were particularly tragic in certain Wyandot and Delaware
settlements. Tenskwatawa's credibility soared in the summer of 1806 when
he predicted a "black sun." He apparently had learned of this celestial occurrence because several teams of scientists were traveling in the mid-West
to observe it. He called his followers to his new village at Greenville and
told them he would use his power to darken the sun in the middle of the
day. When the sky grew dark, he claimed that he had caused the sun to disappear and then to emerge again.

George Catlin, *Ten-squat-a-way* [Tenskwatawa], *The Open Door, Known as The Prophet, Brother of Tecumseh*. Courtesy of the Smithsonian American Art Museum.

The amazing display of spiritual power connected with the eclipse brought more converts to this movement. As in messianic movements everywhere, especially among the dispossessed, someone who preached revitalization and ethnic empowerment was bound to attract followers. It also was likely that the prophetic individual would attract the suspicions of those who might be threatened. Twice in early 1806 the governor of Ohio sent emissaries to confer with Tenskwatawa, but neither set was able to find evidence of a smoking gun in the village. Among the accommodationists at Wapakoneta there was little respect for the one they still regarded as the Noisemaker. Mutual recriminations passed between Wapakoneta and Greenville throughout 1806 and 1807, with each village blaming the other for unexplained deaths. Black Hoof blamed the Prophet for the killings of two of his kinsmen, just as Black Hoof had been blamed for the death of a settler in the spring of 1806 by the Prophet's followers.

Fear of Indian war was heightened in 1807, in part driven by fear of renewed warfare with England in the aftermath of the HMS *Leopard*'s attack on the USS *Chesapeake*. Most American citizens assumed that war with Great Britain would mean conflict with the Native Americans, the former allies of the British. Thus citizens of western Ohio were somewhat nervous about the presence of the Prophet's followers near Greenville. They had become increasingly nervous as numerous "pilgrims" from other tribes came to the Shawnee mecca in order to hear the prophetic words. It was becoming increasingly difficult for moderates like Blue Jacket to account for all the stories swirling about.

While anti-Indian tension rose alarmingly, cooler heads on both sides tried to prevail. Among the Shawnees an increasingly popular option seemed to be relocation of the burgeoning settlement near Greenville to a settlement farther west on the Wabash. That relocation was to take place in the following spring. In the meantime the acting governor of Ohio, Thomas Kirker, tried to calm the waters about the alleged hostility of the people still living at Greenville. He dispatched Thomas Worthington and Duncan McArthur, along with interpreter Stephen Ruddell, to confer with the leaders at Greenville.

The Ohoians reminded the Indians of their past experience in dealing with the British, saying they would be well advised to avoid involvement in the new conflict lest they be harmed once more. Whatever the Native Americans did they were likely to lose. Blue Jacket's answer was that they intended neutrality and would simply do without if the Americans stopped the trade. He blamed the unrest along the frontier of the new state on the agent at Fort Wayne, William Wells, whose dismissal he sought in vain. Nevertheless, the emissaries from Ohio were satisfied. Blue Jacket's biographer reports that the venerable chief and Tecumseh were invited to return to Chillicothe and repeat their assurances of peace.[90] Their words satisfied the acting governor and the assembled crowd that the Shawnees and others gathered at Greenville wanted only peace. Tecumseh reportedly repeated the request for the dismissal of the agent at Fort Wayne and also asked that the interpreter Stephen Ruddell be sent as storekeeper to the site on the Wabash River to which the Prophet intended to relocate.

Although it appeared that tensions had eased between the officials of Ohio and the leaders at the Greenville settlement headed by the spiritual leadership of the Prophet, the western Ohio location was increasingly unsatisfactory. Food was inadequate, the proximity of Ohio settlements unsettling, and the distance to western converts too great. Consequently in April 1808 the Prophet and many of his followers started west. Inspired by his interpretation of the Master of Life's teaching, he intended development of a spiritual community that could follow the Native American way without interference.

At the same time, his biographer points out, the Prophet began to take steps placing him on a collision course with the United States.[91] Although his brother Tecumseh had been convincing in dealing with the Ohioans in 1807, the Prophet took an ominous turn, seeking to open lines of communication with the British. Initially he indicated that he would travel to Canada to meet with British Indian officials, but he sent his brother Tecumseh instead. The official position of the two was to avoid the white man's quarrels, but they likewise did not wish to be encroached upon in their new home.

For the moment, however, Tenskwatawa presented a pacific face to the Americans, largely because the new settlement of Prophetstown in the Indiana Territory had no food supply. Through his representatives he assured the territory's governor, William Henry Harrison, that the Master of Life wanted the Indians to live in peace with everyone. Harrison apparently believed him and thought he could use the Prophet to manage the Indians in the region.[92] To further this illusion the Shawnee visionary planned a highly visible trip to Vincennes, where Harrison lived. He conferred with the governor, assured him of his peaceful intentions, denigrated William Wells, and promised never to support the British. By this ruse Tenskwatawa persuaded the American governor to feed people he himself could not feed; the governor even sent the delegation back with a present of corn, more farming utensils, and a bit of gunpowder.[93] During the winter of 1808–9, however, discussions among the several tribes in the West indicated that Tenskwatawa was less than friendly to the United States. Harrison too lost support among the uncommitted tribes when he bought more land in Indiana and Illinois from the Miami, Delaware, and even the Potawatomies, despite the fact that they had no villages in the area. This purchase only underscored the Prophet's repeated warnings that the Americans planned to purchase all their lands.

By 1810 it was clear that the Prophet's views were decidedly anti-American. As a result, any of his disciples who traveled to Canada were treated well and given presents. Gifts of weapons were tempered with the warning that no action was to be taken prematurely. Both Tenskwatawa and Tecumseh preached the Prophet's message to those unconverted. Among the Shawnees and Wyandots still living in the new state of Ohio there was an almost constant give and take between Tecumseh's appeals on behalf of his brother and attempts by American representatives to counter the Prophet's influence. Both state and federal officials feared the teachings of the holy man would lead the younger warriors away from the path of peace.

Beyond Ohio the crisis was coming to a head. Governor Harrison of the Indiana Territory tried to determine the nature of the Prophet's intentions through the use of both spies and direct communication. Finally in July of 1810 he sent a message to Prophetstown inviting Tenskwatawa and three chiefs to visit Washington and discuss their concerns with their Great Father. He received his answer when Tecumseh, not the Prophet, traveled to Vincennes for a conference in August. As R. David Edmunds points out, this occasion seems to have been the juncture at which Tecumseh emerged as the leader of the pan-Indian movement. Tecumseh explained that he wished to unite all the tribes in opposition to land sales and threatened to execute any chiefs who engaged in land sales without the permission of all. Warning the governor to relinquish land claims, Tecumseh said, "If you do not it will appear as if you wished me to kill all the chiefs that sold you this land. I tell you so because I am authorized by all the tribes to do so. I am the head of them all. . . . If you do not restore the land you will have a hand in killing them."[94] Neither he, "alone the acknowledged chief of all the Indians," nor the Prophet wished to visit the president. Clearly a shift in leadership was taking place inside the movement the Prophet had started, a change Harrison illuminated when he wrote to the secretary of war that Tecumseh was "really the efficient man—the Moses of the family. . . . He [was] described by all as a bold, active, sensible man, daring in the extreme and capable of any undertaking."[95]

Those who lived on the western edge of Ohio were understandably fearful about the activities of the Shawnees under the Prophet and Tecumseh, since there were still Shawnees living within the state. Consequently the Indian agent at Piqua, John Johnston, invited the Ohio Shawnees and Wyandots to a conference in August of 1811. On the twenty-third of that month about fifty delegates gathered for a two-day meeting that the agent later described as a satisfactory gathering that demonstrated there was no danger of war with the Shawnees, Miamis, Wyandots, and Delawares.[96] Nerves were so on edge that the discovery of three bodies at the confluence of the Maumee and Auglaize Rivers led a volunteer company from Miami County to seek revenge by killing and capturing whatever native peoples they could find.

The settlers' apprehensions certainly were not without foundation, for Tecumseh was trying to broaden the political confederacy he envisioned. At the same time, however, the dream of a Native American haven at Prophetstown collapsed. Alarmed by increasing numbers of warriors gathering at the new town and fearful of even more being attracted there, William H. Harrison led his troops from Vincennes into a battle that destroyed the settlement and the charismatic movement that had given birth to it. When Tecumseh returned from the South, he was faced with rebuilding. In the meantime he played the diplomat and allowed Harrison to believe he would journey to Washington in the summer of 1812 as part of an official delegation to settle western Indian difficulties. At the same time, he was cultivating his ties with the British authorities in Canada, who thought war between the United States and Great Britain so imminent that they were looking for allies.

When war came in 1812, the western tribes formerly under the influence of the Prophet once more played diplomatic games, feigning peace with the United States while communicating with the British (who were convinced by Tecumseh that the tribes would rally to them). Tecumseh, along with ten warriors, actually traveled to Fort Malden on the Ontario side of the Detroit River in order to visit the British military officials stationed there. The party had gone primarily to seek the renewal of ties and obtain supplies of guns and ammunition. While the party was there, the long-anticipated war erupted; Tecumseh could demonstrate his commitment by joining the British in their battles at Brownstown and Monguagon. At the latter he sustained a wound in the leg that took some months to heal. This new turn of events meant that American attempts to hold a peace conference at Piqua in Ohio attracted only about 250 Indians. The Prophet held out until late in 1812 before going to Canada, where he found Tecumseh recovering from his injury. By early 1813 the two brothers had returned west on a mission to recruit warriors for a spring offensive. When they did retrace their steps to Canada they arrived in time to participate in the failed attempt to dislodge the Americans from Fort Meigs. When Harrison's counterattacking forces pursued the British and their Indian allies into Canada, Fort Malden was abandoned. The American troops finally overtook the Anglo-Indian force near Moraviantown on October 5. Tecumseh was killed in that battle, thus bringing an end to a struggle that had begun in Ohio in the 1780s.

For the forty years roughly corresponding to Tecumseh's adulthood, the Shawnees and the rest of Ohio's native peoples had struggled valiantly to maintain their way of life. Every avenue had been tried, including withdrawal, resistance, diplomacy, accommodation, conversion to Christianity, and war, but there was no solution. Tecumseh's last battle would also be the last for his people and their neighbors. Small enclaves would cling to parcels of land for another three decades, but in the end their lands would be lost. Ohio would know the native peoples no more, save in memory, records, and place names scattered across a gridlike map of roads, canals, and communities that would bear no resemblance to what once had been the heart of it all for countless Native Americans.

"NO RESTING PLACE"

On January 9, 1789, at Fort Harmar on the west bank of the Ohio River, the Wyandots, along with the Delawares and other native peoples of the Old Northwest, were granted lands on which they could live, hunt, or "otherwise occupy as they shall see fit." The stipulated boundary was to be in effect "forever."[1] Even as the Wyandot leader known as Tarhe (the Crane) marked the agreement, he must have wondered how much faith he could place in this document signed within clear view of the newly established settlement at Marietta. Well might he have puzzled over the permanency of this understanding, for during the next fifty years his people's territory was slowly eroded, despite the frequent assertions that the lands had been granted forever.[2] In 1836, for example, the Wyandots ceded yet another 39,200 acres, leaving them a tract in Crawford County about fourteen miles long and twelve miles wide.[3] Although they had actually discussed removal over the years, they had found no lands to their liking; some tribal members would consider moving if the price for their land was high enough, while others wanted "to get their share of lands in severalty, and become citizens of Ohio."[4] Finally, at the Treaty of Upper Sandusky in 1842 the Wyandots were persuaded to give up their remaining claims in the East, along with "Such Improvements as Add Value," for a new home in the West.[5]

On reflection, one might wonder what "improvements" would be left behind. A journey in 1842 across the landscape of what became Wyandot County, Ohio, would take us past a number of "cleared and fenced" farms. The dwellings on these included fifteen hewed log cabins (as well as five round log cabins), twenty-six hewed log houses, and one each of plank, brick, and frame; many were flanked by spring houses, stables, apple trees, and plowed fields.[6] We would pass Big John Solomon's cabin of hewed logs, George Wright's cabin and house along with the forty-eight acres of plowed fields and twenty apple trees, and then, not far away, Whitecrow's two hewn houses, well, stable, and milk house. To be sure, we would see that Charles Split-the-Log's cabin wasn't worth much and that William Walker's well had brackish water, but there were more good houses in the neighborhood. The Widow Lumpy's improvements included a hewn log house that had been used as a tavern along with a smokehouse and a "good stoned well." This clearly was not a scattering of transients, but a settled agricultural community.

Also on our tour would be the Methodist Mission on the Wyandot reservation, where more than 110 acres had been put into cultivation and the missionaries had built a mission house, a dwelling house, a school-house, and a barn. The entire picture was one of a rural neighborhood marked by the expected activities of farming.[7] As R. Douglas Hurt has written recently in *The Ohio Frontier,* the frontier farmer who had 160 acres, a house, a barn, cultivated fields, and livestock was relatively "well off."[8] Apparently, by the time the missionary James Finley came to live among them, the Wyandots already had acquired livestock, since one of the issues he tried to solve was that of identifying the ownership of cattle, hogs, and horses. Finley's answer was to prepare a book of earmarks in order to register the animals and also to keep a record of brands for the horses.[9] The notations about the presence of fencing in the historical record suggest it was there to contain livestock. To describe the Wyandots as "well off" is no doubt an exaggeration, but they were practicing rudimentary plowed field agriculture. The pioneer Methodist missionary John Stewart observed that the Wyandots had lived in a "savage state" until his arrival,

Between-the-Logs, Wyandot Methodist exhorter.

living in bark huts and practicing "heathenism." Stewart believed it was
Christianity that had prompted the Wyandots to abandon their old ways
and take up plowing their fields and building houses of hewn logs.[10] Indeed
the English traveler Charles Dickens commented that the Wyandots were
"a fine people but degraded and broken down. If you could see any of them
on a race-course in England, you would not know them from gipsies."[11]
Culturally, however, the Wyandots and their Native American neighbors
in northwestern Ohio still tried to maintain some traditional ways. When
the missionaries arrived in the early 1820s the Native Americans were still
using winter hunting camps, and nearly all went in search of sugar maples

(*Acer saccharum*) in February.[12] During the first three decades of the nineteenth century several groups of missionaries attempted to bring more of the outside world to the Wyandots. Perhaps the most unusual approach was that of the drunkard turned Methodist evangelist John Stewart.

Stewart clearly was unique because of his background. Born a free black in Virginia, John Stewart was trained in the cloth-dyeing business, an enterprise he intended to follow in the free state of Ohio. Leaving his home in Virginia, Stewart journeyed westward toward Marietta, Ohio, where he hoped to establish his trade. According to his memoirs, John Stewart was robbed and thereafter fell into dissolution and became a self-described drunkard. One night in 1815 he heard singing and praying through the open window of a Methodist meetinghouse near Marietta. After entering to join the service, Stewart underwent a conversion experience that led him to believe he should become a missionary to the Indians. Since the nearest Indians were northwest of Marietta, he eventually journeyed to the Delaware village of Pipetown (founded by Captain Pipe in 1782 after his withdrawal from the Muskingum-Tuscarawas area), where he attended an Indian dance. He drew the attention of the assembly by singing from his hymnbook. The Delawares introduced him to the Wyandot subagent William Walker. Walker directed him to the home of Jonathan Pointer, a black man who had been taken prisoner by the Wyandots when he was a child. Since Pointer could speak English and Wyandot, he could translate both Stewart's preaching and the hymns that so impressed John Stewart's listeners. Pointer helped to introduce the young missionary to the Wyandots by taking him to a dance and feast. There Stewart invited the Wyandots to come to Pointer's home, where the neophyte missionary preached his first sermon to the Wyandots in November of 1816.

In addition to the difficulty of his inability to speak Wyandot, Stewart faced resistance from traditionalists who did not want the white man's religion and from those in the tribe who still had some ties to Roman Catholicism. A chief named John Hicks assured him that "the Great Spirit" had given the Wyandots their own religion. Hicks explained to Stewart: "We are willing to receive good advice from you, but we are not willing to have the religion and customs of our Fathers assailed and abused."[13] Echoing the response of Red Jacket to missionaries who asked permission to preach in the Seneca towns in the East, John Hicks said John Stewart's message was for the white people only, not the Indians.

Stewart's pioneering work attracted criticism from those who questioned his authority because he was not an ordained minister and those who said that since an African American could not preach to whites, the Indians should not listen to him. Some of this criticism along racial lines came from rival Presbyterian missionaries who wanted to discredit the Methodists at any price. These religious competitors told the Wyandots that if they listened to Stewart they would "disgrace themselves in being taught by blacks."[14] Part of the carping was neutralized when the Methodist Church accepted Stewart as a local preacher in March of 1819, meaning that he could claim status within the Methodist hierarchy. Further support was extended to him in August of 1819, when the Methodist annual conference meeting in Cincinnati assumed responsibility for the Wyandot mission. The Methodist organization donated money to buy Stewart a horse and some clothing. In addition, the Methodist bishop undertook raising separate funds to purchase sixty acres of land for a farm on which John Stewart and his family could live. The sponsoring Methodist conference had been made aware that attempts by Stewart and Pointer to hold the Wyandots to a higher moral standard had brought some criticism upon them; the conference delegates also had been informed about the racist tactics of the men's Presbyterian competitors.[15]

Despite his dramatic abilities as both preacher and gospel singer, John Stewart found that he was opposed by a number of factions. The Americans who traded with the Wyandots feared that Stewart might emphasize personal holiness to the detriment of their business, the Wyandots exposed to Roman Catholic missionaries in Michigan were suspicious of him, and tribal traditionalists like Mononcue and John Hicks resisted his message at first because they feared they would have to abandon tribal practices like face painting. (One of the other missionaries at the time told the Wyandots that wearing gaudy dress was contrary to the Gospel.) John Stewart had received some support against his detractors in his early weeks among the Wyandots when William Walker testified that the missionary's hymnal and Bible were based on true religion. Apparently some of Stewart's enemies asserted that because his Bible was in English, not Latin, it was not legitimate.

Following his initial visit to the Wyandots, Stewart returned briefly to Marietta and then retraced his steps northwestward. Upon his return he found that a young man had died after a drinking bout, the result of the kind of behavior that Stewart had condemned in his sermons. The missionary's opponents blamed his moralistic condemnations for the youth's death. Some of the Wyandots played the race card against him; Two Logs asked why the Indians should listen to him when no congregation of whites would. Furthermore, announced Two Logs, John Stewart should be avoided because Negroes were created by an evil spirit.

Stewart's success among the Wyandots and the uniqueness of his racial background attracted the attention of the African Methodist Episcopal Church, founded by Richard Allen. A group of Allenites actually visited the missionary on the Wyandot reserve and invited Stewart to join their conference. Interestingly, James Finley found no contradiction in Stewart's connection with the Allenites and continued to support him as before. All the backing in the world, however, could not overcome the tuberculosis that John Stewart had contracted. Despite his suffering, he continued to work until the fall of 1823, when he was no longer able. On December 17, 1823, he died at his home, "in great peace." As early as 1821 it was Stewart who was credited with being "the first to open the way to their [the Wyandots'] receiving the gospel."[16]

After the arrival of Stewart, other missionaries came, first James Montgomery, who worked initially among the Wyandots and then among the western Seneca, then James Finley, who worked with the Wyandots for several years.[17] At Finley's invitation several Wyandot chiefs, including Between-the-Logs and Mononcue, attended an annual Methodist conference held in Marietta. Speaking with William Walker as his interpreter, Between-the-Logs expressed his happiness with the presence of the missionaries, especially James Finley, who "is industrious and learns our people to work."[18] Both Wyandot visitors urged Finley's reappointment to their mission. They likewise were glad the Methodists had started a school, an initiative the government had promised but failed to complete.

Others in the Wyandot community were not so pleased with the missionary because of his attempt to enforce personal piety in conformity with the church rules codified in *The Methodist Discipline*.[19] One of the expected codes of conduct was the pledge of abstinence from alcohol. Finley's demand for teetotalism precipitated the birth of an anti-Methodist party and revival of a pro–native religion party. Sobriety was no small challenge for either the missionaries or the Wyandots, since every council held by government representatives with the tribe called for a liberal supply of

Mononcue, Wyandot Methodist exhorter.

"ardent spirits."[20] Finley's overall effort among the Wyandots also may have been diminished by his assumption that "a man must be Christianized, or he can never be civilized."[21] Finley's rhetoric was echoed in the comment of Bishop William McKendree, who visited the Wyandot reserve in 1823: "There is nothing that can civilize a man but religion and its influence."[22] During his June 1823 visit McKendree found at Upper Sandusky "the large national reserve of the Wyandott [sic] tribe of Indians," containing 147,840 acres, plus another reservation "five miles square at Big Spring, head of Blanchard's River." The bishop wanted to credit the advances in civilization to the missionaries, especially the estimated two hundred Wyandots who had rejected "heathenism" and embraced Christianity.

Ohio's First Peoples

Church membership for the Wyandots at the mission was a rigorous affair. An 1829 report indicated that thirteen members had been expelled and one put on trial for "marrying contrary to *Discipline*."[23] In the report for the previous year, a hopeful missionary had observed: "There are a number of pious and established Christians in the Wyandott Nation who are making progress in the divine life and who oppose sin in all its variety of forms. A part of the nation remain wild and heathenish but they are generally in the woods so that we are not much troubled with them."[24] Indeed, this optimistic correspondent believed that there were fewer drunkards and Sabbath breakers on the reservation than in many white settlements of the same size. Some of the Wyandots, on the other hand, wondered why the whites had so many laws!

As the community of Wyandot converts became more active, they sent exhorters (determined lay witnesses) to preach among their Seneca neighbors with some effect: one Seneca chief declared in favor of Christianity. On the other hand, two Seneca chiefs were denounced for immorality—one for drunkenness and the other for both drunkenness and polygamy.[25] Among the most effective of the Christian Wyandot witnesses was Grey Eyes, who traveled through the nation visiting families and holding meetings. The missionaries described Grey Eyes not only as "Blessed of the Lord" but also as "a pious Holy Man very Zealous . . . [who] has the confidence of the Brethren, and nation at large, and we doubt not if he should be continued he will yet be more abundantly useful."[26]

One troublesome aspect of the Methodist mission activity was James Finley's blatant anti-Catholicism. His initial characterization of the Wyandots was as "sunk in the most degrading vices, such as Drunkenness, lewdness, and gambling, till many of them became the most degraded and worthless of their race." He blamed their condition on their longtime association with Roman Catholicism.

They had been under the religious instruction of the Roman Catholics for many years. But it appears, both from their morals and from the declarations of many who professed to be Catholics, that they did them little or no good. To carry a silver cross, and to count a string of beads, to worship the Virgin Mary, to go to church and hear mass said in Latin, and be taught to believe that for a beaver-skin or its value, they could have all their sins pardoned, comprised the sum total of their Christianity, and served but to encourage them in their superstition and vice.[27]

Finley, like Stewart, found that the Wyandots and their neighboring villages still followed some traditional ways. The missionaries were startled to hear the sounds of the Wyandots racing through the woods on horseback toward the church; the galloping hoofbeats of their horses were accompanied by the noise from the jangling bunches of earrings and nose tassels worn by the riders. On one occasion James Finley traveled with three Wyandot chiefs and the tribal agent to visit a nearby village of Mohawks, only to find that they had left to attend a "great Seneca feast." On Sunday morning the five visitors went to the Seneca council house, where a meeting was going on inside while outside between fifty and one hundred were playing ball accompanied by shouts that were "truly terrifying." The Wyandot delegation had to wait at the door of the council house for more than two hours until a missing principal chief arrived. The passing of a peace pipe and a ladleful of hominy then welcomed them. Knowing that the Wyandots wanted permission to preach among the Senecas, one of the Seneca chiefs answered that the Great Spirit not only had sent four angels to take care of them but also had called visionaries like the Seneca prophet. The Wyandot chief Between-the-Logs responded by speaking of his new religion and chastising the Senecas for engaging in the ball play; when he knelt to pray at the end of his speech, several of his listeners left the council house, while others "raised the Indian yell." Since there was a fair amount of disorder and levity during the speech, the audience may not have been paying close attention.[28]

Finley and the Methodists tried to continue the Wyandots along the path of change by establishing a farm in conjunction with the mission and the school. At the school the children learned to "read, write, and spell with proficiency," although they had some trouble with arithmetic; nevertheless one of the scholars excelled sufficiently to help the schoolmaster with teaching in 1827.[29] The farm would provide food for the missionaries and the teachers, offer work to the schoolchildren, and set an example of successful field agriculture for the Wyandots. Cornfields that yielded sixty bushels to the acre and twelve acres of potatoes, cabbage, and turnips no doubt would impress farmers accustomed to less-intensive Native American methods of planting and harvesting.[30] The manual labor system popular in educational circles at the time required the boys to work at least one day a week as field hands and for the girls to do chores like sewing, knitting, spinning, and cooking.[31] In order to ensure maximum exposure to these new cultural expectations the children lived at the mission house. They could not leave to go home without the permission of the missionary.[32]

Methodist missionaries also undertook educating the Wyandots who lived at the Big Spring reservation, twelve miles from Sandusky, where a school was constructed in 1829. The opening of the Big Spring school reduced the number enrolled at Sandusky, putting the total number of Wyandot scholars attending both schools at about forty.[33] In summer the number of attendees declined to thirty.[34] At the Wyandot mission school, when one of teachers resigned shortly after the beginning of the term, one of the local preachers filled in, thus enabling the mission to save money. The savings would not have been great, however, since a schoolteacher was paid only $8 a month.[35] Given the pittance teachers were paid, it was of some assistance that they were provided room and board. Life for a teacher in such a frontier school must have been demanding indeed, since the schoolmaster was expected to have the pupils up and ready for school each day.[36] Education had been a high priority with the Wyandots since the War of 1812, but the government had delayed opening a school, leaving the field open to the missionaries. In the missionary community there was rivalry over implementing education even before the Wyandot mission school opened. The Presbyterians attempted to undermine the Methodists among the Wyandots by spreading the rumor that the Methodists had no intention of opening the school.[37]

The Wyandot mission farm, like farms everywhere, had both good years and bad. By 1834 hired hands were doing most of the work on the farm. Crop yields had fallen, especially the harvest of corn, oats, and wheat; the insufficient returns prompted the farm overseer to buy one hundred bushels of wheat as well as corn and oats.[38] The year's difficulty was intensified by the death of a Wyandot child as well as one of the superintendent's, not to mention the fact that the farm spent more than it received. The mission received $800 from a missionary society and $400 from the War Department, but its expenditures amounted to $1,348.40.[39]

The Wyandots did seek Finley's help in communicating with the War Department of the United States government to obtain money supposedly set aside for assistance to the Native Americans. Although the secretary of war issued an order for an appropriation of $500, it never came. Acting in the manner of many applicants for government aid, Finley then journeyed to Washington, consulted with Secretary of War John C. Calhoun, and received enough government money to build a thirty-by-forty-foot lime-stone church near Upper Sandusky.[40] Calhoun would have granted this money under the terms of the "civilization fund" created by congress in 1819.[41]

What James Finley could not alter, however, was the determination of the government to remove the Wyandots westward. According to the treaty negotiations of 1818 attended by the Wyandots, Delawares, and Miamis, the official policy of the federal government was to remove all these peoples west of the Mississippi, but the native peoples showed "such strong symptoms of disapprobation" that the government dared not proceed farther. For the moment they granted large tracts in present-day Ohio to the Wyandots, Shawnees, and Senecas as reservations.[42] The Indian commissioners appointed by the Continental Congress believed that "as our settlements gradually surround them, their minds will be better prepared to receive this proposition, and we do not doubt but that a few years will accomplish what could not now be accomplished except at an expense greatly dispropor-tioned to the object."[43]

By the time of Finley's appointment to the Wyandot mission, the pressure was on again, with the Wyandots still resisting. The U.S. secretary of war responded by urging them to continue on the path of civilization by following the teaching of their missionary. The secretary did assure them that they would never be removed by force.[44] Finley brought up with the Wyandots the idea of dividing land into individual properties as well as the idea of moving west, but as before, the tribe rejected the idea.[45] James Finley did send a letter to Secretary of War Lewis Cass on December 15, 1825, asking once more that the Wyandots be allowed to remain. Two long-time leaders of the tribe who had converted to Christianity even accompa-nied Finley on a tour eastward in 1825. Between-the-Logs and Mononcue appeared before missionary societies not only in behalf of fund-raising efforts for the Wyandot mission but also in an attempt to make whatever positive impressions they might on the voting public. At a camp meeting in Baltimore, Between-the Logs spoke without an interpreter with such power that the crowd was greatly impressed. Between-the-Logs took this trip despite his advanced tuberculosis, from which he died on January 1, 1827.[46] The pressure on the Wyandots and their neighbors was inexorable as Ohio farmers plowed their way westward. After Ohio attained state-hood in 1803 increasing numbers of farmers wanted more land. The first lands settled in southeastern Ohio had now declined in value, as the rich, rolling acres in the western part of the state promised higher yields and greater profits. Lands held by the Wyandots and their neighbors were in great demand, since they had never been extensively farmed and, if brought to market either through a federal land office or a speculator, they could be obtained for reasonable prices. Farmers from New England to Virginia cast covetous eyes westward on land selling for far less than the several hundred dollars per acre they might have to pay for farmland east of the mountains. Thus the more than one hundred thousand acres eventually given up by the Wyandots in Ohio were eagerly sought.

Pressure for removal had increased with each passing year after 1815. The Treaty of Ghent had removed even the faintest hope of British backing, while the more westerly tribes also were being removed to prevent their being used as places of refuge in time of conflict. Ohio counties marched inexorably westward, pushed by the demands of land-crazed farmers. By 1833 the National Road had opened to Columbus, Ohio, lying some fifty miles south of the Wyandot lands; five years later it had reached Springfield, Ohio.[47] The area that became Wyandot County in 1845 already was surrounded by five counties established in 1820: Marion, Crawford, Seneca, Hancock, and Hardin. Whenever a tribal group elected to move west, Ohio farmers were not far behind, ready to buy up former reservation lands for as little as $5 an acre.[48] Ohio's population increased from 231,000 people in 1810 to 938,000 people in 1830, a growth rate of some 400 percent.[49] By 1840, on the eve of Wyandot removal, the population had reached 1,519,000, an increase of over 60 percent in ten years.[50] As six Seneca chiefs had written to President John Quincy Adams as early as 1828, they were "now surrounded by a dense white population, which has brought so many evils upon them, that they can no longer reside there."[51] Several of the Ohio groups wanted to visit Washington in 1828 in order to explain their plight to the president himself. Agent John Johnston wrote to Indian Commissioner Thomas McKenney on September 14 explaining that the Indians of his agency were perplexed by their situation and the "pressure of the white population upon them." Many wanted to visit the nation's capital: "I believe that nothing will satisfy them short of the indulgence asked for; and as they have not been troublesome in this way, and most of them being tried friends of the United States, in all times of danger and difficulty, I earnestly recommend that permission may be granted that three Wyandots, two Shawanoese, two Senecas, and one Delaware, be permitted to visit the President of the United States, at the seat of government, during the ensuing Winter."[52] On May 28, 1830, the Congress passed the long-debated removal bill.[53] Indian-held lands in the East would be exchanged for designated lands in the West, improvement on eastern lands would be paid for, the removal would be paid for, and those who migrated would be supported for a year.

Among the non-Indian neighbors who actually stood to lose from the removal of the tribes from Ohio were Indian traders like George C. Johnston, who operated a trading house on the Shawnee reservation at Wapakoneta. It is clear from his records that he was part storekeeper and part moneylender. His job-printed ledger book produced by the *Piqua Gazette* was boldly labeled WAPAUGHKONNETTA. Each page had two printed forms that were in effect simple promissory notes, so that when Wewellapee came to Johnston on November 12, 1829, he signed a note for $7.00.[54] Between November 8, 1829, and April 8, 1830, Wewellapee charged for himself or his wife items amounting to $350.00! Included were andirons at $2.50, a tea kettle at $1.25, a tin bucket for his wife at $1.00, two bridles at $5.00, an axe at $2.37, vest pattern lining and buttons at $1.37, five pounds of coffee at $1.00, and a pair of shoes at $2.00.

By the time John Johnston wrote his letter to Commissioner McKenney requesting permission to bring a delegation from the Ohio tribes to Washington, he was working with the issue of removal for several tribes. Some Ohio peoples had already begun to relocate, with bands of Delawares and Shawnees leaving between 1820 and 1828. In 1828 Johnston attempted to help one small band of Senecas and Mohawks, along with about twenty Wyandots, relocate westward. His memo to McKenney explained the need for $5,000 to buy their lands, make improvements, and pay for moving expenses, an exigency created in part by the fact that the Senecas wanted to wait until April, six months later, when the weather would be more favorable but of course at increased cost. More money was needed because the Senecas wanted horses and travel funds along with an interpreter paid to accompany them.[55] By the fall of 1828 negotiations were proceeding to move the Delawares from their 5,760 acres adjoining the Wyandots at Upper Sandusky. Johnston's estimates of expenses were beginning to grow. About 450 people were to be moved at a cost of $13,000: $6,000 to buy their lands, $5,000 to remove other Ohio Indians, $1,539.24 for damages committed by U.S. citizens—"compensation claimed under the law of intercourse"—and $500 for the interpreter to accompany the Senecas.[56]

A few of Ohio's non-Indian citizens demonstrated some sympathy toward the Indians about the removal question, at least as it pertained to the Cherokee. In 1830, 210 citizens of Brown County signed a memorial "in Relation to the Cherokee Indians." The memorialists did not think it right to force the Cherokee to leave their tribal lands. Such a measure was "cruel, unjust and disgraceful to our Government," which should "turn a deaf ear to such solicitations."[57] The concerned citizens of Brown County were in a decided minority, as most Ohioans wanted the tribes finally removed in order to obtain their lands. Others were eager to capitalize on the profits to be made in assisting with the removal. If a farmer turned teamster could provide a driver, a wagon, and a two-horse team, all the expenses for the journey would be paid, both coming and going. It would be a tedious journey, it was understood, but "those who live to come back without meeting serious accidents may do tolerable well by going." The "tolerable well" was predicated on the fact that the would-be escorts believed the per diem being paid was $250![58] The actual amount listed in Henry C. Brish's expense account at the end of December 1831 was $4.75 a day for the wagons.[59] Brish was the agent hired to accompany the Senecas west.

The first group to be moved after the 1830 Removal Act was the Senecas of Sandusky.[60] When they finally set out in the fall of 1831, it was far too late in the season for a cross-country journey. The plan called for two parties, one traveling by canal boat and steamer to St. Louis and the other overland with the horses that the tribe would need in its new home. Under the guidance of Brish they left for the West on October 16, moving overland toward the canal stop at Dayton on the Miami and Erie Canal. At Bellefontaine, Ohio, the horse herd and its escort headed toward Indiana. By November 16 the people traveling by boat were on board the steamer *Ben Franklin* off St. Louis. That group, led by subagent Brish, included chiefs Comstock, Seneca Steel, Captain Goodhunter, Hard Hickory, and 228 other Senecas from Sandusky.[61] Henry Brish was frustrated not only by the lateness of the season but also because Ohio Indian agent John McElwain had failed to provide the blankets and rifles specified in the migration agreement. The overland party in the meantime fared even worse. At Munseetown, Indiana, an outbreak of distemper left eighteen horses dead and the rest weak. Four of the Senecas died, so dispiriting the remainder that some went no farther and others returned to Ohio.[62] The stresses of trying to guide such a large party finally convinced subagent Brish that he needed the aid of three friends to help him with the "blood-thirsty dispositions" of the Senecas under his direction.[63] Henry Brish probably engaged in hyperbole because of the difficulty of the journey; the issue primarily was that many of the Senecas lamented the move and, without the vigilant supervision of the escort, probably would have quickly returned to the sanctuary of their Wyandot friends in Ohio.[64] Brish finally arranged for the advance party to encamp near St. Louis for the duration of the winter, because the bitter cold in Missouri had left many sick and several dead and had rendered travel impossible.[65] At least one official in St. Louis was unhappy with this winter camp, urging Brish to get the Senecas to their lands and contract for someone to supply them throughout the required period of transition.[66] Part of the reason for urging them onward was the expense of providing food. Between November 26 and December 31, 1831, Henry Brish distributed 8,352 rations of bread and meat for 232 Senecas for thirty-six days, not to mention finding twenty wagons to convey the elderly, women, and children along with their baggage and provisions.[67]

After a wintertime trip back to Ohio, Henry Brish traveled through Indiana, found those who had stayed there, conveyed them to St. Louis, trekked to the camp of the overland party, and then pushed on to the new lands in the Indian Territory, arriving there on July 4, 1832. Three hundred fifty-two had survived the trip, thirty had died en route, and forty-eight more were still on the trail somewhere between Indiana and the Indian territory.[68] In a letter written to Clark a few days later, Brish lamented: "I charge myself with cruelty in forcing these unfortunate people on, at a time when a few days delay might have prevented some deaths, and rendered the sickness of others more light, and have to regret this part of my duty, which together with the extreme to which I have been subjected, and the sickness consequent upon it, have made the task of removing the Senecas excessively unpleasant to me."[69]

The Wyandots managed to postpone removal for another decade, but after the treaty of 1842 was signed, they could delay no more. They moved west, leaving behind the "improvements" on their lands, appraised at a value of $125,937.24.[70] By the time of their removal, those in charge of these forced migrations had enough experience to schedule the journeys in the summer and concentrate the emigrants on boats. Accordingly, the Wyandots left the Grand Reserve on July 12, 1843, and spent the next week trekking southward to Cincinnati, where they boarded two river steamers for the West. At St. Louis they transferred to two Missouri River boats, and they reached the mouth of the Kansas River by the last week in July.

Observers of their movement through Ohio must have wondered what was happening to these people. When they passed through Xenia, Ohio, on Sunday, July 16, a reporter for the *Xenia Torch-Light* reported reflectively on them.

> The remains of this once flourishing tribe of Indians passed through our town on Sunday morning last. They encamped about three miles north of town on Saturday evening, where they had intended to remain over the Sabbath, but some person or persons, having injudiciously furnished the intemperate among them with ardent spirits, it was thought best to leave in the morning, for fear that their peace would be seriously disturbed by those few who had become intoxicated. The general appearance of these Indians was truly prepossessing. Every one of them, we believe, without an exception, was decently dressed, a large proportion of them in the costume of the whites. Their deportment was quite orderly and respectful. We are informed that nearly one-half of them make a profession of the Christian religion. They appeared to be well fitted out for their journey, having a convenient variety of cooking utensils, and provisions in abundance. The whole number of persons in the company, so far was we could learn, was about 750. The number of wagons, carriages and buggies owned by the tribe, about 80. Hired wagons 55. Horses and ponies near 300.[71]

Still without specific tribal territory in the West, the Wyandots settled on lands near their former Ohio neighbors the Delawares, an arrangement formalized in an agreement for purchase in late 1843. Other matters relating to payments for their Delaware lands and for their improvements dragged on for some years. Unhappy with their settlement from the United States over their Ohio "improvements," a delegation journeyed to Washington in early 1846.[72] The complaint of the principal chief and his delegation was that the government had paid them only $20,000 for their Ohio "improvements," when these were worth almost $126,000. The Wyandots suspected that they were being defrauded by speculators who wanted to devalue their lands and improvements in order to buy them more cheaply.

They reminded the government of the treaty's terms about paying for their improvements by quoting the article of the treaty under which the original arrangements had been made.[73]

With the final approval by the Congress of an agreement between the Delawares and the Wyandots for land in the West amounting to about twenty-five thousand acres, the Wyandot transition from Ohio was complete. All their claims in the East were renounced in lieu of a settlement of $185,000 in cash and annuities, $46,080 of which would have to be paid to the Delawares.

Ohio's first peoples had passed from the scene, leaving behind a rich legacy of place names and long-ignored artifacts. Modern Ohioans would do well to remember them, their appreciation for the land, and their ability to survive and adapt to change.

OHIO'S FIRST PEOPLES

A Bicentennial Afterthought

As Ohioans contemplate the absence of a visible Native American population in our state today, we might ask ourselves the reason for that absence. When the pioneers arrived in April of 1788 there were forty-eight of them and several thousand Native Americans living within the present boundaries of Ohio. Today there are several million inhabitants of Ohio, none who are readily visible Native Americans and only a few thousand who identify themselves as such to the United States Bureau of the Census.

Part of the reason may lie in the cultural baggage that came west to Ohio in the late eighteenth century. When the Europeans arrived to establish the first permanent settlement in 1788, the possibility of a shared landscape was highly unlikely. Their ancestors had brought with them across the Atlantic an ethnocentrism grounded in hatred for peoples of color, peoples of lesser technological accomplishment, and peoples who were not Christian (at least according to their definition). More than two hundred years of contact between Europeans and native peoples in North America had established an invidious pattern of violence that bred violence until warfare was the norm; peace was merely an interlude of truce before fighting broke out once more. This is not to say that there were not individuals who wanted the bloodshed to stop, even those who labored without rest and at the risk of their lives to stop the fighting, but *the issue was the land*. In the European view, to borrow the words of John Donne, the Indians "doe live like deer in herds and waste the land." No matter how civilized a tribe or a tribesperson might become, Indians were still regarded as savages who should melt away into the distant wasteland, leaving framed homes, plowed fields, and crops ripe for harvest to the "civilized" conqueror, who would properly manage and manure the ground. No matter, indeed, how much a single Delaware like Captain White Eyes, or an entire tribe like the Cherokees, lived in a "civilized" manner; they were always barbarians in the eyes of their white beholders. Even Christianity could not baptize an Indian into acceptability—witness the slaughtered Moravian converts in 1782. Bearing Christian names and singing the hymns of their church, they were clubbed to death by their executors, who had voted to kill them rather than be bothered with taking them prisoners.

In 2003 we cannot turn back time, nor could we adequately compensate present-day persons of Native American descent (or any other groups) for past treatment. What we might do is regard our present neighbors with more tolerance. Because their looks, dress, smell, or beliefs are different from ours, are they less worthy of our regard? Before we judge them so, perhaps we should take a day trip to the site of Gnadenhutten and contemplate the place where more than ninety human beings were murdered because they were different.

Notes

Introduction

1. Susan L. Woodward and Jerry N. McDonald, *Indian Mounds of the Middle Ohio Valley: A Guide to Adena and Ohio Hopewell Sites* (Newark, Ohio: The McDonald and Woodward Publishing Company, 1986).

2. Personal communication with Wesley Clarke, Registered Professional Archaeologist, January 21, 2002. A Middle Fort Ancient site was recently excavated just two miles up the Muskingum River from the Hopewellian hamlet. It too has lain relatively undisturbed, between a boat ramp and playing fields, only inches beneath the surface. Known as the Indian Acres site (33WN39), it has been radiocarbon dated at A.D. 1320. Wesley Clarke to James O'Donnell, personal communication to author, April 15, 2001.

3. Jeff Carskadden and James Morton, "Living on the Edge: A Comparison of Adena and Hopewell Communities in the Central Muskingum Valley of Eastern Ohio," in *Ohio Hopewell Community Organization,* ed. William S. Dancey and Paul J. Pacheco (Kent, Ohio: Kent State University Press, 1997), 365–401. In particular see table 14.1, "Radiocarbon Dates from Adena, Hopewell and Early Late Woodland Sites in the Muskingum Valley," 389–90.

4. Paul J. Pacheco, "Ohio Middle Woodland Intracommunity Settlement Variability," in *Ohio Hopewell Community Organization,* ed. William S. Dancey and Paul J. Pacheco (Kent, Ohio: Kent State University Press, 1997), 41–84. In particular see table 2.6, "Assemblage Size, Estimated Surface Area, and Density," 77. See also Mark F. Seeman, *The Locust Site (33Mu160): The 1983 Test Excavation of a Multicomponent Workshop in East Central Ohio,* Kent State Research Papers in Archaeology, no. 7 (Kent, Ohio: Kent State University Press, 1985).

5. David Brose, "Archaeological Investigations at the Paleo Crossing Site, a PaleoIndian Occupation in Medina County, Ohio," in William S. Dancey, ed., *The First Discovery of America: Archaeological Evidence of the Early Inhabitants of Ohio* (Columbus: Ohio Archaeological Council, 1994); Daniel C. Fisher, Bradley T. Lepper, and Paul E. Hooge, "Evidence for the Butchery of the Burning Tree Mastodon," in ibid. Additional information about the earliest Ohioans may be found in Olaf H. Prufer and Dana A. Long, *The Archaic of Northeastern Ohio,* Kent State Research Papers in Archaeology, no. 6 (Kent, Ohio: Kent State University Press, 1986); and in Olaf H. Prufer, Dana A. Long, and Donald J. Metzger, *Krill Cave: A Stratified Rockshelter in Summit County, Ohio,* Kent State Research Papers in Archaeology, no. 8 (Kent, Ohio: Kent State University Press, 1989).

6. Richard White, *The Middle Ground: Indians, Empires, and Republics in the Great Lakes Region, 1650–1815* (Cambridge: Cambridge University Press, 1991); on the extensive influence of the Madisonville culture see Penelope B. Drooker, *The View from Madisonville: Protohistoric Western Fort Ancient Interaction Patterns* (Ann Arbor: Museum of Anthropology, University of Michigan, 1997). With regard to the axhead see E. Thomas Hemmings, "Neale's Landing: An Archeological Study of a Fort Ancient Settlement on Blennerhassett Island, West Virginia" (submitted to the West Virginia Antiquities Commission and the Office of Archeology and Historic Preservation, Department of the Interior—National Park Service in fulfillment of contracts for Archeological Research at Blennerhassett Island, West Virginia, National Park Service project number 54-73-00020-00), West Virginia Geological and Economic Survey, Morgantown, West Virginia, 1977.

7. David S. Brose, "Penumbral Protohistory on Lake Erie's South Shore," in *Societies in Eclipse: Archaeology of the Eastern Woodland Indians, A.D. 1400–1700* (Washington, D.C.: Smithsonian Institution Press, 2001).

8. Bruce Trigger, "Early Iroquoian Contacts with Europeans," in *Handbook of North American Indians,* ed. William C. Sturtevant (Washington, D.C.: Smithsonian Institution Press, 1978), 15:344–56; hereafter *HNAI.* There is a voluminous literature on this subject, including the classic twentieth-century account written by George T. Hunt, *The Wars of the Iroquois* (Madison: University of Wisconsin Press, 1940). Other accounts of interest include William N. Fenton, *The Great Law and the Longhouse: A Political History of the Iroquois Confederacy* (Norman: University of Oklahoma Press, 1998); Elizabeth Tooker, "Three Aspects of Northern Iroquoian Culture Change," *Pennsylvania Archaeologist* 30 (2): 65–71; Allen W. Trelease, *Indian Affairs in Colonial New York: The Seventeenth Century* (Ithaca, N.Y.: Cornell University Press, 1960); and Bruce Trigger, *The Children of Aataentsic: A History of the Huron People to 1660* (Montreal: McGill-Queen's University Press, 1976).

9. Elizabeth Tooker, "Wyandot," in *HNAI,* 15:398–406.

10. Rufus Putnam letter, Marietta College Special Collections, Dawes Memorial Library, Marietta College, Marietta, Ohio.

11. William F. Romain, *Mysteries of the Hopewell: Astronomers, Geometers, and Magicians of the Eastern Woodlands* (Akron: University of Akron Press, 2000). In modern dictionaries the first definition of "earthwork" still includes the meaning of fortification. Cf. *American Heritage College Dictionary,* third edition (1993), 431, and *Compact OED* (1971), 826.

12. Clarke, personal communication to the author, April 15, 2001.

13. Ephraim G. Squier and Edwin H. Davis, *Ancient Monuments of the Mississippi Valley,* edited by David J. Meltzer (Washington, D.C.: Smithsonian Institution Press, 1998).

14. Robert Silverberg, *Mound Builders of Ancient America: The Archaeology of a Myth* (Greenwich: New York Graphic Society, 1968), 6.

15. Randolph C. Downes, *Council Fires on the Upper Ohio: A Narrative of Indian Affairs in the Upper Ohio Valley until 1795* (Pittsburgh: University of Pittsburgh Press, 1940); James H. Howard, *Shawnee! The Ceremonialism of a Native Indian Tribe and Its Cultural Background* (Athens: Ohio University Press, 1981); Clinton A. Weslager, *The Delaware Indians: A History* (New Brunswick: Rutgers University Press, 1972); R. David Edmunds, *The Shawnee Prophet* (Lincoln: University of Nebraska Press, 1983); R. David Edmunds, *Tecumseh and the Quest for Indian Leadership* (Boston: Little, Brown, 1984); and Allan W. Eckert, *A Sorrow in Our Heart: The Life of Tecumseh* (New York: Bantam, 1992). All of Eckert's works are stories well told, with only a genuflection toward historical sources. My review essay analyzing Eckert's documentation was published in the *Northwest Ohio Quarterly* 65 (1993): 50–54. On Downes as a historian of the frontier see James H. O'Donnell, "Randolph C. Downes," in *Historians of the American Frontier: A Bio-Bibliographical Sourcebook,* ed. John R. Wunder (New York: Greenwood Press, 1988), 249–61.

16. For a summary of Abraham Maslow's ideas and a useful chart, see H. Dan O'Hair, James S. O'Rourke, and Mary John O'Hair, *Business Communication: A Framework for Success* (Cincinnati: South-Western Publishing, 2001), 332–34.

17. James H. O'Donnell, "Captain Pipe's Speech: A Commentary on the Delaware Experience, 1775–1781," *Northwest Ohio Quarterly* 64 (1992): 126–33.

Chapter 1

1. This is the phrase used by Jennings in his argument that when the Europeans arrived on the Atlantic shore, "They did not settle a virgin land. They invaded and displaced a resident population." Francis Jennings, *The Invasion of America: Indians, Colonialism, and the Cant of Conquest* (Chapel Hill, N.C.: Institute of Early American History and Culture, 1975), 15.

2. In the Rufus Putnam Papers in the Special Collections of the Marietta College Library are Putnam's records of his encounter with the mounds. See in particular his "Plan of part of the city of Marietta at the confluence of the Rivers Ohio and Muskingum together with the remains of ancient works found therein, surveyed by the Ohio Company, 1788"; a manuscript map to accompany the "Plan"; and Rufus Putnam to "Dear Sir," n.d. [1788]. The last is a letter apparently meant to accompany the other two items, intended to inform one of his correspondents in the East about the natural curiosities on the western frontier.

3. Putnam to "Dear Sir," ibid. Even a traveler who came fifteen years after Putnam remarked, "These works are scattered over the whole face of the country. You

cannot ride twenty miles in any direction without finding some of the mounds, or vestiges of ramparts." Thaddeus M. Harris, *The Journal of a Tour . . . 1803* (Boston: Manning and Loring, 1805), 148.

4. Harris, *Journal*. According to Manasseh Cutler's journal for 1788 on Saturday, September 6, "The Directors ordered yesterday that this day the surveyors be directed to measure the Ancient Works; . . . examined the elevated squares, Sacra Via, measured the great mound, ditch, etc." William P. Cutler and Julia P. Cutler, eds., *Life, Journals, and Correspondence of Rev. Manasseh Cutler, LL.D.* (Athens: Ohio University Press, 1987), 1:418.

5. Cutler and Cutler, *Life, Journals.*

6. Ibid. Putnam is using "covered" in the military sense, that is, the persons within its walls would be sheltered from enemy projectiles.

7. Rufus Putnam was aware of the potential for flooding in such a location, since he had visited the lower Mississippi River searching for western lands in 1773 and had noted the presence of flood debris entangled high in the tree branches along the river banks. Putnam was not the first to map the mounds. A map of them, drawn by Captain Jonathan Heart, who was stationed with the First American Regiment across the Muskingum River at Fort Harmar, was published as a "Plan of the Remains of some Ancient Works on the Muskingum" in the *Columbian Magazine* for May 1787. This map is reproduced in an unpublished paper prepared for the Ohio Historic Preservation Office in June 2001 by archaeologist Wesley Clarke entitled "The Marietta Earthwork Complex, Washington County, Ohio." Both the Putnam manuscript map and the published Heart map show similar features, including the peculiarly lobed side of the mound on which the Washington County Library now rests.

8. Interview with Ray Zoerkler, Certified Professional Geologist, January 2, 2002.

9. William S. Dancey and Paul J. Pacheco, "A Community Model of Ohio Hopewell Settlement," in *Ohio Hopewell Community Organization,* ed. Dancey and Pacheco (Kent, Ohio: Kent State University Press, 1997), 9–10. Similar but more comparative information may be found in the same authors' "The Ohio Hopewell Settlement Pattern Problem in Historical Perspective" (paper presented at the fifty-seventh annual meeting of the Society for American Archaeology, Pittsburgh, Pa., 1992). I am indebted to Wesley Clarke for a copy of this paper. For inhabitants of modern communities it would be much like two churches at two corners of an intersection, the first, older, smaller, and of less pretentious architecture, now housing a congregation of a different denomination, while the newer, larger, more architecturally ambitious structure has become the home of the older congregation, which moved "up" from across the street.

10. Harris, *Journal*, 152.

11. Ibid. Harris also reports finding "plates of copper rivetted together, cop-

per beads, various implements of stone and a very curious . . . of porcelain." Ibid., 159.

12. Brian Fagan, *Ancient North America: The Archaeology of a Continent* (New York: Thames and Hudson, 1991), 364.

13. Elliot M. Abrams, "Woodland Settlement Patterns in the Southern Hocking River Valley, Southeastern Ohio," in *Cultural Variability in Context: Woodland Settlements of the Mid-Ohio Valley,* ed. Mark F. Seeman, *Midcontinental Journal of Archaeology Special Papers* (Kent, Ohio: Kent State University Press, 1992), 20. For evidence of Glacial Kame usage see Prufer, Long, and Metzger, *Krill Cave,*75.

14. Don W. Dragoo, *Mounds for the Dead: An Analysis of Adena Culture* (Pittsburgh: Carnegie Museum of Natural History, 1963), 3.

15. Dee Anne Wymer, "Trends and Disparities: The Woodland Paleoethnobotanical Record of the Mid-Ohio Valley," in *Cultural Variability in Context: Woodland Settlements of the Mid-Ohio Valley,* ed. Mark F. Seeman, Midcontinental Journal of Archaeology Special Papers (Kent, Ohio: Kent State University Press, 1992), 65–66.

16. Ibid., 68.

17. Ibid.

18. Ibid., 66.

19. Romain, *Mysteries of the Hopewell,* 129–42.

20. Brad Lepper, "The Great Hopewell Road and the Role of Pilgrimage in the Hopewell Interaction Sphere" (paper presented at "Perspectives on Middle Woodland at the Millennium," a conference held at the Center for American Archaeology, Kampsville, Ill., July 2000). See also his earlier article, "Tracking Ohio's Great Hopewell Road," *Archaeology* 48, no. 6 (1995): 52–56. My thanks to Dr. Lepper for these.

21. Brad Lepper, "Newark Earthworks and the Geometric Enclosures of the Scioto Valley: Connections and Conjectures," in *A View from the Core: A Synthesis of Ohio Hopewell Archaeology,* ed. Paul J. Pacheco (Columbus: Ohio Archaeological Council, 1996), 238.

22. E. B. Andrews, "Reports on the Exploration of a Cave and of Mounds in Ohio," *Tenth Annual Report of the Peabody Museum* (Salem, Mass.: Salem Press, 1877), 55.

23. Lepper, "The Great Hopewell Road," 9.

24. Dee Anne Wymer, "The Hopewell Econiche: Human-Land Interaction in the Core Area," in *A View from the Core: A Synthesis of Ohio Hopewell Archaeology,* ed. Paul J. Pacheco (Columbus: Ohio Archaeological Council, 1996), 39.

25. Ibid., 45.

26. Ibid., 47.

27. Ibid.

28. See Olaf Prufer, "How to Construct a Model: A Personal Memoir," in *Ohio Hopewell Community Organization,* ed. William S. Dancey and Paul J. Pacheco (Kent, Ohio: Kent State University Press, 1997).

29. See figure 2.3, Pacheco, "Ohio Hopewell Regional Settlement Patterns," in *A View from the Core: A Synthesis of Ohio Hopewell Archaeology,* ed. Pacheco (Columbus: Ohio Archaeological Council, 1996), 24.

30. Penelope B. Drooker and C. Wesley Cowan, "Transformation of the Ft. Ancient Cultures of the Central Ohio Valley," in *Societies in Eclipse: Archaeology of the Eastern Woodland Indians,* A.D. *1400–1700,* ed. David S. Brose, C. Wesley Cowan, and Robert C. Mainfort Jr. (Washington, D.C.: Smithsonian Institution Press, 2001), 83–106.

31. Ibid., 90.

32. Ibid. It appears that there was a long-term movement away from upland and open foraging locales toward relatively permanent village sites in rich bottomlands from the Archaic through the Fort Ancient periods, apparently tied to an increasing dependence on agriculture, particularly as maize, beans, and squash became the dominant vegetable foodstuffs of the Ohio Valley tribes. Additional recent commentary on this evolution may be seen in Flora Church and John P. Nass, Jr., "Central Ohio Valley during the Late Prehistoric Period: Subsistence-Settlement Systems' Responses to Risk," in *Northeast Subsistence-Settlement Change,* A.D. *700–1300,* ed. John P. Hart and Christina B. Rieth (Albany, N.Y.: New York State Museum Bulletin 496, 2002), 11–42.

33. In the twentieth century the island became a West Virginia state park; the lack of natural predators or licensed hunting has created a population crisis for the deer there. Forcibly relocating the animals to the mainland solves no problems either, since deer can swim!

34. Drooker and Cowan, "Transformation," 90.

35. Arthur F. Goss, "Astronomical Alignments at the Incinerator Site," in *A History of 17 Years of Excavation and Research: A Chronicle of the 12th-Century Human Values and the Built Environment,* ed. James M. Heilman, Malinda C. Lilias, and Christopher A. Turnbow (Dayton, Ohio: Dayton Museum of Natural History, 1988), 314–34.

36. Hemmings, "Neale's Landing."

37. Drooker, *View from Madisonville,* 245, 263.

38. Drooker and Cowan, "Transformation," 96.

39. Ibid., 94. The Calumet ceremony and the Black Drink ceremony are examples of the required diplomatic introductions practiced by Native Americans and Europeans during the historic period.

40. Drooker, *View from Madisonville,* quoted in ibid. These conclusions are entirely hypothesized from the interpretation of artifactual evidence by contemporary archaeologists.

41. Drooker, *View from Madisonville,* and Drooker and Cowan, "Transformation," 94.

42. Drooker, *View from Madisonville,* 278, for the latter.

43. Ibid., 262.

44. Ibid., 263.

45. Ibid., 269.

46. Ibid., 281, 332.

47. Ibid., 260.

48. Brose, "Archaeological Investigations."

49. Ibid., 164.

50. Ibid., 165.

51. Ibid., 182–83.

52. Carskadden and Morton, "Living on the Edge," 159.

53. Ibid.

54. Ibid., 170.

Chapter 2

1. See Tooker, "Wyandot," 398–406, and Conrad Heidenreich, "Huron," in *HNAI,* 15:368–88.

2. For a diagram of the village at Detroit and its fortification see Tooker, "Wyandot," 400.

3. Weslager, *Delaware Indians,* 243.

4. Ibid.

5. Quoted in ibid., 189. A full-page reproduction of Gustavus Hesselius's portrait of "Lapowinsa" is printed on page 181 in *The American Heritage Book of Indians,* ed. Alvin M. Josephy Jr. (New York: American Heritage Publishing, 1961). The Historical Society of Pennsylvania owns the original. On the involvement of Lappawinzo in the Walking Purchase see Francis Jennings, *The Ambiguous Iroquois Empire: The Covenant Chain Confederation of Indian Tribes with English Colonies from Its Beginning to the Lancaster Treaty of 1744* (New York: W. W. Norton and Company, 1984), 336.

6. For a more detailed discussion of the Walking Purchase, see Jennings, *Ambiguous Iroquois Empire,* 325ff. and appendix B.

7. By virtue of their strategic location, their conquests during the "beaver wars," and their alliance with the British, the Iroquois tried to claim hegemony over all the tribes within their orbit from the St. Lawrence to the Carolinas and from the Atlantic to the Mississippi. For an extended discussion of the emergence and decline of Iroquois power, not to mention the fragile base on which it rested, see Francis Jennings's trilogy: *The Invasion of America: Indians, Colonialism and*

the *Cant of Conquest* (Chapel Hill, N.C.: Institute of Early American History and Culture, 1975); *Ambiguous Iroquois Empire;* and *Empire of Fortune: Crowns, Colonies, and Tribes in the Seven Years War in America* (New York: W. W. Norton and Company, 1988).

8. William Hunter, "History of the Ohio Valley," in *HNAI,* 15:592. Frontier usage was to label the Ohio Iroquois peoples as the "Mingo," but since that carries a certain pejorative connotation, I will not use it routinely.

9. For general information about a complex pattern of movements, see Hunter, "History of the Ohio Valley," and Charles Callender, "Shawnee," in *HNAI,* 15:622–35. By the 1770s the tribe was the nemesis of the Virginians, who labeled every hostile action the work of the "dreaded Shawnee" and constantly called for punitive actions against them. The Virginians even tarred with that brush the reputation of villages in Ohio that were not Shawnee. The frequent raids by George Rogers Clark, later Virginia's leader in conquering the Illinois country, and the Kentuckians are an extension of this attitude.

10. Ebenezer Denny, *Military Journal of Major Ebenezer Denny, an Officer in the Revolutionary and Indian Wars, with an Introductory Memoir* (Philadelphia: J. B. Lippincott, for the Historical Society of Pennsylvania, 1859), 59. Denny reports that men as well as women made use of the structure for purposes of diplomacy.

11. Christopher Gist, *Christopher Gist's Journals with Historical, Geographical, and Ethnological Notes and Biographies of His Contemporaries,* ed. William M. Darlington (Pittsburgh: J. R. Weldin and Company, 1893).

12. Weslager, *Delaware Indians,* 243.

13. Ibid., 291.

14. With regard to the profits derived from the deerskin trade in South Carolina see Verner W. Crane, *The Southern Frontier, 1670–1732* (Ann Arbor: University of Michigan Press, 1956).

15. On the question of multiethnic individuals see James Clifton, *On Being and Becoming Indian: Biographical Studies of North American Frontiers* (Chicago: Dorsey Press, 1989). With regard to captives see James Axtell, *The Invasion Within: The Contest of Cultures in Colonial North America* (New York: Oxford University Press, 1985). In 1773 would-be missionary David Jones visited a village in central Ohio where a Maryland emigrant named Conner lived; the town's chief was Conner's brother-in-law, as the two men had married sisters who were white captives, "likely from childhood, for they have the very actions of Indians, and speak broken English." See Emily Foster, ed., *The Ohio Frontier: An Anthology of Early Writings* (Lexington: University Press of Kentucky, 1996), 33. Foster's work will be referred to as *Ohio Frontier Writings* to avoid confusion with R. Douglas Hurt's *The Ohio Frontier.*

16. The maps in *Atlas of Great Lakes Indian History* illustrate the frequency with which towns, whether Delaware, Shawnee, or Western Iroquois, were relo-

cated, especially during the period from 1775 to 1790. Helen H. Tanner, ed., *Atlas of Great Lakes Indian History* (Norman: University of Oklahoma Press, 1988).

17. It is clear from the Charles Stuart captivity narrative that horses (as well as cattle and hogs) were desirable prizes. See note 19, below. Canines, it has recently been argued, may have been with native peoples from before they crossed the Bering Straits. See a summary of these ideas in the *Wall Street Journal* for November 22, 2002, and the articles on which it is based in *Science* for the same date, especially Peter Savolainen, Ya-ping Zhang, Jing Luo, Joakim Lundeberg, and Thomas Leitner, "Genetic Evidence for an East Asian Origin of Domestic Dogs," *Science*, November 22, 2002, 1610–13.

18. See the Treaty of 1778 with the Delaware, the first between the United States and an Indian tribe, in Wilcomb Washburn, *The American Indian and the United States: A Documentary History*, 4 vols. (New York: Random House, 1973), 3:2263; hereafter Washburn.

19. Beverley W. Bond Jr., "The Captivity of Charles Stuart, 1755–57," *Mississippi Valley Historical Review* 13 (1926–27): 63.

20. Jennings, *Empire of Fortune*, 158. Jennings's description could be applied to St. Clair's defeat: "From the trees the Indians poured forth a devastating fire while the British fired back aimlessly at targets they could not see" (157).

21. Bond, "Captivity," 64.

22. Ibid.

23. Ibid., 59.

24. The episode of Old Briton, who moved his Miami followers to Pickawillany in search of better trading connections, is a case in point. Old Briton relocated closer to the British traders both to improve his people's material well-being and to escape the dominance of the French. He paid dearly for this rebellion, being killed and then cooked for eating by the French-allied Indians who captured him. See R. David Edmunds, "Old Briton," in *American Indian Leaders: Studies in Diversity*, ed. Edmunds (Lincoln: University of Nebraska Press, 1980), 1–20.

25. Charles Stuart's report of his visit to the Choctaw country, July 1, 1778, British Public Record Office, Colonial Office, ser. 5, vol. 79:196–202, microfilm; hereafter Co5/vol:page. For purposes of clarification I should point out that the writer of this report from the British Public Record Office was a deputy in the British Southern Indian Department, not the person captured in Pennsylvania.

26. Stuart evidently believed that he and his wife were most fortunate to have been brought together and relatively unharmed to Detroit. In his narrative he claimed that "the constant orders given by the French government and French priests at Detroit to the Indian parties they send against the English is to kill, burn and destroy all, save none unless it be one for their own use." Bond, "Captivity," 79. Charles Stuart and his wife were the only couple spared by the raiders; in total, however, twenty-two men, women, and children were taken captive, while

four men and two women were killed during the raid itself, at least according to Stuart's enumeration. Some scholars argue that raiders usually killed twice as many as they captured, but the reverse is true here. The landmarks indicated by Stuart are sufficient to allow the modern reader to retrace the route followed from their farm near McConnellsburg, Pennsylvania; to Fort Duquesne (Pitt) and into Ohio via the Great Trail that ran west from Logstown to Beaver Town; on to Mohican John's Town and thence to Sandusky. For the towns see Tanner, *Atlas;* for the trails see Paul W. A. Wallace, *Indian Paths of Pennsylvania* (Harrisburg: Pennsylvania Historical and Museum Commission, 1965), 142–47; and Frank N. Wilcox, *Ohio Indian Trails: A Pictorial Survey of the Indian Trails of Ohio,* ed. William A. McGill (Kent, Ohio: Kent State University Press, 1970). Most of the individual captives would have been adopted into the tribes living where the captives were left. For an account of the adoption ritual, see the selection from James Smith's captivity reprinted in Foster, *Ohio Frontier Writings,* 19–20.

27. Interpretations of the role played by Neolin's message vary. It is central in Gregory Dowd, *A Spirited Resistance: The North American Indian Struggle for Unity, 1745–1815* (Baltimore: Johns Hopkins University Press, 1992) and secondary in Jennings, *Empire of Fortune.*

28. Jennings, *Empire of Fortune,* 447 n. 26. Ironically, some of the Moravian Delawares taken into protective custody and housed in Philadelphia public buildings during the war also contracted smallpox, from which fifty-six of them died. Weslager, *Delaware Indians,* 248. One recent biographer of David Zeisberger says the fifty-six constituted 40 percent of those who had taken refuge in Philadelphia. See Earl Olmstead, *David Zeisberger: A Life among the Indians* (Kent, Ohio: Kent State University Press, 1997), 130.

29. Ibid., 442.

30. Quoted in Weslager, *Delaware Indians,* 249.

31. William Smith, *Historical Account of Bouquet's Expedition against the Ohio Indians in 1764* (Cincinnati: Robert Clarke and Company, 1868), 63.

32. The engraving is between pages 78 and 79 of ibid. It is poorly reproduced in James Axtell, *Invasion Within,* 305. Axtell's illuminating discussion of the emotional plight of the captives follows on pages 306–8.

33. Smith, *Historical Account,* 76.

34. Ibid., 76, 80. R. Douglas Hurt identifies two of these women as Rhonda Boyd and Elizabeth Studebaker. See Hurt, *The Ohio Frontier: Crucible of the Old Northwest, 1720–1830* (Bloomington: Indiana University Press, 1996), 53.

35. Treaties for the South and the North are tabulated separately in Dorothy V. Jones, *License for Empire: Colonialism by Treaty in Early America* (Chicago: University of Chicago Press, 1982), 53, 70.

36. For discussions of these issues see Jones, *License;* Jennings, *Ambiguous Iroquois Empire;* Jennings, *Empire of Fortune;* Daniel K. Richter and James H. Merrell, *Beyond the Covenant Chain: The Iroquois and Their Neighbors in In-*

dian North America, 1600–1800 (Syracuse, New York: Syracuse University Press, 1987); and William N. Fenton, *The Great Law and the Longhouse: A Political History of the Iroquois Confederacy* (Norman: University of Oklahoma Press, 1998). More on Iroquois treaties may been found in Francis Jennings, William N. Fenton, Mary A. Druke, and David R. Miller, eds., *The History and Culture of Iroquois Diplomacy: An Interdisciplinary Guide to the Treaties of the Six Nations and Their League* (Syracuse, N.Y.: Syracuse University Press, 1985).

37. This must have been a curious sight early in the return journey to the Indian country, when the caravan included ninety raiders, nineteen captives, one hundred horses, eighteen cattle, and a mixed pack of dogs and hogs! It is no wonder that they moved only a few miles a day. See Bond, "Captivity."

38. Ibid., 62. Given the number of captives and amount of plunder, the size of the party, and the recent escape of two frontiersmen, one suspects this council decision to kill two captives in a prescribed, gory way may have been a bit of psychological warfare designed to cow the others. Given that there were only four adult males in the entire party of captives, this certainly would have had a chilling impact. A later artist's depiction of how such a death was carried out in the burning of William Crawford in 1782 has been reprinted in Paul O'Neill, ed., *The Frontiersmen* (Alexandria, Va.: Time-Life Books, 1977). The original of the painting is owned by the Seneca County Museum in Tiffin, Ohio.

39. For a recently reprinted documentary account of the attack on Logan's family see Foster, *Ohio Frontier Writings*, 38–40. For a chart of the incidents along the Ohio in 1774, see James H. O'Donnell, "'Who is There to Mourn for Logan? No One!': The Native American Crisis in the Ohio Country, 1774–1783," in *Ohio in the American Revolution*, ed. Thomas H. Smith (Columbus: Ohio Historical Society, 1976), 21.

40. Excerpts from Heckewelder's diary can be found in Foster, *Ohio Frontier Writings*, 35. Hurt estimates there were fifty thousand whites "on the transAppalachian frontier . . . by 1774." See his *Ohio Frontier*, 55.

41. Foster, *Ohio Frontier Writings*.

42. A table of the incidents and their sources is found in O'Donnell, "Who is There to Mourn," 21. Henry Jolley's narrative is reprinted in part in Foster, *Ohio Frontier Writings*, 38–39. The assassins appear to have spared the infant and kept it.

43. Thomas Jefferson, *Notes on the State of Virginia*, ed. William Peden (New York: W. W. Norton and Company, 1954), 63 and appendix 4. About Logan's oration and related issues see James H. O'Donnell III, "Logan's Oration: A Case Study of Ethnographic Authentication," *Quarterly Journal of Speech* 65 (1979): 150–56.

44. Lieutenant John Penn to the Shawnees, August 6, 1774, in Foster, *Ohio Frontier Writings*, 41.

45. Quoted in Hurt, *Ohio Frontier*, 55.

46. About William Crawford see James H. O'Donnell, "William Crawford," in *American National Biography,* ed. John Garraty (New York: Oxford University Press, 1999 [hereafter *ANB*]), 5:710–11. Washington asked Crawford to locate a tract of fifteen hundred to two thousand acres, but it had to be done without informing others of their motives; once approval was given by the king or the governor, others would "flock there in shoals." Quoted in John Shy, "Dunmore, the Upper Ohio Valley, and the American Revolution," in *Ohio in the American Revolution: A Conference to Commemorate the Two Hundredth Anniversary of the Ft. Gower Resolves,* ed. Thomas H. Smith (Columbus: Ohio Historical Society, 1976), 15.

47. Shy, "Dunmore," 15.

48. O'Donnell, "Logan's Oration." For comments about Dunmore's motives see Shy, "Dunmore," 13–16.

Chapter 3

1. July 1775 Miscellaneous Papers, Convention Papers, Virginia State Library; hereafter VSL. The manuscript material also is available in printed form in volumes 3 to 7 of Robert L. Scribner and Brent Tartar, eds., *Revolutionary Virginia: The Road to Independence* (Richmond: University Press of Virginia, 1977), passim.

2. Speech of White Eyes, summer, 1775, Co5/1353:196; Dunmore to White Eyes, August 9, 1775, Leven Powell Papers, Swem Library, College of William and Mary.

3. Deposition of Garet Pendergrass before John Gibson, July 20, 1775, Misc. Papers, Convention Papers, VSL.

4. July 1775 Resolutions, Convention Papers, VSL.

5. Lord Dunmore to Captain White Eyes, August 9, 1775, Leven Powell Papers, Swem Library, College of William and Mary. Dunmore's speech was included on the back of a message from John Connolly to John Gibson.

6. American Conference with the Western Indians, Fort Pitt, October 1775, Public Archives of Canada, M.G. 12, B ser., W.O. 28, vol. 10, pt. 1; hereafter PAC.

7. William Trent to "Dear Sir," October 15, 1775, Co5/40:51–53.

8. Adam Stephen to R. H. Lee, September 23, 1775, Lee Papers, 1:155, American Philosophical Society.

9. Worthington C. Ford, et al., eds., *Journals of the Continental Congress, 1774–1789,* 34 vols. (Washington, D.C.: Government Printing Office, 1905–1937), 3:433; hereafter *JCC.*

10. Richard Butler Journal, 1775, 26, Historical Society of Pennsylvania; hereafter HSP. At the Fort Pitt negotiations White Eyes indicated he would keep the peace even if a tomahawk was sticking in the heads of the Delawares! This truly prophetic statement is printed in Scribner and Tartar, *Revolutionary Virginia,*

3:262. See also Logan to the Continental commissioners about the difficulty of keeping the peace. See August 19, 1776, *JCC*, 5:668–69.

11. Logan to the Continental commissioners, August 19, 1776, *JCC*, 5:668–69.

12. Tachnechdorus to the Continental commissioners for the Middle Indian Department, August 19, 1776, *JCC*, 5:668–69.

13. Supplies Distributed to Western Seneca Prisoners in jail at Fort Pitt, April 3 to May 17, 1775, Daniel Claus Papers, I, Public Archives of Canada.

14. Minutes of the Pittsburg Conference, May–July, Convention Papers, July 1775, Miscellaneous Papers, Virginia State Library; White Eyes to Connolly, June 6, 1775, Co5/1353:296; Minutes of the American Conference at Fort Pitt, October 7–9, 1775, M.G. 12, B ser., W.O. 28, vol. 10, pt. 1, Public Archives of Canada.

15. August 1775, John Connolly to George Rootes, Virginia Convention Papers, August 1775, Miscellaneous Papers, Virginia State Library.

16. Minutes of American Conference . . . Fort Pitt, October 1775, and William Trent to "Dear Sir," October 15, 1775, Co5/40:51–53. Trent's position may have been a little uncertain given the accusation published in the *Virginia Gazette* that he had been funded by Lord North to incite the Indians. See *The Virginia Gazette,* Purdie's, September 8, 1775, s2. Trent was a trader who was no friend of the Native Americans. He had participated in the germ warfare scheme at Fort Pitt during its siege by the Delawares.

17. On the issue of captives who did not wish to return see James Axtell, "The White Indians of Colonial America," *William and Mary Quarterly*, 3rd ser., 32 (January 1975): 55–88, or his longer work, *Invasion Within*. An earlier popular treatment of this issue is Conrad Richter's novel *Light in the Forest* (New York: Knopf, 1953).

18. April 1776, *JCC*, 4:269–70.

19. Ibid.; Report on Letters Received, April 16, 1776, Papers of the Continental Congress, The National Archives, 21,1, 21 (hereafter PCC); Instructions to George Morgan, April 19, 1776, *JCC*, 4:294–95.

20. April 1776, *JCC*, 4:267.

21. John Nevill to the President of the Virginia Convention, Convention Papers, Letters, May 1776, Virginia State Library.

22. Henry Hamilton to Lord Dartmouth, August 29 and September 2, 1776, Co5/7:342–43.

23. Ibid. Hamilton, like his commander General Gage, did not have a high opinion of colonials.

24. See Wythe, Morris, and Wolcott to Morgan, April 11, 1776, George Morgan Papers, Library of Congress (hereafter LC); and Wilson, Wolcott, and Duane to Morgan, May 14, 1776, ibid.

25. On these tensions and related matters see Jasper Yeates to Edward Shippen, August 13, 1776, Burd-Shippen Family Collection, Pennsylvania Historical and Museum Commission Library; James Burd to Edward Shippen, November 13,

1776, Mills Collection, Peale Papers, American Philosophical Society Library, Philadelphia; August 19, 1776, *JCC,* 5:668–69; Walter, Harvie, Montgomery, and Yeates to Colonel Dorsey Pentecost, September 1, 1776, Executive Papers, Virginia State Library; and John Page to Colonel William Fleming, September 9, 1776, in H. R. McIlwaine, ed., *Official Letters of the Governors of the State of Virginia,* 3 vols. (Richmond, Va.: Division of Purchase and Printing, 1926–29) 1:38–39; hereafter *LGV.*

26. Warrant for public expense of conveying Indian captives, May 7, 1776, H. R. McIlwaine, ed., *Journal of the Council of State of Virginia, 1776–1781,* 2 vols. (Richmond: Virginia State Library, 1931–32) 2:500; Supplies for Indian Captives, June 27, 1776, in William P. Palmer et al., eds., *Calendar of Virginia State Papers and Other Manuscripts, 1652–1781,* 11 vols. (Richmond, Va.: R. F. Walker, 1875–93), 3:226 (hereafter *CVSP*); *Va. Gazette,* July 20, 1776, page 4, col. 1. See also Scribner and Tartar, *Revolutionary Virginia,* 7, pt. 1:51.

27. September 1776, *JCC.*

28. December 7, 1776, *JCC,* 6:1011; December 9, 1776, ibid., 6:1013.

29. See Scribner and Tartar, *Revolutionary Virginia,* 3:238. The entry is headed "Sweat, Dust, Ears and Tears" indicating the traditional steps in a welcoming speech.

30. John Killbuck to George Morgan, April 27, 1777, Morgan Papers, LC; George Washington to Morgan, May 11, 1777, ibid. General Washington actually received the Delawares on May 12.

31. George Morgan to John Hancock, January 4, 1777, Ayer Collection, Newberry Library.

32. January 8, 1777, *JCC,* 7:21–22; Patrick Henry to Richard Henry Lee, January 9, 1777, William W. Henry Papers, box 1, Virginia Historical Society; February 12, 1777, *LGV,* 1:104–5; Journal of the Council of Virginia, March 12, 1777, *LGV,* 1:118–19.

33. On the matter of punishing the inhabitants of Pluggy's Town see the Journal of the Council of Virginia, March 12, 1777, *LGV,* 1:118–19; Resolves of the council, March 12, 1777, Morgan Papers, LC; Virginia Council to George Morgan and John Neville, March 12, 1777, ibid.; Patrick Henry to Morgan and Neville, ibid.; Henry to Colonel David Shepherd, April 12, 1777, *LGV,* 1:138; Henry to Morgan and Neville, April 15, 1777, ibid., 1:139; Henry to Edward Hand, July 3, 1777, Hand Papers, 7E, 1, LC; and Henry to Colonel David Rogers, March 27, 1777, *LGV,* 1:128.

34. Conference at Detroit, June 17, 1777, American Philosophical Society.

35. Ibid. On the question of using the forest warriors for raiding, see George Germain to Guy Carleton, March 26, 1777, in "Haldimand Papers," in *Michigan Pioneer and Historical Collections,* 40 vols. (Lansing, Mich.: State Printer, 1877–1929), 9:347; hereafter *MPC.*

36. David Zeisberger to George Morgan, July 7, 1777, Hand Papers, 7E 1, LC.

37. Résumé of Parties going out from Detroit, July–September 1777, July 27, 1777, M.G. 12, B ser., W.O. 28, vol. 10, pt. 1, PAC.

38. Samuel Moorhead to Edward Hand, August 19, 1777, Force Papers, 7E, Hand, 1, LC; Deveraux Smith to Edward Hand, September 2, 1777, ibid.

39. Matthew Arbuckle to Edward Hand, July 26, 1777, Force Papers, 7E, Hand, 4 LC; David Zeisberger to Hand, July 29, 1777, Force Papers, 7E, Hand, 1, LC.

40. Zeisberger to Hand, July 29, 1777, ibid.

41. Lt. Gov. John Page to Edward Hand, September 17, 1777, *LGV,* 1:189; Edward Hand to the Delawares, September 17, 1777, Force Papers, 7E, Hand, 2, LC. On the hatred of the frontier folk toward the Delawares and all other Indians see Hand to Jasper Yeates, August 25, 1777, ibid., 3, LC; Joseph Ogle to Hand, August 2, 1777, ibid., 1, LC; and John Gibson to Hand, August 1, 1777, ibid., 1, LC.

42. David Zeisberger to Edward Hand, September 22, 1777, Force Papers, 7E, Hand, 2, LC.

43. White Eyes to Congress, September 22, 1777, ibid., 2, LC.

44. George Morgan to "Dear Sir," May 1784, George Morgan Papers, LC.

45. Matthew Arbuckle to Edward Hand, October 6, 1777, Force Papers, 7E, Hand, 4, LC.

46. Deposition of John Anderson, William Ward, and Richard Thomas, November 10, 1777, Force Papers, 7E, Hand, 4, LC; Edward Hand to Patrick Henry, December 9, 1777, ibid., and Hand to Richard Peters, December 9, 1777, ibid.

47. Journal of the Council, March 27, 1778, *LGV,* 1:256.

48. A Talk from the Shawnees to Edward Hand, n.d. [early 1778], Force Papers, 7E, Hand, 2, LC; Edward Hand to Colonel Daniel McFarland, April 13, 1778, ibid., 4, LC; John Evans to Hand, April 18, 1778, ibid., 2, LC; Sampson Mathews to the Commandant at Fort Pitt, May 1778, ibid.

49. *Purdie's Virginia Gazette,* March 27, 1778. For a recent account of this captivity see John Mack Faragher, *Daniel Boone, the Life and Legend of an American Pioneer* (New York: Henry Holt and Company, 1992), 155–76.

50. Henry Hamilton to Alexander McKee, April 23, 1778, Claus Papers, II, PAC. McKee along with Simon Girty and several other western Loyalists familiar with the Indians had broken with the Americans and fled either into the Indian country of Ohio or to Detroit. Edward Hand to Horatio Gates, March 30, 1778, Force Papers, 7E, Hand, 4, LC. McKee's career has most recently been explored in Larry Nelson, *A Man of Distinction among Them: Alexander McKee and the Ohio Country Frontier, 1754–1799* (Kent, Ohio: Kent State University Press, 1999).

51. Virginia Council to Colonel William Fleming, February 19, 1778, *LGV,* 1:243; Journal of the Council of Virginia, March 27, 1778, *LGV,* 1:256; and Patrick Henry to Preston and Fleming, March 27, 1778, *LGV,* 1:257.

52. Virginia Council to Colonel George Rogers Clark, January 14, 1778, *LGV,* 1:227.

53. Edward Hand to Horatio Gates, March 7, 1778, Force Papers, 7E, Hand, 4, LC; Hand to Colonel Alexander Barr, March 5, 1778, ibid.; Hand to Colonel John Pipes, March 7, 1777, ibid.; Hand to Colonel David Shepherd, March 7, 1778, ibid.

54. For Captain Pipe's clear-eyed vision of the realities of frontier rivalries see his speech to the council at Detroit in O'Donnell, "Captain Pipe's Speech."

55. See Ideas of George Morgan on the Indian Expedition, January 1778, Morgan Papers, LC; George Clymer, Sampson Matthews, and Samuel McDowell to Edward Hand, March 19, 1778, Force Papers, 7E, Hand, 2, LC; McDowell to Hand, April 28, 1778, ibid. Clymer, Matthews, and McDowell hoped for a treaty conference at Fort Pitt in July.

56. Hand to the Delawares, July 12, 1778, Force Papers, 7E, Hand, 4, LC.

57. George Washington to Colonel William Russell, May 19, 1778, in *Writings of George Washington,* ed. John C. Fitzpatrick, 39 vols. (Washington, D.C.: Government Printing Office, 1931–44) 10:422; hereafter *Writings.* McIntosh was being posted westward to put him out of arm's reach of those Georgians furious over his celebrated duel with Button Gwinnett, in which Gwinnett had been killed.

58. One of the recurrent difficulties in the frontier wars was the notorious lack of discipline on the part of volunteer militia, who often broke and ran if attacked. Such behavior was instrumental in the defeats of both Harmar and St. Clair in the 1790s.

59. Hand to the Delawares, June 1778, Force Papers, 7E, Hand, 4, LC.

60. Zeisberger to Morgan, July 19, 1778, Force Papers, 7E, Hand, 4, LC.

61. Ibid.

62. Captain White Eyes and John Killbuck to Morgan, June 9, 1778, Force Papers, 7E, Hand, 4, LC; Delaware Council to Morgan, ibid.; and Hand to Captain White Eyes and John Killbuck, June 17, 1778, ibid.

63. Zeisberger to Morgan, June 9, 1778, Force Papers, 7E, Hand 4, LC.

64. Treaty with the Delawares, September 12, 1778, Force Papers, 9, LC. This is printed in Washburn, 3:2263. There is also a copy of the treaty in the Indian File at the Henry E. Huntington Library, San Marino, California; hereafter HEHL.

65. Washburn, 3:2265.

66. Ibid., emphasis added.

67. For varying opinions on the Detroit expedition see Minutes of the Virginia Council, October 2, 1778, *LGV,* 1:312; id., October 5, 1778, *LGV,* 1:313; Patrick Henry to Henry Laurens, July 8, 1778, *LGV,* 1:296–98; Patrick Henry to the county lieutenant of Monongalia, August 6, 1778, *LGV,* 1:303.

68. "Robert McCready's Orderly Book," 1778, LC.

69. George Morgan to "Dear Sir," May 1784, Morgan Papers, LC.

70. "Robert McCready's Orderly Book," LC.

71. For a discussion of this Ohio frontier outpost, see Thomas I. Pieper and

James B. Gidney, *Fort Laurens, 1778–79: The Revolutionary War in Ohio* (Kent, Ohio: Kent State University Press, 1976).

72. George Rogers Clark to the Speaker of the House, March 10, 1779, British Headquarters Papers, no. 1816, microfilm; hereafter BHQ.

73. Two Ottawas, a Huron, and four Miamis secretly witnessed the bludgeoning of the warriors and quickly reported it. See Account Brought in from Post St. Vincent's by Captain Chene, BHQ, no. 1932.

74. Bird to Lernoult, March 12, 1778, BHQ, no. 1818; Haldimand to Clinton, August 29, 1778, BHQ, no. 2234.

75. Daniel Brodhead to John Jay, October 26, 1779, Clark Papers, box 8, VSL. The experienced westerner Daniel Brodhead had replaced the unhappy Lachlan McIntosh early in 1779. See Washington to Brodhead, March 22, 1779, *Writings*, 16:280.

76. Washington to Brodhead, November 21, 1779, *Writings*, 17:157.

77. John Heckewelder, *Narrative of the Mission of the United Brethren among the Delaware and Mohegan Indians* (Philadelphia: McCarty and Davis, 1820), 333.

78. DePeyster to Brown, April 5, 1780, BHQ, no. 2672 (1).

79. DePeyster to McKee, June 22, 1780, Claus Papers, II, PAC; Guy Johnson to McKee, April 6, 1780, ibid.

80. Michael Francklin to Clinton, August 21, 1780, BHQ, no. 2873.

81. John Heckewelder to Daniel Brodhead, March 30, 1780, film at American Philosophical Society, Philadelphia, of the Harvard original; hereafter APS film.

82. Gilbert Narrative, 30ff., HEHL.

83. DePeyster to McKee, April 4, 1780, Claus Papers, II, PAC; DePeyster to McKee, May 8, 1780, ibid.

84. DePeyster to McKee, April 4, 1780, Claus Papers, II, PAC.

85. DePeyster to McKee, May 8, 1780, Claus Papers, II, PAC.

86. The most recent account of this expedition is in Larry Nelson's *Man of Distinction*, 113–17. Nelson describes the conquest of the two outposts and the capture of some three hundred Kentuckians. When General Haldimand reported the campaign to General Henry Clinton, he inflated the accomplishments to three stockade forts and four hundred prisoners. Haldimand to Clinton, August 28, 1780, BHQ, no. 2595 (7). On the difficulty of recovering and ransoming the prisoners see DePeyster to McKee, September 8, 1780, Claus Papers, II, PAC; and The Autobiography of Colonel Cave Johnson, Filson Club Historical Society Library, Louisville, Kentucky. My thanks to Dr. Patricia Watlington of Lexington, Kentucky, for bringing the Johnson piece to my attention.

87. Bird to McKee, August 16, 1780, Claus Papers, II, PAC.

88. Bowman to Brodhead, May 27, 1780, William H. English collection, Indiana Historical Society; Worthing to Bowman, May 19, 1780, ibid.

89. Jefferson to Clark, January 29, 1780, *LGV*, 2:90.

90. These land grants to potential soldiers had been urged by western leaders for some time. See Clark to Captain John Todd, March 1780, Clark Papers, VSL.

91. Jefferson to Clark, March 19, 1780, Julian P. Boyd, et al., eds., *The Papers of Thomas Jefferson*, 16 vols. (Princeton, N.J.: Princeton University Press, 1950–61), 3:316–17; hereafter *TJP*.

92. William Homan to Captain Bird, August 15, 1780, British Museum Additional Manuscripts, 21781, 76, 82, microfilm; McKee to DePeyster, August 22, 1780, ibid.

93. Jefferson to Clark, September 29, 1780, *LGV*, 2:213.

94. Guy Johnson to McKee, April 6, 1780, Claus Papers, II, PAC.

95. Heckewelder, *Narrative,* 347–60.

96. Ibid.

97. See Heckewelder to Brodhead, August 14, 1780, APS film.

98. See Heckewelder to Brodhead, ibid.; William Homan to Captain Bird, August 15, 1780, British Museum Additional Manuscripts, 21781, 76, 82; McKee to DePeyster, August 22, 1780, ibid.

99. DePeyster to McKee, June 22, 1780, Claus Papers, II, PAC.

100. See Brodhead to Washington, November 2, 1780, Brodhead Letterbook, 1780–81, HSP.

101. Linctot to Jefferson, January 30, 1781, *CVSP*, 1:474.

102. John Todd Jr. to Jefferson, January 24, 1781, *CVSP*, 1:460. Logan also was dead, adding to the loss of leadership in the western tribes.

103. Heckewelder to Brodhead, February 26, 1781, APS film.

104. Brodhead to Washington, March 27, 1781, Brodhead Letterbook, 1780–81, HSP.

105. Brodhead to Joseph Reed, April 3, 1781, Brodhead Letterbook, HSP; Brodhead to the County Lieutenant of Greenbrier, August 24, 1781, ibid. For a detailed discussion of the predicament of the Moravians throughout the conflict see Olmsted, *David Zeisberger.*

106. On Brant's activities in the West see Isabel Kelsay, *Joseph Brant, 1783–1807: Man of Two Worlds* (Syracuse, N.Y.: Syracuse University Press, 1984). Simon Girty's activities are discussed in Colin Calloway, "Simon Girty: Interpreter and Intermediary," in *On Being and Becoming Indian,* ed. James Clifton (Chicago: Dorsey Press, 1989), 38–58.

107. Andrew Thompson and Alexander McKee to Arents DePeyster, August 29, 1781, BHQ, no. 3747; DePeyster to McKee, September 7, 1781, Claus Papers, II, PAC; and John Macomb to Claus, September 14, 1781, ibid., III, PAC. The episode also is treated in Nelson, *Man of Distinction,* and in Kelsay, *Joseph Brant.*

108. Ibid.

109. Heckewelder Narrative, APS film; Captain Pipe to Arents DePeyster, November 9, 1781, ibid. The speech has been published in *Northwest Ohio Quarterly,*

64 (1992):126–33, and reprinted in Colin Calloway, *The World Turned Upside Down: Indian Voices from Early America* (Boston: Bedford Books, 1994).

110. Calloway, *World Turned Upside Down*. The parenthetical remarks and italicized emphases were included by John Heckewelder in his "Remarks on Captain Pipe's Spirited Speech to the Commandant at Detroit on the 9th Day of November, 1781," APS. About the first paragraph of the speech, Heckewelder's marginal comment was: "Note this sentence or part he spoke with a low voice as if addressing himself principally to those present, casting sarcastic looks around."

111. Heckewelder, *Narrative,* APS film.

112. Representative accounts may be found in the Relation of Frederick Lineback, April 8, 1782, *CVSP,* 1:122; Lineback in PCC, 59:3, 49; Depeyster to [?], May 13, 1782, British Museum Additional Manuscripts, no. 21781 (78); McKee to DePeyster, April 10, 1782, ibid., John Etwin to [?], March 31, 1782, PCC, 59:3, 81; and *The Murder of the Christian Indians in North America in the Year 1782, A Narrative of Facts* (Dublin, 1823). In an effort to capitalize on this episode and deny American culpability, the missionary to the Oneidas, Samuel Kirkland, initiated the rumor that the massacre actually was carried out by British troops! See Joseph Chew to Maurice Morgan, July 6, 1782, BHQ, no. 5019. Governor Harrison of Virginia described this as a "Shocking and cruel murder" and hoped the killers could be brought to justice. See Harrison to Duval, Crawford, and Evans, April 30, 1782, *LGV,* 3:200.

113. DePeyster to [?], May 13, 1782, ibid.

114. See indication of the origin of the attacks in John Evans to the Governor of Virginia, March 9, 1782, box 21, Executive Papers, VSL; Benjamin Wilson to Colonel William Davis, May 2, 1782, ibid.

115. "A Remarkable Narrative of an Expedition against the Indians with an Account of the Barbarous Execution of Colonel Crawford and Dr. Knight's Escape from Captivity," HEHL. On Crawford's career see O'Donnell, "William Crawford," *ANB,* 5:710–11.

116. Estimates of the Native American numbers range from 300 to 600 and their opponents from 132 to 182. Representative descriptions of this conflict may be found in Andrew Steele to the Governor of Virginia, August 26, 1782, Executive Papers, VSL; Levi Todd [who lost a brother in the battle] to Robert Todd, ibid.; Daniel Boone to the Governor of Virginia, August 30, 1781, box 15, Executive Papers, VSL; and Benjamin Logan to Governor Harrison, August 31, 1782, ibid. Nelson's account of the battle places the number of Native Americans at three hundred. See Nelson, *Man of Distinction,* 127.

117. George Walls to Colonel William Davis, December 16, 1782, box 28, Executive Papers, VSL; George Rogers Clark to "Sir"(Governor of Virginia), November 13, 1782, film at Colonial Williamsburg research library of Chicago Historical Society original; DePeyster to McKee, November 21, 1782, Claus Papers, III, PAC; Clark to the Governor of Virginia, November 27, 1782, box 43,

Clark Papers, VSL; John Crittenden to Colonel William Davis, November 29, 1782, box 27, Executive Papers, VSL; and Clark to the Governor of Virginia, November 30, 1782, box 43, Clark Papers, VSL.

Chapter 4

1. For a discussion of the Ohio River zone of conflict during the American Revolution see O'Donnell, "The Ohio River as Interface of Conflict: The Ohio River Indian Frontier, 1774–1784" (paper presented at the Ohio River Odyssey Symposium, Huntington, W.Va., September 19, 1987).

2. Proceedings of the Virginia Commissioners with the Cherokee, April 1777, Draper Collections, Preston Papers, 4:122–49, quoted in James H. O'Donnell III, *Southern Indians in the American Revolution* (Knoxville: University of Tennessee Press, 1973), 56.

3. Randolph Downes described this as the major bone of contention from 1768 to 1795. See *Council Fires,* 184.

4. Washburn, 4:2269.

5. Reginald Horsman, "United States Indian Policies, 1776–1815," in *HNAI,* 4:29.

6. Philip R. Shriver and Clarence E. Wunderlin, Jr., eds., *Documentary Heritage of Ohio* (Athens: Ohio University Press, 2000), 52.

7. Ibid., 54.

8. Ibid., 56. On the matter of these lands and their resolution, see Weslager, *Delaware Indians.*

9. Weslager, *Delaware Indians,* 348.

10. Nelson, *Man of Distinction,* 149.

11. Even as late as 1812 one writer invited a friend to go on an amusing "scout" against the Indians; if his correspondent felt "somewhat indisposed, driving them off, burning their towns, and cutting up their corn is fine sport." Samuel Swearingen to Abraham Shepherd Jr., December 9, 1812, Ohio Historical Society; hereafter OHS. This attitude of Indian raiding as "fine sport" cost the United States dearly, especially in the disastrous campaigns led by Harmar and St. Clair. As the regular army officers testified, especially in some of the courts martial proceedings, the untrained militia broke and ran, giving the field to the forest soldiers and leaving the trained troops to be overwhelmed. About this issue see James H. O'Donnell, "John Armstrong," "William Crawford," "David Ziegler," *American National Biography,* ed. John Garraty (New York: Oxford University Press, 2002), 1:616–17; 5:710–11; and 24:240–42.

12. George W. Knepper, *Ohio and Its People* (Kent, Ohio: Kent State University Press, 1989), 59; Denny, *Military Journal,* 59. According to Denny that post was finished on November 8, 1785.

13. Denny, *Journal*, 59.

14. Ibid., 60.

15. Ibid., 63.

16. Ibid., 69, 71.

17. Ibid., 72.

18. Ibid., 73.

19. Ibid.

20. Ibid., 76.

21. Ibid., 77.

22. This was one of fourteen attacks launched into Ohio country between 1774 and 1786. See "Expeditions into the Northwest Indian Country," map 14 in Tanner, *Atlas*, 71–73.

23. Hurt, *Ohio Frontier*, 99.

24. Brant's speech quoted in Hurt, *Ohio Frontier*, 100; a copy of the Speech of the United Indian Nations, at their Confederate Council, December 18, 1786, is printed in Shriver and Wunderlin, *Documentary Heritage of Ohio*, 74–75. This official message smacks of Joseph Brant's literary style; Brant, a former student at Eleazer Wheelock's Indian School, had served as an interpreter in the British Indian department before emerging as a military leader during the war. See James H. O'Donnell, "Joseph Brant" in *American Indian Leaders: Studies in Diversity*, ed. R. David Edmunds (Lincoln: University of Nebraska Press, 1980); and Kelsay, *Joseph Brant*.

25. Hurt's summary is on pages 100–101 of *Ohio Frontier;* see also Nelson, *Man of Distinction*, 155.

26. There were already numerous schemes afoot to divide the Ohio country for settlement. Connecticut and Virginia both lay claim to large swaths of the Ohio country. Speculators too, like the Ohio Company of Associates, planned the acquisition of thousands of acres in Ohio; many of that group's leaders were men with military backgrounds who would be well prepared to defend themselves and crush the Indians if needed. The background of the Ohio Company of Associates may be explored in full in the company's papers held in the archives at Marietta College. A brief statement about the company's organization may be found in Shriver and Wunderlin, *Documentary Heritage of Ohio*, 62–63.

27. Shriver and Wunderlin, *Documentary Heritage of Ohio*, 60–61.

28. Ibid., 61.

29. Ibid., 63.

30. Putnam was a friend and political ally of George Washington who regarded his former commander-in-chief as "so great and good a man." General Washington had signed himself in a 1776 letter as Putnam's "asured frind." See Rufus Putnam, *The Memoirs of Rufus Putnam and Certain Official Papers and Correspondence*, ed. Rowena Buell (Boston: Houghton Mifflin and Company,

1903); and Washington to Putnam, August 11, 1776, Marietta College Special Collections.

31. James H. O'Donnell, "Armchair Adventurers and Horseback Botanists: Explorations of Florida's Natural History, 1763–1800," *Gulf Coast Historical Review* 8 (1992): 85–94.

32. See the excerpt from Joseph Barker's reminiscences in Shriver and Wunderlin, *Documentary Heritage of Ohio,* 63. Putnam's military perspective led him to envision the sacred enclosures at Marietta as part of an elaborate fortification. See the introduction to this volume regarding Rufus Putnam's description of the mounds. Putnam did purchase the northeast corner of the former Campus Martius along with unused timber from the fort itself in order to double the size of his home. The original size of his dwelling within the fort is retained by the Ohio Historical Society as part of the Campus Martius Museum in Marietta, Ohio.

33. Washburn, 4:2279. A part of any general frontier peace was a stipulation about the return of all captives taken by any of the tribes, whether white or black, young or old, male or female, willing or unwilling. European ethnocentrism assumed that no one would like to remain among the "savages." Mary Jemison was not the only white captive who chose to remain with her adopted people. See Axtell, *Invasion Within;* and Richter, *Light in the Forest.*

34. Washburn, 4:2279. Emphasis mine.

35. Ibid., 4:2280.

36. Ibid. Native hunters crossing into land sold to the United States took the risk of themselves becoming the hunted, given the attitude of most frontiersmen about the worth of Indian life. In his play about the American frontier, Robert Rogers has one of his characters reflect, "It's no more murder to crack a Louse" than it is to kill an Indian. See Robert Rogers, *Ponteach; or, the Savages of America: A Tragedy,* ed. Allan Nevins (1914; reprint, New York: Burt Franklin, 1971), 186.

37. Washburn, 4:2282, Article IX.

38. Ibid., 4:2281.

39. Ibid., 4:2282–83.

40. Ibid., 3:2266; and ibid., 4:2284. See also O'Donnell, "Captain Pipe's Speech."

41. See Olmstead, *David Zeisberger,* 313ff., on this.

42. See John Heckewelder, *History, Manners, and Customs of the Indian Nations Who Once Inhabited Pennsylvania and the Neighbouring States* (Philadelphia: Historical Society of Pennsylvania, 1876), 285–89, for the rather lachrymose passage in which the missionary historian recounts Wingenund's explanation to William Crawford of why he cannot save him from the stake. Even Alexander McKee, the British agent who had a residence nearby, knew that he could not extricate the American officer. See Nelson, *Man of Distinction,* 125–26. Despite Wingenund's inability to rescue the doomed captive, he was described favorably

by John Heckewelder: "This great and good man was not only one of the bravest and most celebrated warriors, but one of the most amiable men of the Delaware Nation." Heckewelder also explains that his name means "the well beloved." Heckewelder, *History*, 285. His opinion may rest in part on the Delaware's action in escorting Heckewelder safely to Pittsburgh during the tensions of 1777. Ibid., 279. Although Wingenund may have relocated to the Upper Sandusky area about the time Captain Pipe did, he was part of the escort party guarding the missionaries and their converts when they were forced to leave the Muskingum area. He joined Captain Pipe in delivering the British ultimatum to David Zeisberger that he appear before them in Detroit. On the latter matters see Weslager, *Delaware Indians*, 295, 313; and Olmstead, *David Zeisberger*, 290, 312–13, 320, 328.

43. Washburn, 4:2284.

44. Ibid.

45. Horsman, "United States Indian Policies," 31. George Washington was to the point: "there is nothing to be obtained by an Indian War but the soil they live on and this can be had by purchase at less expense." Quoted in Hurt, *Ohio Frontier*, 98.

46. The expedition that resulted in the death of William Crawford had to delay its departure until the soldiers were satisfied with the leadership. See O'Donnell, "William Crawford," *ANB*, 5:710–11. George Washington, the experienced commander-in-chief, knew the nature of the militia, too. In a diary entry for July 9, 1790, noting Harmar's difficulties in the West, he mentioned the militia, which, "according to custom, getting tired, and short of provisions, became clamorous to go home." *Writings*, 4:141.

47. Leroy Eid, "'A Kind of Running Fight': Indian Battlefield Tactics in the Late Eighteenth Century," *Western Pennsylvania Historical Magazine* 71 (1988): 147–71.

48. See John Sugden, *Blue Jacket, Warrior of the Shawnees* (Lincoln: University of Nebraska Press, 2000); and Kelsay, *Joseph Brant*.

49. Meals on the hoof, bawling along behind the army, would be far more difficult to transport than the Meals ready to eat (MRE) consumed by modern soldiers.

50. "Diary of John Armstrong," *Cist's Cincinnati Miscellanies*, 1:195–97.

51. See ibid. For accounts of the expedition and specific insights into the plight of the regular army officers like Captain Armstrong and Major David Ziegler, see Hurt, *Ohio Frontier*, 105–11; Sugden, *Blue Jacket*, 99–105; Sword, *George Washington's Indian War*, 79–122; and O'Donnell, "John Armstrong" and "David Ziegler," *ANB*, 1:616–17 and 24:240–41.

52. McBride, *Pioneer Biography*, 1:127.

53. "Diary of John Armstrong."

54. Court Martial of General Harmar, *American State Papers: Military Affairs*, 1:25–27.

55. Ibid., 25.

56. Quoted in Hurt, *Ohio Frontier,* 111. For more on Armstrong see O'Donnell, "John Armstrong," *ANB,* 1:616–17.

57. Quoted by Sugden, *Blue Jacket,* 117, and cited by Nelson, *Man of Distinction,* 222n. 22.

58. James Smith, *An Account of the Remarkable Occurrences in the Life and Travels of Colonel James Smith,* 150. For a discussion of Smith's ideas and native American battlefield tactics see Leroy V. Eid, "The Indian Explanation for Braddock's Defeat" (paper presented at the Duquesne History Forum, Pittsburgh, Pa., October 31, 1987); and also Eid's articles, "'A Kind of Running Fight'" and "'Their Rules of War': James Smith's Summary of Indian Woodland War," the latter in *Selected Papers from the 1985 and 1986 George Rogers Clark Trans-Appalachian Frontier History Conferences,* ed. Robert J. Holden (Vincennes, Ind.: Eastern National Park and Monument Association and Vincennes University, 1988), 63–76.

59. Winthrop Sargent Diary, 256.

60. Ibid., 258; St. Clair to Knox, November 9, 1791, *Documentary Heritage of Ohio,* 77.

61. St. Clair to Knox, November 9, 1791, ibid., 79.

62. Denny, *Military Journal,* 165.

63. Winthrop Sargent Diary, 271. Compare a postbattle account of Antietam in 1862: "in about seven or eight acres of wood there is not a tree which is not full of bullets and bits of shell. It is impossible to understand how anyone could live in such a fire as there must have been there." Quoted in James McPherson, *Ordeal by Fire* (New York: Alfred Knopf, 1982), 288. The firefight at St. Clair's camp took place in about a five-acre area. Given the smoke from black powder ammunition, it is amazing that anyone could see a target, unless they simply fired at the flashes of the opponent's weapons.

64. Denny, *Military Journal,* 165.

65. Ibid.

66. During the furious assault on the camp, the women had attempted to rally the slackers hiding underneath the wagons by poking them with firebrands and upbraiding them as cowards. See Winthrop Sargent Diary, 269.

67. Hurt, *Ohio Frontier,* 120.

68. Ibid., 130. See also Helen H. Tanner, "The Glaize in 1792: A Composite Indian Community," *Ethnohistory* 25 (1978): 15–39.

69. Tanner, "Glaize in 1792."

70. Hurt, *Ohio Frontier,* 120–21.

71. Anthony Wayne to Nathanael Green, June 14, 1782, PCC no. 155, 2:491–95, quoted in O'Donnell, *Southern Indians,* 123.

72. "Account Brought in from Post St. Vincents by Captain Chene," BHQ, no. 1932. Also see O'Donnell, "'National Retaliation': Thomas Jefferson's Brief for

the Imprisonment of Henry Hamilton," in *Selected Papers from the 1985 and 1986 George Rogers Clark Trans-Appalachian Frontier Conference,* ed. Robert J. Holden (Vincennes, Ind.: Eastern National Park and Monument Association and Vincennes University, 1988), 93–106. Clark's confrontation with the so-called Hair Buyer, Henry Hamilton, was rather ironic, given the actual blood still on the Virginian's hands from his execution of the captured Indians.

73. Wayne's campaign and the policies followed by the parties involved have been explored in detail by Hurt, *Ohio Frontier;* Nelson, *Man of Distinction;* Sugden, *Blue Jacket;* and Knopf, *George Washington's Indian War.* The general narrative here follows the path blazed in those publications.

74. Hurt, *Ohio Frontier,* 132.

75. O'Donnell, "Captain Pipe's Speech."

76. Sugden, *Blue Jacket,* 181.

77. Washburn, 4:2295–303.

78. Ibid., 4:2302–03.

79. The following general discussion of Tecumseh, Tenskwatawa, and Blue Jacket is based on Edmunds's *Shawnee Prophet* and *Tecumseh* and Sugden's *Blue Jacket.* While Allan Eckert has also published a book about Tecumseh, it is another work of the historical fiction for which the author is famous. On Eckert's sources see O'Donnell, review essay of *A Sorrow in Our Heart.*

80. Washburn, 4:2299.

81. Sugden, *Blue Jacket,* 208.

82. Cf. Bernard Sheehan, *Seeds of Extinction: Jeffersonian Philanthropy and the American Indian* (Chapel Hill, N.C.: Institute of Early American History and Culture, 1973).

83. A discussion of this is in Edmunds, *Tecumseh,* 68–69.

84. The general outlines of the discussion about Blue Jacket follow Sugden, *Blue Jacket.*

85. Sugden, *Blue Jacket,* 210.

86. Charles C. Sellers, *Mr. Peale's Museum: Charles Willson Peale and the First Popular Museum of Natural Science and Art* (New York: W. W. Norton and Company, 1980), 92. Peale lost no chance to attract visitors in search of exotic forms. While Blue Jacket and Red Pole were there he took the information necessary to construct wax portraits of them in their native costume. Although these ephemeral constructions have not come down to the present, one can capture the spirit of his Indian paintings in the gartered and rouged "museum portrait" that he painted of Joseph Brant when the famous Mohawk visited Philadelphia in 1797. Ibid., 93.

87. George Washington to Chiefs and Warriors . . . , November 29, 1796, *Writings,* 35:302. The president must have thought it was Native American week in Philadelphia; he reportedly dined with four groups of Indians in four days during the week of November 28. See ibid., 35:302n. 56.

88. On the nature of the political connections between the two, see Sudgen, *Blue Jacket*.

89. Lalawethika's experiences are described in both of Edmunds's books about the two brothers.

90. This discussion follows Sugden's reconstruction in *Blue Jacket,* 251–53. Readers should be advised that since Sugden's narrative depends on reminiscences, it may not be wholly accurate.

91. Edmunds, *Shawnee Prophet,* 70.

92. Ibid., 73.

93. Ibid., 75.

94. Ibid., 91.

95. Quoted in ibid., 93.

96. Hurt, *Ohio Frontier,* 325.

Chapter 5

1. Treaty of Fort Harmar, January 9, 1789, in Washburn, 4:2279, 2280.

2. In 1817 the Wyandots, Senecas, and Shawnees ceded 3,360,000 acres, the Chippewas, Ottawas, and Potawatomies gave up 512,000 acres, and the Delawares 8,820. See Carl Klopfenstein, "The Removal of the Indians from Ohio," in *The Historic Indian in Ohio,* ed. Randall Buchman (Columbus: Ohio Historical Society, 1976), 30.

3. T. Hartley Crawford to Joel R. Poinsett, May 13, 1840, PA box 44, OHS.

4. Ibid.

5. See Hurt, *Ohio Frontier,* 1–2, and for the comment about "improvements" see Removal Act, May 28, 1830, Washburn, 2:2170. Between 1789 and 1842 the Native Americans in northwestern Ohio ceded more than twenty-five million acres of land. At the $5 an acre paid by one settler for part of "an Indian reservation" in 1840, the land would have been worth $125,000,000. See Ansel Blossom to Matthias Blossom, April 29, 1840, Ansel Blossom Papers, ms. 682, box 1, folder 1, OHS.

6. Lonny L. Honsberger, ed. *A Book of Diagrams and Index of Indian Landholders on the Wyandot Reservation, Wyandot County, Ohio, at the Time of Cession* (Sandusky, Ohio: L. L. Honsberger, 1989).

7. Honsberger, *Book of Diagrams,* passim. Although the Reverend Mr. James Finley is not especially complimentary of the Wyandot lifestyle (for his own reasons), his *Life among the Indians* is another snapshot of this community. See James B. Finley, *Life among the Indians; or, Personal Reminiscences and Historical Incidents Illustrative of Indian Life and Character,* ed. Rev. D. W. Clark. (Cincinnati, Ohio: Cranston and Stowe, 1857).

8. Hurt, *Ohio Frontier,* 362.

9. Finley, *Life,* 368–69.

10. Ibid., 354–55.

11. Dickens to John Forster, April 24, 1842, *The Letters of Charles Dickens,* ed. Madeline House, Graham Storey, and Kathleen Tillotson (Oxford: Clarendon Press, 1965–2002), 3:207.

12. Stanley W. Baker, *Acculturation and Evolutionary Change in the Historic Settlement/Subsistence Practices in the Southern Lake Erie Basin: The Wyandot Example* (Tiffin, Ohio: Mineral and Geology Museum, Heidelberg College, 1985), 13. For this information the author draws on the reports of James Finley.

13. Finley, *Life,* 243.

14. Report from the Wyandot Mission, 1821, Moses Henkle Sr., OHS, Methodist Episcopal Church Records, collection 231, box 1, folder 9.

15. Report from the Wyandot Mission, OHS. Stewart had served his apprenticeship by being admitted to the Ohio Conference on trial in 1817. See Cole, *Lion of the Forest,* 43.

16. Cole, *Lion of the Forest: The Life of James B. Finley* (Lexington, University Press of Kentucky, 2000.

17. Cole, *Lion of the Forest,* is the most recent biography of Finley.

18. Finley, *Life,* 321–22.

19. This handbook, published quadrennially, expressed the current state of Methodist expectations for the members of the church. For an example of strictures about abstinence from alcohol and following the proper rules on marriage, both issues raised by Finley with the Wyandots, see Methodist Episcopal Church, *The Doctrines and Discipline of the Methodist Episcopal Church,* 1829, 76, 85, 89. These remonstrances were steeped in the eighteenth-century emphasis on holiness practiced by John Wesley and his followers.

20. Report from the Wyandot Mission, OHS.

21. Finley, *Life,* 277.

22. Ibid., 363.

23. Report from the Wyandot Mission, OHS.

24. Ibid.

25. Ibid.

26. Undated report from Thomas Thompson, Missionary, OHS; Finley would conclude that by 1833 about 25 percent of the Wyandots were Christians and by 1843, on the eve of removal, perhaps 50 percent, but there always seemed to be a conservative core of people who were unwilling to abandon their traditional ways. See Baker, *Acculturation,* 19.

27. Finley, *Life,* 233. Jesuit missionaries had labored among the Wyandots in earlier days but there had been no resident missionary among them for several decades. On this see Tooker, "Wyandot," 401.

28. Finley, *Life,* 342.

29. Report from the Wyandot Mission for 1827, Moses Henkle, Sr. OHS, Methodist Episcopal Church Records, collection 231, box 1, folder 9, OHS.

30. Finley, *Life,* 363.

31. Ibid., 349.

32. Charles Elliott, *Indian Missionary Reminiscences, Principally of the Wyandot Nation* (New York: T. Mason and J. Lane, 1837), 70.

33. Report from the Wyandot Mission for 1829, Moses Henkle, Sr., Methodist Episcopal Church Records, collection 231, box 1, folder 9, OHS.

34. Report from the Wyandot Mission for 1829, ibid., undated report from Thomas Thompson, Missionary, OHS.

35. Ibid.

36. Ibid.

37. Ibid.

38. Report from the Wyandot Mission by H. O. Sheldon, Superintendent, in Methodist Episcopal Church Records, collection 231, box 1, folder 9, OHS.

39. Report from the Wyandot Mission, OHS.

40. A picture of this 1824 structure may be found in Leonard U. Hill, *John Johnston and the Indians in the Land of the Three Miamis* (Piqua, Ohio, 1957), 54.

41. See Horsman, "United States Indian Policies," 43.

42. Washburn, 4:2366.

43. Ibid., 4:2367.

44. That might have been so while John Quincy Adams was president but was not so once his successor, Andrew Jackson, came into office in early 1829.

45. A delegation sent westward in 1832 on an exploratory mission was "decidedly of opinion that the interests of the nation will not be promoted, nor their condition ameliorated by removal . . . [instead they should] cease all contention, bickerings and party strifes; settle down and maintain their position in the state of Ohio." Quoted in Klopfenstein, "Removal," 32.

46. Finley, Life; Both well-known Wyandot leaders, Between-the-Logs and Mononcue had signed the 1814 treaty of alliance between the Wyandots and the United States. Washburn, 4:2346. See pictures on pages 112 and 116.

47. Knepper, *Ohio and Its People,* 118.

48. Ansel Blossom to Matthias Blossom, April 29, 1840, Ansel Blossom Papers, ms. 682, box 1, folder 1, OHS.

49. Knepper, *Ohio and Its People,* 112.

50. *Historical Statistics of the United States.*

51. Removal of the Seneca from Ohio, Petition of Six Seneca Chiefs to the President of the United States, December 18, 1828, OHS.

52. John Johnston to Thomas McKenney, Wapaghkonetta, September 14, 1828, PA box 92B, OHS.

53. Horsman, "United States Indian Policies," 45.

54. Johnston Record Book, vol. 338, OHS.

55. John Johnston to Thomas McKenney, January 29, 1828, PA box 92B, OHS. Johnston later explained to McKenney that the cost for sending an interpreter named Lane would be $500. See Johnston to McKenney, December 18, 1828, PA box 92B, OHS.

56. Johnston to McKenney, December 18, 1828, PA box 92B, OHS. For other estimates by Johnston relating to the Delawares, Senecas, and Mohawks see his note attached to the Petition of the Delawares to Thomas McKenney, September 2, 1828, PA box 92B, OHS.

57. Memorial of the Inhabitants of Brown County, in the State of Ohio, in Relation to the Cherokee Indians, February 22, 1830, PA box 726, folder 9, OHS.

58. Ansel Blossom to Matthias Blossom, n.d., Ansel Blossom Papers, ms. 682, box 1, folder 1, OHS.

59. See Provision Report, November 26 to December 31, 1831, Brish Papers, OHS.

60. A brief account of this story may be found in Klopfenstein, "Removal," 28–38.

61. Henry C. Brish to William Clark, Brish Papers, OHS.

62. Brish to Clark, December 14, 1831, Brish Papers, OHS; and Brish to Samuel Hamilton, January 20, 1832, ibid.

63. Brish to Clark, November 26, 1831, Brish Papers, OHS.

64. See Brish to an unspecified correspondent, ibid.

65. Ibid.

66. See Ruland to Brish, November 1831, Brish Papers, OHS.

67. See Provision Report, undated, unsigned, Brish Papers, OHS.

68. Klopfenstein, "Removal," 34.

69. Quoted by Klopfenstein, ibid. See also Brish's letter to William Clark of January 26, 1832, describing the rheumatism and exhaustion that plagued him once he returned to Ohio. Brish Papers, OHS.

70. Klopfenstein, "Removal," 35.

71. Shriver and Wunderlin, *Documentary Heritage of Ohio,* 169.

72. Memorial of Chiefs and Delegates of the Wyandot Indians asking payment for the value of their improvements, January 17, 1846, PA box 44, folder 17, OHS.

73. Ibid.

Works Cited

Unpublished Sources

Blossom, Ansel. Papers. Ohio Historical Society, Columbus.
Brish, Henry C. Papers. Ohio Historical Society, Columbus.
British Museum Additional Manuscripts. Microfilm. Omohundro Institute of Early American History and Culture, Williamsburg, Virginia.
British Public Record Office, Colonial Office. Series 5. Microfilm. Colonial Williamsburg Research Library and the Library of Congress.
Brodhead, Daniel. Letterbook, 1780–81. Historical Society of Pennsylvania, Philadelphia.
Burd-Shippen Family Collection. Pennsylvania Historical and Museum Commission Library, Harrisburg.
Butler, Richard. Journal. Historical Society of Pennsylvania, Philadelphia.
Clark, George Rogers. Papers. Virginia State Library, Richmond.
Claus, Daniel. Papers. Public Archives of Canada, Ottawa.
Executive Papers. Virginia State Library, Richmond.
English, William H. Collection. Indiana Historical Society, Indianapolis.
Hand, Edward. Papers. Manuscripts Division. Library of Congress.
Headquarters Papers of the British Army in North America. Microfilm. Omohundro Institute of Early American History and Culture, Williamsburg, Virginia.
Heckewelder, John. Letters. Film at American Philosophical Society, Philadelphia.
———. "Remarks on Captain Pipe's Spirited Speech to the Commandant at Detroit on the 9th Day of November 1781." American Philosophical Society, Philadelphia.
Henry, William W. Papers. Virginia Historical Society, Richmond.
Indian File. Henry E. Huntington Library, San Marino, California.
Johnson, Cave. The Autobiography of Colonel Cave Johnson. Filson Club Historical Society Library, Louisville, Kentucky.
Lee, R. H. Papers. American Philosophical Society Library, Philadelphia.
McCready, Robert. "Robert McCready's Orderly Book." Manuscripts Division. Library of Congress.
Methodist Episcopal Church Papers. Ohio Historical Society, Columbus.
Morgan, George. Letters. Ayer Collection. The Newberry Library, Chicago.
Morgan, George. Papers. Manuscripts Division. Library of Congress.
Papers of the Continental Congress, 1774–1789. National Archives, Washington, D.C.

Peale, C. W. Papers. Mills Collection. American Philosophical Society Library, Philadelphia.

Powell, Leven. Papers. Swem Library Special Collections. College of William and Mary, Williamsburg, Virginia.

Public Archives of Canada. Manuscript group 12, B series. War Office, Ottawa.

Putnam, Rufus. Papers. Dawes Memorial Library Special Collections. Marietta College, Marietta, Ohio.

Virginia Convention Papers. Miscellaneous Papers, July 1775. Virginia State Library, Richmond.

Published Sources

Abrams, Elliot M. "Woodland Settlement Patterns in the Southern Hocking River Valley, Southeastern Ohio." In *Cultural Variability in Context: Woodland Settlements of the Mid-Ohio Valley,* ed. Mark F. Seeman. Midcontinental Journal of Archaeology Special Papers. Kent, Ohio: Kent State University Press, 1992.

Andrews, E. B. "Reports on the Exploration of a Cave and of Mounds in Ohio." *Tenth Annual Report of the Peabody Museum.* Salem, Mass.: Salem Press, 1877.

Armstrong, John. "Diary of John Armstrong." *The Cincinnati Miscellany.* 2 vols. (Cincinnati: Charles Cist, 1846), 1:195–97.

Axtell, James. *The Invasion Within: The Contest of Cultures in Colonial North America.* New York: Oxford University Press, 1985.

———. "The White Indians of Colonial America." *William and Mary Quarterly,* 3rd ser., 32 (January 1975): 55–88.

Baker, Stanley W. *Acculturation and Evolutionary Change in the Historic Settlement/Subsistence Practices in the Southern Lake Erie Basin: The Wyandot Example.* Tiffin, Ohio: Mineral and Geology Museum, Heidelberg College, 1985.

Bond, Beverley W. "The Captivity of Charles Stuart." *Mississippi Valley Historical Review* 13 (1927): 52–81.

Brose, David. "Archaeological Investigations at the Paleo Crossing Site, a Paleo-Indian Occupation in Medina County, Ohio." In *The First Discovery of America: Archaeological Evidence of the Early Inhabitants of Ohio,* ed. William S. Dancey. Columbus: Ohio Archaeological Council, 1994.

———. "Penumbral Protohistory on Lake Erie's South Shore." In *Societies in Eclipse: Archaeology of the Eastern Woodland Indians, A.D. 1400–1700,* ed. David S. Brose, C. Wesley Cowan, and Robert C. Mainfort Jr. Washington, D.C.: Smithsonian Institution Press, 2001.

Burnett, Edmund C. *Letters of the Members of the Continental Congress.* Washington, D.C.: Carnegie Institution of Washington, 1921–36.

Callender, Charles. "Shawnee." In *Handbook of North American Indians,* vol. 15, ed. William C. Sturtevant. Washington, D.C.: Smithsonian Institution Press, 1978.

Calloway, Colin. "Simon Girty: Interpreter and Intermediary." In *On Being and Becoming Indian,* ed. James Clifton. Chicago: Dorsey Press, 1989.

———. *The World Turned Upside Down: Indian Voices from Early America.* Boston: Bedford Books, 1994.

Carskadden, Jeff, and James Morton. "Living on the Edge: A Comparison of Adena and Hopewell Communities in the Central Muskingum Valley of Eastern Ohio." In *Ohio Hopewell Community Organization,* ed. William S. Dancey and Paul J. Pacheco. Kent, Ohio: Kent State University Press, 1997.

Church, Flora, and John P. Nass Jr. "Central Ohio Valley during the Late Prehistoric Period: Subsistence-Settlement Systems' Responses to Risk." In *Northeast Subsistence-Settlement Change,* A.D. *700–1300,* ed. John P. Hart and Christina B. Rieth. Albany: New York State Museum Bulletin 496, 2002.

Clarke, Wesley. "The Marietta Earthwork Complex, Washington County, Ohio." Unpublished paper prepared for the Ohio Historic Preservation Office in June 2001.

Clifton, James, ed. *On Being and Becoming Indian: Biographical Studies of North American Frontiers.* Chicago: Dorsey Press, 1989.

Cole, Charles C. *Lion of the Forest: The Life of James B. Finley.* Lexington: University Press of Kentucky, 2000.

Crane, Verner. *The Southern Frontier, 1670–1732.* Ann Arbor: University of Michigan Press, 1956.

Cutler, William P., and Julia P. Cutler. *Life, Journals, and Correspondence of Reverend Manasseh Cutler, LL.D.* 2 vols. Athens: Ohio University Press, 1987.

Dancey, William S., and Paul J. Pacheco. "A Community Model of Ohio Hopewell Settlement." In *Ohio Hopewell Community Organization,* ed. William S. Dancey and Paul J. Pacheco. Kent, Ohio: Kent State University Press, 1997.

———. "The Ohio Hopewell Settlement Pattern Problem in Historical Perspective." Paper presented at the fifty-seventh annual meeting of the Society of American Archaeology, Pittsburgh, Pa., April 1992.

Denny, Ebenezer. *Military Journal of Major Ebenezer Denny, an Officer in the Revolutionary and Indian Wars, with an Introductory Memoir.* Philadelphia, Pa.: J.B. Lippincott for the Historical Society of Pennsylvania, 1859.

Dickens, Charles. *Letters of Charles Dickens.* Ed. Madeline House, Graham Storey, and Kathleen Tillotson. 12 vols. Oxford: Clarendon Press, 1965–2002.

Dowd, Gregory. *A Spirited Resistance: The North American Indian Struggle for Unity, 1745–1815.* Baltimore: Johns Hopkins University Press, 1992.

Downes, Randolph C. *Council Fires on the Upper Ohio: A Narrative of Indian Affairs in the Upper Ohio Valley until 1795.* Pittsburgh: University of Pittsburgh Press, 1940.

Dragoo, Don W. *Mounds for the Dead: An Analysis of Adena Culture*. Pittsburgh: Carnegie Museum of Natural History, 1963.

Drooker, Penelope B. *The View from Madisonville: Protohistoric Western Fort Ancient Interaction Patterns*. Ann Arbor: Museum of Anthropology, University of Michigan, 1997.

Drooker, Penelope B., and C. Wesley Cowan, "Transformation of the Ft. Ancient Cultures of the Central Ohio Valley." In *Societies in Eclipse: Archaeology of the Eastern Woodland Indians, A.D. 1400–1700,* ed. David S. Brose, C. Wesley Cowan, and Robert C. Mainfort Jr. Washington, D.C.: Smithsonian Institution Press, 2001.

Eckert, Allan W. *A Sorrow in Our Heart: The Life of Tecumseh*. New York: Bantam, 1992.

Edmunds, R. David. "Old Briton." In *American Indian Leaders: Studies in Diversity,* ed. R. David Edmunds. Lincoln: University of Nebraska Press, 1980.

———. *The Shawnee Prophet*. Lincoln: University of Nebraska Press, 1983.

———. *Tecumseh and the Quest for Indian Leadership*. Boston: Little, Brown, 1984.

Eid, Leroy V. "The Indian Explanation for Braddock's Defeat." Duquesne History Forum, October 31, 1987, Pittsburgh, Pa.

———. "'A Kind of Running Fight': Indian Battlefield Tactics in the Late Eighteenth Century." *Western Pennsylvania Historical Magazine* 71 (1988): 147–71.

———. "'Their Rules of War': James Smith's Summary of Indian Woodland War." In *Selected Papers from the 1985 and 1986 George Rogers Clark Trans-Appalachian Frontier History Conferences,* ed. Robert J. Holden. Vincennes, Ind.: Eastern National Park and Monument Association and Vincennes University, 1988.

Elliott, Charles. *Indian Missionary Reminiscences, Principally of the Wyandot Nation*. New York: T. Mason and J. Lane, 1837.

Fagan, Brian. *Ancient North America: The Archaeology of a Continent*. New York: Thames and Hudson, 1991.

Faragher, John Mack. *Daniel Boone, the Life and Legend of an American Pioneer*. New York: Henry Holt and Company, 1992.

Fenton, William N. *The Great Law and the Longhouse: A Political History of the Iroquois Confederacy*. Norman: University of Oklahoma Press, 1998.

Finley, James. *Life among the Indians; or, Personal Reminiscences and Historical Incidents Illustrative of Indian Life and Character*. Ed. Rev. D. W. Clark. Cincinnati, Ohio: Cranston and Stowe, 1857.

Fisher, Daniel C., Bradley T. Lepper, and Paul E. Hooge. "Evidence for the Butchery of the Burning Tree Mastodon." In *The First Discovery of America: Archaeological Evidence of the Early Inhabitants of Ohio,* ed. William S. Dancey. Columbus: Ohio Archaeological Council, 1994.

Ford, Worthington C., et al., eds. *Journals of the Continental Congress, 1774–1789*. 34 vols. Washington, D.C.: Government Printing Office, 1905–37.

Foster, Emily, ed. *The Ohio Frontier: An Anthology of Early Writings.* Lexington: University Press of Kentucky, 1992.

Gist, Christopher. *Christopher Gist's Journals with Historical, Geographical, and Ethnological Notes and Biographies of His Contemporaries.* Ed. William M. Darlington. Pittsburgh: J. R. Weldin and Company, 1893.

Goss, Arthur F. "Astronomical Alignments at the Incinerator Site." In *A History of 17 Years of Excavation and Research: A Chronicle of 12th-Century Human Values and the Built Environment,* ed. James M. Heilman, Malinda C. Lilias, and Christopher A. Turnbow. Dayton: Dayton Museum of Natural History, 1988.

Haldimand, Frederic. "Haldimand Papers." Vols. 9, 10, 19, 20 of *Michigan Pioneer and Historical Collections.* 40 vols. Lansing, Mich.: State Printer, 1877–1929.

Harmar, Joseph. "Court of Inquiry on General Harmar," in *American State Papers: Military Affairs* (Washington, D.C.: Gales and Seaton, 1790), 1:20–27.

Harris, Thaddeus M., *The Journal of a Tour . . . 1803.* Boston: Manning and Loring, 1805.

Hart, John P., and Christina B. Rieth, eds. *Northeast Subsistence-Settlement Change, A.D. 700–1300.* Albany: New York State Museum Bulletin 296, 2002.

Heart, Jonathan. "A Plan of the Remains of Some Ancient Works on the Muskingum." *Columbian Magazine,* May 1787.

Heckewelder, John. *History, Manners, and Customs of the Indian Nations Who Once Inhabited Pennsylvania and the Neighbouring States.* Philadelphia: Historical Society of Pennsylvania, 1876.

———. *Narrative of the Mission of the United Brethren among the Delaware and Mohegan Indians.* Philadelphia: McCarty and Davis, 1820.

Heidenreich, Conrad. "Huron." In *Handbook of North American Indians,* vol. 15, ed. William C. Sturtevant. Washington, D.C.: Smithsonian Institution Press, 1978.

Hemmings, E. Thomas. "Neale's Landing: An Archeological Study of a Fort Ancient Settlement on Blennerhassett Island, West Virginia." Submitted to the West Virginia Antiquities Commission and the Office of Archeology and Historic Preservation, Department of the Interior—National Park Service in fulfillment of contracts for Archeological Research at Blennerhassett Island, West Virginia, National Park Service Project number 54-73-00020-00. West Virginia Geological and Economic Survey, Morgantown, West Virginia, 1977.

Hill, Leonard U. *John Johnston and the Indians in the Land of the Three Miamis.* Piqua, Ohio, 1957.

Historical Statistics of the United States, 1790–1970. Ed. Donald B. Dodd and Wynelle S. Dodd. University: University of Alabama Press, 1973.

Honsberger, Lonny, ed. *A Book of Diagrams and Index of Indian Landholders on the Wyandot Reservation, Wyandot County, Ohio, at the Time of Cession.* Upper Sandusky, Ohio: L. L. Honsberger, 1989.

Horsman, Reginald. "United States Indian Policies, 1776–1815." In *Handbook of*

North American Indians, vol. 4, ed. William C. Sturtevant. Washington, D.C.: Smithsonian Institution Press, 1988.

Howard, James. *Shawnee! The Ceremonialism of a Native Indian Tribe and Its Cultural Background.* Athens: Ohio University Press, 1972.

Hunt, George T. *The Wars of the Iroquois.* Madison: University of Wisconsin Press, 1940.

Hunter, William. "History of the Ohio Valley." In *Handbook of North American Indians,* vol. 15, ed. William C. Sturtevant. Washington, D.C.: Smithsonian Institution Press, 1978.

Hurt, R. Douglas. *The Ohio Frontier: Crucible of the Old Northwest, 1720–1830.* Bloomington: Indiana University Press, 1996.

Jefferson, Thomas. *Notes on the State of Virginia.* Ed. William Peden. New York: W. W. Norton and Company, 1954.

———. *The Papers of Thomas Jefferson.* Ed. Julian P. Boyd et al. 16 vols. Princeton, N.J.: Princeton University Press, 1950–61.

Jennings, Francis. *The Ambiguous Iroquois Empire: The Covenant Chain Confederation of Indian Tribes with English Colonies from Its Beginnings to the Lancaster Treaty of 1744.* New York: W. W. Norton and Company, 1984.

———. *Empire of Fortune: Crowns, Colonies, and Tribes in the Seven Years War in America.* New York: W. W. Norton and Company, 1988.

———. *The Invasion of America: Indians, Colonialism, and the Cant of Conquest.* Chapel Hill, N.C.: Institute of Early American History and Culture, 1975.

Jennings, Francis, William N. Fenton, Mary A. Druke, and David R. Miller, eds. *The History and Culture of Iroquois Diplomacy: An Interdisciplinary Guide to the Treaties of the Six Nations and Their League.* Syracuse, N.Y.: Syracuse University Press, 1985.

Jones, Dorothy V. *License for Empire: Colonialism by Treaty in Early America.* Chicago: University of Chicago Press, 1982.

Josephy, Alvin M. *The American Heritage Book of Indians.* New York: American Heritage Publishing Company, 1961.

Kelsay, Isabel. *Joseph Brant, 1783–1807: Man of Two Worlds.* Syracuse, N.Y.: Syracuse University Press, 1984.

Klopfenstein, Carl. "The Removal of the Indians from Ohio." In *The Historic Indian in Ohio,* ed. Randall Buchman. Columbus: Ohio Historical Society, 1976.

Knepper, George W. *Ohio and Its People.* Kent, Ohio: Kent State University Press, 1989.

Knopf, Richard. "'Cool Cat George' and the Indian Wars in Ohio." In *The Historic Indian in Ohio,* ed. Randall Buchman. Columbus: Ohio Historical Society, 1976.

Lepper, Brad. "The Great Hopewell Road and the Role of Pilgrimage in the Hopewell Interaction Sphere." Paper presented at "Perspectives on Middle

Woodland at the Millennium," Center for American Archaeology, Kampsville, Ill., July 2000.

———. "Newark Earthworks and the Geometric Enclosures of the Scioto Valley: Connections and Conjectures." In *A View from the Core: A Synthesis of Ohio Hopewell Archaeology*, ed. Paul J. Pacheco. Columbus: Ohio Archaeological Council, 1996.

———. "Tracking Ohio's Great Hopewell Road." *Archaeology* 48, no. 6 (1995): 52–56.

McIlwaine, H. R., ed. *Journal of the Council of State of Virginia, 1776–1781*. 2 vols. Richmond: Virginia State Library, 1931–32.

———. *Official Letters of the Governors of the State of Virginia*. 3 vols. Richmond: Division of Purchase and Printing, 1926–29.

McPherson, James. *Ordeal by Fire*. New York: Alfred Knopf, 1982.

Methodist Episcopal Church. *The Doctrines and Discipline of the Methodist Episcopal Church*. 1829.

The Murder of the Christian Indians in North America in the Year 1782, A Narrative of Facts. Dublin, 1823.

Nelson, Larry. *A Man of Distinction among Them: Alexander McKee and the Ohio Country Frontier, 1754–1799*. Kent, Ohio: Kent State University Press, 1999.

O'Donnell, James H. "Allan W. Eckert's *A Sorrow in Our Heart: The Life of Tecumseh*, A Review Essay." *Northwest Ohio Quarterly* 65 (1993): 50–54.

———. "Armchair Adventurers and Horseback Botanists: Explorations of Florida's Natural History, 1763–1800." *Gulf Coast Historical Review* 8 (1992): 86–94.

———. "Captain Pipe's Speech: A Commentary on the Delaware Experience, 1775–1781." *Northwest Ohio Quarterly* 64 (1992): 126–33.

———. "John Armstrong," "William Crawford," "David Ziegler." In *American National Biography*, vols. 1, 5, and 24, ed. John Garraty. New York: Oxford University Press, 2002.

———. "Joseph Brant." In *American Indian Leaders: Studies in Diversity*, ed. R. David Edmunds. Lincoln: University of Nebraska Press, 1980.

———. "Logan's Oration: A Case Study of Ethnographic Authentication." *Quarterly Journal of Speech* 65 (1979): 150–56.

———. "'National Retaliation': Thomas Jefferson's Brief for the Imprisonment of Henry Hamilton." In *Selected Papers from the 1985 and 1986 George Rogers Clark Trans-Appalachian Frontier Conferences*, ed. Robert J. Holden. Vincennes, Ind.: Eastern National Park and Monument Association and Vincennes University, 1988.

———. "The Ohio River as Interface of Conflict: The Ohio River Indian Frontier, 1774–1784." Paper presented at the Ohio River Odyssey Symposium, Huntington, W.Va., September 19, 1987.

———. "The Plight of the Ohio Indians during the American Revolution." In *The Historic Indian in Ohio,* ed. Randall Buchman. Columbus: Ohio Historical Society, 1976.

———. "Randolph C. Downes." In *Historians of the American Frontier: A Bio-Bibliographical Sourcebook,* ed. John R. Wunder. New York: Garland Press, 1988.

———. *Southern Indians in the American Revolution.* Knoxville: University of Tennessee Press, 1973.

———. "'Who is There to Mourn for Logan? No One!': The Native American Crisis in the Ohio Country, 1774–1783." In *Ohio in the American Revolution,* ed. Thomas H. Smith. Columbus: Ohio Historical Society, 1976.

Olmstead, Earl. *David Zeisberger: A Life among the Indians.* Kent, Ohio: Kent State University Press, 1997.

O'Neill, Paul, ed. *The Frontiersmen.* Alexandria, Va.: Time-Life Books, 1977.

"The Origins of Canines." *Wall Street Journal,* November 22, 2002.

Pacheco, Paul J. "Ohio Hopewell Regional Settlement Patterns." In *A View from the Core: A Synthesis of Ohio Hopewell Archaeology,* ed. Paul J. Pacheco. Columbus: Ohio Archaeological Council, 1996.

———. "Ohio Middle Woodland Intracommunity Settlement Variability." In *Ohio Hopewell Community Organization,* ed. William S. Dancey and Paul J. Pacheco. Kent, Ohio: Kent State University Press, 1997.

Palmer, William P., et al., eds. *Calendar of Virginia State Papers and Other Manuscripts, 1652–1781.* 11 vols. Richmond, Va.: R. F. Walker, 1875–93.

Pieper, Thomas I., and James B. Gidney. *Fort Laurens, 1778–79: The Revolutionary War in Ohio.* Kent, Ohio: Kent State University Press, 1976.

Prufer, Olaf H. "How to Construct a Model: A Personal Memoir." In *A View from the Core: A Synthesis of Ohio Hopewell Archaeology,* ed. Paul J. Pacheco. Columbus: Ohio Archaeological Council, 1996.

Prufer, Olaf H., and Dana A. Long. *The Archaic of Northeastern Ohio.* Kent State Research Papers in Archaeology, no. 6. Kent, Ohio: Kent State University Press, 1986.

Prufer, Olaf H., Dana A. Long, and Donald J. Metzger. *Krill Cave: A Stratified Rockshelter in Summit County, Ohio.* Kent State Research Papers in Archaeology, no. 8. Kent, Ohio: Kent State University Press, 1989.

Putnam, Rufus. *The Memoirs of Rufus Putnam and Certain Official Papers and Correspondence.* Ed. Rowena Buell. Boston: Houghton Mifflin and Company, 1903.

Richter, Conrad. *Light in the Forest.* New York: Alfred Knopf Publishers, 1953.

Richter, Daniel K., and James H. Merrell. *Beyond the Covenant Chain: The Iroquois and Their Neighbors in Indian North America, 1600–1800.* Syracuse, N.Y.: Syracuse University Press, 1987.

Rogers, Robert. *Ponteach; or, the Savages of America: A Tragedy.* Ed. Allan Nevins. 1914. Reprint, New York: Burt Franklin, 1971.

Romain, William F. *Mysteries of the Hopewell: Astronomers, Geometers, and Magicians of the Eastern Woodlands*. Akron, Ohio: University of Akron Press, 2000.

Sargent, Winthrop. The Diary of Winthrop Sargent. Winthrop Sargent Papers, Ohio Historical Society, Columbus.

Savolainen, Peter, Ya-Ping Zhang, Jing Luo, Joakim Lundeberg, and Thomas Leitner. "Genetic Evidence for an East Asian Origin of Domestic Dogs." *Science*, November 22, 2002, 1610–13.

Scribner, Robert L., and Brent Tartar, eds. *Revolutionary Virginia: The Road to Independence*. Richmond: University Press of Virginia, 1977.

Seeman, Mark F. *The Locust Site (33Mu160): The 1983 Test Excavation of a Multicomponent Workshop in East Central Ohio*. Kent State Research Papers in Archaeology, no. 7. Kent, Ohio: Kent State University Press, 1985.

Sellers, Charles C. *Mr. Peale's Museum: Charles Willson Peale and the First Popular Museum of Natural Science and Art*. New York: W. W. Norton and Company, 1980.

Sheehan, Bernard. *Seeds of Extinction: Jeffersonian Philanthropy and the American Indian*. New York: W. W. Norton and Company, 1973.

Shriver, Philip R., and Clarence E. Wunderlin, Jr., eds. *The Documentary Heritage of Ohio*. Athens: Ohio University Press, 2000.

Shy, John. "Dunmore, the Upper Ohio Valley, and the American Revolution." In *Ohio in the American Revolution: A Conference to Commemorate the Two Hundredth Anniversary of the Ft. Gower Resolves,* ed. Thomas H. Smith. Columbus: Ohio Historical Society, 1976.

Silverberg, Robert. *Mound Builders of Ancient America: The Archaeology of a Myth*. Greenwich: New York Graphic Society, 1968.

Smith, James. *An Account of the Remarkable Occurrences in the Life and Travels of Colonel James Smith: during his captivity with the Indians in the years 1755, . . . written by himself*. Philadelphia: J. Grigg, 1831.

Smith, Thomas H., ed. *Ohio in the American Revolution*. Columbus: Ohio Historical Society, 1976.

Smith, William. *Historical Account of Bouquet's Expedition against the Ohio Indians in 1764*. Cincinnati: Robert Clarke and Company, 1868.

Squier, Ephraim G., and Edwin H. Davis. *Ancient Monuments of the Mississippi Valley*. Ed. David J. Meltzer. Washington, D.C.: Smithsonian Institution Press, 1998.

Sugden, John. *Blue Jacket, Warrior of the Shawnees*. Lincoln: University of Nebraska Press, 2000.

Sword, Wiley. *President Washington's Indian War: The Struggle for the Old Northwest, 1790–1795*. Norman: University of Oklahoma Press, 1985.

Tanner, Helen H. "The Glaize in 1792: A Composite Indian Community," *Ethnohistory* 25 (1978): 15–39.

Tanner, Helen H., ed. *Atlas of Great Lakes Indian History*. The Civilization of the American Indian Series, vol. 174. Norman: University of Oklahoma Press, 1987.

Tooker, Elizabeth. "Three Aspects of Northern Iroquoian Culture Change." *Pennsylvania Archaeologist* 30 (2): 65–71.

————. "Wyandot." In *Handbook of North American Indians,* vol. 15, ed. William C. Sturtevant. Washington, D.C.: Smithsonian Institution Press, 1978.

Trelease, Allen W. *Indian Affairs in Colonial New York: The Seventeenth Century.* Ithaca, N.Y.: Cornell University Press, 1960.

Trigger, Bruce. *The Children of Aataentsic: A History of the Huron People to 1660.* Montreal: McGill-Queen's University Press, 1976.

————. "Early Iroquoian Contacts with Europeans." In *Handbook of North American Indians,* vol. 15, ed. William C. Sturtevant. Washington, D.C.: Smithsonian Institution Press, 1978.

Virginia Gazette. Microfilm from Colonial Williamsburg, Inc. Editions are identified by editor, such as Purdie in 1778 or Dixon and Hunter in other periods. A set of the microfilm is owned by the Marietta College Library.

Wallace, Paul W. A. *Indian Paths of Pennsylvania.* Harrisburg: Pennsylvania Historical and Museum Commission, 1965.

Washburn, Wilcomb. *The American Indian and the United States: A Documentary History.* 4 vols. New York: Random House, 1973.

Washington, George. *Writings of George Washington.* 39 vols. Ed. John C. Fitzpatrick. Washington, D.C.: Government Printing Office, 1931–44.

Weslager, C. A. *The Delaware Indian Westward Migration.* Wallingford, Pa.: Middle Atlantic Press, 1978.

————. *The Delaware Indians: A History.* New Brunswick: Rutgers University Press, 1981.

White, Richard. *The Middle Ground: Indians, Empires, and Republics in the Great Lakes Region, 1650–1815.* Cambridge: Cambridge University Press, 1991.

Wilcox, Frank N. *Ohio Indian Trails: A Pictorial Survey of the Indian Trails of Ohio.* Ed. William A. McGill. Kent, Ohio: Kent State University Press, 1970.

Woodward, Susan L., and Jerry N. McDonald. *Indian Mounds of the Middle Ohio Valley: A Guide to Adena and Ohio Hopewell Sites.* Newark, Ohio: The Woodward and McDonald Publishing Company, 1986.

Wymer, Dee Anne. "The Hopewell Econiche: Human-Land Interaction in the Core Area." In *A View from the Core: A Synthesis of Ohio Hopewell Archaeology,* ed. Paul J. Pacheco. Columbus: Ohio Archaeological Council, 1996.

————. "Trends and Disparities: The Woodland Paleoethnobotanical Record of the Mid-Ohio Valley." In *Cultural Variability in Context: Woodland Settlements of the Mid-Ohio Valley,* ed. Mark F. Seeman. Midcontinental Journal of Archaeology Special Papers. Kent, Ohio: Kent State University Press, 1962.

Zoerkler, Ray. Interview with Ray Zoerkler, Certified Professional Geologist, January 2, 2002.

Index

Page numbers in italics refer to illustrations.

Adams, John Quincy, 121, 156n44
Adena culture, 4, 6, 8, 12, 14–18, 25, 82
African Methodist Episcopal Church, 115
alcohol and alcoholism, 5, 77, 100, 103, 115. *See also* rum
Allen, Richard, 115
Amherst, Jeffrey, 36–37
Andrews, Ebenezer Baldwin, 20–21
anti-Catholicism, 117
Antietam, Battle of, 91
Armstrong, John, 87–89
astronomical observatories, 19–20, *25*
Athens, Ohio, 20

Baubee, 65
Beaver's Town (Shingas' village), 32
beaver wars, 4
Becker, Carl, 47
Belpre, Ohio, 25
Between-the-Logs, *112*, 115, 118, 120
Big Spring (Wyandot reservation), 119
Blackfish, 56, 64
Black Hoof, 101, 105
Blennerhassett Island, 4, 24–26
Blue Jacket, 86, 89–90, 92–93, 98, 101–2, 105–6
Blue Licks, Battle of the, 71, 86
Bolivar, Ohio, 32
Boone, Daniel, 56, 71, 78
botanical remains, 2, 18, 21–22, 26
Bouquet, Henry, 38–39

Boyd, Rhonda, 138n34
Braddock, Edward, 33–34
Bradstreet, John, 38
Brant, Joseph, 65, 78, *79*, 82, 86, 92–94, 153n86
Brish, Henry C., 123–24
British relations with Native Americans, 36–38, 41, 75, 80, 89, 92, 94–98, 101–2, 106. *See also specific wars (e.g.,* Revolutionary War)
Brodhead, Daniel, 60, 64–65
Brose, David, 2, 27
Brown County, Ohio, 123
Bryan's Station (Ky. settlement), 71
Buckongahelas, 77
building styles, 25–26, 29, 31–33, 111
burial practices, 16–17, 25–26

Calhoun, John C., 119–20
Camp Deposit, 97
Campus Martius, *81*, 81–82
Canadian relations with Native Americans, 75
captives, 32, 34–36, 39, *40*, 48, 50, 74, 83
Carleton, Guy, 1st baron Dorchester, 95–96, 98
Carskadden, Jeff, 27
Cayugas, 5, 30
ceremonial centers, 16, 19, 22–24
Cherokees, 51, 78, 89–92, 123, 128
Chillicothe, Ohio, 19
Chillicothe (Shawnee village), 63–64, 71, 88

Chippewas: diplomatic missions of, 51, 61, 73–74, 78; lands ceded by, 154n2; Resistance of 1763 and, 37–38; Revolutionary War and, 51, 63, 68; treaties with, 74, 82–83

Cincinnati, Ohio, 75, 87, 92–93

Clark, George Rogers, 42, 57, 60–65, 71, 78, 94, 136n9

Clarke, Wesley, 6

Columbus, Ohio, 121

Comstock, 123

Conessaway, 49

Connolly, John, 47–50

Continental Congress, 48–52, 65, 76, 94, 120

Coquethagechton. See White Eyes, Captain

Cornstalk, 44, 52, 56–57

Coshocking (Delaware village), 65

Coshocton, Ohio, 38

Cowan, Wesley, 24

Crawford, William, 44, 69–70, 71, 84

Crawford County, Ohio, 110, 121

Creeks, 31, 93

Creoles, 64

Croghan, George, 30

Cuyahoga (Seneca/Cayuga village), 30, 57

Dancey, William S., 11

Davis, Edwin H., 7

Dayton, Ohio, 25

Declaration of Independence, 51

Delawares, 6, 11, 13, 29–34; building styles of, 32–33; Continental Congress and, 49–50, 52–53; diplomatic missions of, 46–51, 53, 55, 58–59, 61, 66–68, 73–74, 76–78, 86, 95; education of, 49–50; Gnadenhutten massacre of, 68–70, 84, 128; land sales and cessions by, 154n2; Lord Dunmore's War and, 44; missionaries to, 33, 42, 49–50, 55, 63, 66; peace desired by, 93; raids against, 57, 64, 68–69, 84, 87, 128; raids by, 34–38, 61, 89–92; Resistance of 1763 and, 37–38; Revolutionary War and, 46–53, 55–61, 63–69; settler encroachment and, 29, 56, 60–61, 68–69; trade and, 29, 51; treaties with, 29–30, 38, 58–60, 65, 74, 78, 82–84, 110, 120; western removal of, 66, 84, 122

Denny, Ebenezer, 82, 91

DePeyster, Arents, 65–66

Detroit, 28–29; Clark's advances on, 60–61, 65; diplomatic missions to, 46–47, 49, 51, 53, 58, 61, 66–68; Jay's Treaty and, 102; Resistance of 1763 and, 37–38

Dickens, Charles, 112

diplomats and diplomacy, Native American, 5; communication among, 18, 64; confederation and, 78, 84, 86, 92–97; half kings as, 30; protocols of, 38, 52, 102. See also individual groups (e.g., Chippewas, diplomatic missions of)

disease outbreaks, 29, 38, 59, 100

Dorchester. See Carleton, Guy, 1st baron Dorchester

Downes, Randolph, 11

Dragoo, Don W., 17–18

Drooker, Penelope, 24–26

Dunmore, Lord. See Murray, John, 4th earl of Dunmore

Dutch settlers/traders, 5

"earthworks," 5–7, 14–15

Eastern Agricultural Complex, 18

Eckert, Allan, 11

Edmunds, R. David, 11, 107

Egushaway, 93

Eid, Leroy, 86

Emistisiguo, 93
English settlers/traders, 4–5, 37. *See also* settler encroachment

Fallen Timbers, Battle of, 97, 99
Finley, James, 111, 115–20
Five Nations. *See* Iroquois League
food sources, 18, 21, 23–25, 26, 29
Fort Adams, 96
Fort Ancient culture, 4, 8, 12, 23–27, 31
Fort Defiance, 96–97
Fort Finney, 31, 76–78
Fort Greenville, 95
Fort Hamilton, 92
Fort Harmar, 75, 76, 80, 82–84, 93–94, 110
Fort Jefferson, 92
Fort Laurens, 59–60
Fort Malden, 109
Fort McIntosh, 59, 82–83
Fort Miamis, 96–97, 102
Fort Pitt: diplomatic missions to, 46–48, 52, 58–60; raids on, 38, 64; Virginia seizure of, 50
Fort Pontchartrain, 28
Fort Randolph, 56
Fort Recovery, 95–96
Fort St. Clair, 92
Fort Stanwix, 41, 73, 78, 82, 95
Fort Steuben, 76, 80
Fort Wayne, 87, 97
French and Indian Wars, 33–36
French Margaret's Town (Delaware village), 31
French settlers/traders, 4–5, 28–29, 34, 36
fur/skins trade, 4–5, 28–29, 32, 37, 75, 80, 100

Gage, Thomas, 43
Genheimer, Robert A., 11

Ghent, Treaty of (1814), 121
Gibson, John, 44, 50, 58
Girty, Simon, 65, 90, 143n50
Glacial Kame peoples, 17
Glaize (village), 92, 96
Gnadenhutten, Ohio, 68–70, 74, 84, 128
Goodhunter, Captain, 123
Gratz family, 51
grave goods, 17, 25–26
Great Hopewell Road, 19–21
Greenville, Ohio, 89
Greenville, Treaty of (1795), 98–100, 102–3
Greenville (Shawnee village), 103, 105
Grey Eyes, 117

Half King, 55, 61, 63, 66, 76–77
Hamilton, Henry, 51, 53, 55, 60, 153n72
Hancock County, Ohio, 121
Hand, Edward, 57
Hard Hickory, 123
Hardin County, Ohio, 121
Hard Labor, Treaty of (1768), 41
Harmar, Josiah, 82, 86–88, 93, 148n11
Harrison, William Henry, 106–9
Heckewelder, John, 42, 52, 63–64, 66–68, 151n42
Henry, Patrick, 53, 57, 60
Hicks, John, 113–14
High Banks works, 19
Hively, Ray, 19
Hopewell culture, 2–4, 6, 8, 12, 14–23, 25, 82
Horn, Robert, 19
horses, return of, 48, 50, 83
hostages, 39, 44, 52, 74, 77, 83
Howard, James, 11
Hurons, 5–6, 28
Hurt, R. Douglas, 111

Incinerator site, 25
Indian commissioners, 50, 52, 76, 94, 120
intermarriages, 32, 39
Iroquois, 28, 30, 41; diplomatic missions of, 47, 94; hunting grounds of, 4; Lord Dunmore's War and, 44; raids by, 70–71; Revolutionary War and, 47–48, 53, 61; settler encroachment and, 63
Iroquois League, 5, 30, 41, 47, 63

Jackson, Andrew, 156n44
Jay's Treaty (1794), 98, 102
Jefferson, Thomas, 43, 62–64, 74
Jemison, Mary, 150n33
Jennings, Francis, 14, 38
Johnny, Captain, 76–77
John Peter, Captain, 35
Johnson, William, 37
Johnston, George C., 122
Johnston, John, 108, 121–22
John's Town, Ohio, 2

Kayashota, 47, 61, 64
Kekionga, 87, 97
Kenton, Simon, 78
Kentucky relations with Native Americans, 31, 41, 44, 56, 61, 71, 75, 78
Kickapoos, 51
Killbuck, Captain John, 47, 53, 58, 65
Kirk, William, 101
Kirker, Thomas, 105
Kirkland, Samuel, 147n112
Knox, Henry, 84

Lalawethika, 99–100, 103. See also Tenskwatawa (The Prophet)
Lappawinzo (a.k.a. Lapowinsa), 30, 30
Lasselle, Antoine, 98

Le Gris, 87
Lepper, Brad, 19–21
Lewis, Andrew, 50
Licking River valley, 2, 21
Linctot, Godefrey de, 64
Little Turtle, 87, 87–89, 92
Lochry, Archibald, 65
Logan, 12–13, 42–45
Logan, Benjamin, 78
Logan's Town (Shawnee village), 64
Logstown (Seneca/Cayuga village), 30–31
Lord Dunmore's War (1774), 43–45, 50, 52, 90
Lower Shawnee Town, 31
Lumpy, Widow, 111

Madisonville (Fort Ancient site), 25
Maguck (Delaware village), 31
maize, 18, 21, 23–24
Marietta, Ohio, 1–2, 5–8, 14–17, 19, 22, 82, 86, 110
Marion County, Ohio, 121
Martin's Station (Ky. settlement), 62
Maslow, Abraham, 12
McArthur, Duncan, 105
McCleland, David, 35
McDonald, Jerry, 1
McElwain, John, 123
McGary, Hugh, 78
McIntosh, Lachlan, 57–58
McKee, Alexander, 94, 98, 143n50, 150n42
McKendree, William, 116
Medina County, Ohio, 2
Methodist Discipline, The, 115, 117
Methodist missionaries, 111–19
Methodist Mission (Wyandot reservation), 111, 114
Miamis, 6; diplomatic missions of, 46, 51, 61, 78, 82; land sales by, 107; raids against, 87–89; raids by,

89–92; Revolutionary War and, 46, 51, 60; treaties with, 120

Miamitown (Shawnee village), 92

Miami Village, 87

Michilimackinac, 38

militia groups, frontier, 44, 57–58, 64, 68–69, 75, 78, 86–90, 108

Mingoes, 86; Continental Congress and, 52; diplomatic missions of, 47–48, 61; missionaries to, 115; raids by, 34, 56, 89–92; settler encroachment and, 42; treaties with, 38

mission towns/missionaries, 33, 63, 111–19

Mohawks, 5, 65, 93–94, 122

Molunthy, 77, 78

Mononcue, 114–16, *116*, 120

Montgomery, James, 115

Montour, John, 51, 58

Moravians, 33, 42, 55, 63, 66, 68, 128

Moraviantown, 109

Morgan, George, 56, 59

Morris, Lewis, 50

Morton, James, 27

Mound City, Ohio, 19

mounds, 1–2, 5–8, 7, 11, 14–17, 19–24, 82

Murphy site, 21

Murray, John, 4th earl of Dunmore, 44, 47. *See also* Lord Dunmore's War

Muskingum County, Ohio, 2

Muskingum Valley, 27

Nanticokes, 92

National Road, 121

Neale's Landing (Fort Ancient site), 25

Neolin, 37

Netawatwees, 32

Newark, Ohio, 1–3, 19, 21–23

Newcomer's Town, 32

Northwest Ordinance (1787), 80

Ohio Company of Associates, 6, 80–81, 149n26

Ojibwas, 82, 89–92

Old Briton, 137n24

Oneidas, 5

Onondagas, 5

Ordinances: (1784), 74; (1785), 74; (1787), 80

Ottawas, 6, 28–29; diplomatic missions of, 46, 51, 61, 73–74, 78; lands ceded by, 154n2; peace desired by, 93; raids against, 88; raids by, 64, 89–92; Resistance of 1763 and, 37–38; Revolutionary War and, 46, 51, 61; treaties with, 74, 82–83

Ouiatenons, 51

Pacane, 55

Pacheco, Paul J., 11, 22–23

Paleoindians, 2

Paris, Treaty of (1783), 75, 80, 96

Peale, C. W., 102

Penn, John, 43

Pennsylvania relations with Native Americans, 29–30, 50–51, 57, 61, 65, 68–70

Philo Archaeological District, 2, 3

Piankashaws, 64, 78

Pickaway (Shawnee village), 63–64

Pipe, Captain, 12–13, 57–59, 61, 63, 66–68, 76–77, 83–84, 97, 113

Pipetown (Delaware village), 113

Pittsburgh, 49–52

Pluggy's Town (Shawnee village), 53

Pointer, Jonathan, 113–14

Point Pleasant attack (1774), 44, 90, 100

Pontiac, 37

Potawatomies, 28; diplomatic missions of, 51, 61, 78; land sales and cessions by, 107, 154n2; raids by, 89–92; Resistance of 1763 and, 37–38; Revolutionary War and, 51, 63; treaties with, 82–83

Presbyterian missionaries, 114, 119

Proclamations (1763), 41, 44

Prophetstown (Ind. Shawnee village), 106, 108

Prufer, Olaf, 22

Putnam, Rufus, 5–6, 14–17, 19, 81

Quakers, 101

Red Jacket, 94, 113

Red Ocher peoples, 17

Red Pole, 93, 101–2

removal. *See* western migration/removal

Removal Act (1830), 122–23

Resistance of 1763, 37–41

Revolutionary War, 46–53, 55–72, 74–75

Romain, William F., 11, 19

Roman Catholic missionaries, 114, 117

Ross County, Ohio, 17, 20

Ruddell, Stephen, 105–6

Ruddell's Station (Ky. settlement), 62

rum, 32, 37, 65, 100

Sacs, 82–83

St. Clair, Arthur, 34, 82–83, 89–91, 93, 148n11

Salem, Ohio, 74

Sandusky Bay, Ohio, 29

Sargent, Winthrop, 90–91

Sasterasszee, 61

Sauwauseekau, 99

Scaroyady, 30

Schoenbrunn, Ohio, 69, 74

Seneca County, Ohio, 121

Senecas, 6, 30; diplomatic missions of, 51, 94; French and Indian War and, 37; Iroquois League and, 5; lands ceded by, 154n2; missionaries to, 113, 117–18; peace desired by, 93; raids against, 42; reservations for, 120; Resistance of 1763 and, 38; Revolutionary War and, 51; settler encroachment and, 121; western removal of, 122–24. *See also* Mingoes

Seneca Steel, 123

settler encroachment, 13, 29, 37, 41–45, 48, 56, 60–64, 73–76, 80–81, 92, 121. *See also* militia groups, frontier

Shawnee Prophet (Tenskwatawa), 11, 31

Shawnees, 6, 11, 13, 30–31; ancestor cultures of, 4, 31; building styles of, 31; Continental Congress and, 52–53, 76; diplomatic missions of, 46, 48, 51–53, 56, 61, 76–78, 82, 86–87, 93–95, 98, 101–2, 105–8; land sales and cessions by, 107–8, 154n2; Lord Dunmore's War and, 44, 52; missionaries to, 101; raids against, 31, 53, 62–64, 71, 78, 87–89; raids by, 34–38, 44, 48, 53, 56, 61–62, 89–92; reservations for, 120; Resistance of 1763 and, 37–38; Revolutionary War and, 46–53, 56–57, 60–64; settler encroachment and, 42, 48, 56, 61–64, 75; treaties with, 38, 44, 77–78, 99–100; War of 1812 and, 108–9; western removal of, 84, 105–6, 109, 122

Shebosh, 52

Shingas, 30–35

Silverberg, Robert, 11

Simcoe, John Graves, 75, 94, 98

skins, animal. *See* fur/skins trade

slaves, return of, 48, 50, 58

smallpox, 38, 59

Smith, James, 90

Solomon, Big John, 111

South Park site, 26–27

Split-the-Log, Charles, 111

Springfield, Ohio, 121

"Squaw campaign" (1778), 57–58

Squier, Ephraim G., 7

Standing Stone (Shawnee village), 71

Stephen, Adam, 50

Steubenville, Ohio, 76

Stewart, John, 111–15

Stuart, Charles, 34–36, 39, 41–42

Studebaker, Elizabeth, 138n34

Sun Watch site, 25

Swedish settlers, 32

Tanaghrisson, 30

Tanner, Helen, 84

Tarhe, 76, 97–98, 110

Tecumseh, 11, 13, 31, 74, 99, 99–100, 103, 106–9; father of, 44, 100

Tenskwatawa (The Prophet), 11, 31, 103–9, *104*. *See also* Lalawethika

Tewas, 51

Thames, Battle of the, 74, 109

Thayendanegea. *See* Brant, Joseph

trade and trade goods, 4–5, 18, 21, 27, 32, 34, 37, 48, 50–51, 100. *See also* fur/skins trade

treaties: (1737) Walking Purchase, 29–30; (1763) Proclamation, 41, 44; (1764) Mingoes, etc., 38; (1768) Hard Labor/Fort Stanwix, 41, 73, 95; (1774) Shawnees at Camp Charlotte, 44; (1778) Delawares at Fort Pitt, 58–60, 65, 83; (1783) Paris Peace, 75, 80, 96; (1784) Six Nations at Fort Stanwix, 78, 82; (1785) Wyandots, etc. at

Fort McIntosh, 74, 78, 82–83; (1786) Shawnees at Fort Finney, 77–78; (1789) Wyandots, etc./Six Nations at Fort Harmar, 82–84, 93–94, 110; (1794) Jay's, 98, 102; (1795) Greenville, 98–100, 102–3; (1814) Ghent, 121; (1842) Wyandots at Upper Sandusky, 111, 124, 126. *See also* Ordinances

Trent, William, 50

Tseendattong, 53

Two Logs, 115

Upper Sandusky, Treaty of (1842), 111, 124, 126

Virginia relations with Native Americans, 41–45, 47–48, 50, 53, 56–57, 61–62. *See also* Lord Dunmore's War

Wabash, 82

Wakatomika, 44

Walker, John, 50

Walker, Thomas, 50

Walker, William, 111, 113–15

Walking Purchase (1737), 29–30

Wapakoneta (Shawnee village/reservation), 101, 105, 122

War of 1812, 105, 108–9, 121

Washington, George, 43–44, 57, 92, 102

Wayne, Anthony, 93, 95–98, 102

Weas, 78

Wells, William, 106–7

Wendocalla, 29, 31

Weslager, C. A., 11

West, Benjamin, 39

western migration/removal, 13, 66, 84, 105–6, 109, 111, 120–26

Western Senecas. *See* Mingoes

Wewellapee, 122

white attitudes toward Native Americans, 5–6, 11, 13, 29, 97, 116
Whitecrow, 111
White Eyes, Captain, 33, 47–51, 53, 55–56, 58–59, 65, 128; son of, 76
Whittlesey, Charles, 26
Whittlesey tradition sites, 26–27
Wilson, James, 50
Wingenund, 76, 84
Wood, James, 50
Woodland cultures, 3, 3–4, 20
Woodward, Susan, 1
Worthington, Thomas, 105
Wright, George, 111
Wyandot County, Ohio, 111, 121
Wyandots, 6, 13, 28–29; ancestor cultures of, 5; building styles of, 29, 111; diplomatic missions of, 46, 48–49, 51, 53, 61, 73–74, 76, 78, 98, 108; education of, 115, 118–19; lands ceded by, 110–11; missionaries to, 111–19; raids by, 55, 61, 89–92; reservations for, 120; Resistance of 1763 and, 37–38; Revolutionary War and, 46, 48–49, 51, 53, 55, 60–61, 63–64; settler encroachment and, 48–49, 69, 120–22; trade and, 28–29; treaties with, 74, 78, 82–84, 110–11, 120, 124, 126; western removal of, 111, 120–22, 124–26
Wymer, Dee Anne, 18, 21–22

Xenia, Ohio, 125

Yellow Creek incident (1774), 43

Zeigler, David, 88
Zeisberger, David, 42, 55, 58, 63–66
Zoar, Ohio, 59